T0417969

Isaiah Shembe's Hymns and the Sacred Dance in Ibandla LamaNazaretha

Studies of Religion in Africa

SUPPLEMENTS TO THE JOURNAL OF RELIGION IN AFRICA

Edited by

Benjamin Soares (*African Studies Center, Leiden, The Netherlands*)
Asonzeh Ukah (*University of Cape Town, South Africa*)
Shobana Shankar (*Stony Brook University, New York, USA*)

VOLUME 45

The titles published in this series are listed at *brill.com/sra*

Isaiah Shembe's Hymns and the Sacred Dance in Ibandla LamaNazaretha

By

Nkosinathi Sithole

BRILL

LEIDEN | BOSTON

Cover illustration: Isaiah Shembe washing feet of worshippers. Courtesy of the Killie Campbell Collections, University of KwaZulu-Natal, Durban.

Library of Congress Cataloging-in-Publication Data

Names: Sithole, Nkosinathi, author.
Title: Isaiah Shembe's hymns and the sacred dance in Ibandla LamaNazaretha / by Nkosinathi Sithole.
Other titles: Studies on religion in Africa ; v. 45.
Description: Boston : Brill, 2016. | Series: Studies of religion in Africa ; volume 45 | Includes bibliographical references and index.
Identifiers: LCCN 2016013905 (print) | LCCN 2016014017 (ebook) | ISBN 9789004317222 (hardback : alk. paper) | ISBN 9789004320628 (E-book)
Subjects: LCSH: Church of the Nazarites—Hymns. | Church of the Nazarites—Rituals. | Dance—Religious aspects—Church of the Nazarites. | Shembe, Isaiah, -1935. | Zulu (African people)—Rites and ceremonies.
Classification: LCC BX7068.7.Z5 S58 2016 (print) | LCC BX7068.7.Z5 (ebook) | DDC 289.93—dc23
LC record available at http://lccn.loc.gov/2016013905

Typeface for the Latin, Greek, and Cyrillic scripts: "Brill". See and download: brill.com/brill-typeface.

ISSN 0169-9814
ISBN 978-90-04-31722-2 (hardback)
ISBN 978-90-04-32062-8 (e-book)

Contents

Acknowledgements

I am grateful to my late mother, Zithulele MaMchunu Sithole, who, after leaving Ibandla lamaNazaretha to marry my non-Nazaretha father, re-converted to the Church before I was born. I am grateful to her also for the stories she told us about her life and about Shembe and her father, the late INkosi Pewula Mchunu of Mdubuzweni, who was very devoted to the Nazaretha faith. I am particularly grateful for her prayers that her children become AmaNazaretha. I am thankful to my late father who allowed our mother to raise us as AmaNazaretha, even though he only converted towards the very end of his life, (when he was in his late 60s) and demanded that we be 'strengthened' by Sangomas and herbalists every now and then, something that is against the grain of Nazaretha faith. Had I not been a member of Ibandla lamaNazaretha, I doubt I would have written this book and I am quite certain that I would not have written it as it is.

I am very grateful for the financial assistance from the National Research Foundation which enabled me to complete a research project from which this book has been developed. I am particularly grateful to Professor Duncan Brown (Dean of the Faculty of Arts at the University of the Western-Cape) for his unending support and guidance from the inception of the aforementioned research project right to the end when he was still Professor of English at the University of KwaZulu-Natal. The same gratitude goes to Professor Gerald West (Professor of Biblical Studies at the University of KwaZulu-Natal) for taking me under his wing as my supervisor when Duncan left for The University of the Western Cape.

All the members of Ibandla lamaNazaretha who have been part of this work through interviews and in other ways are hereby acknowledged, and many thanks to all for allowing me to record performances at weddings, competitions, overnight meetings of twenty-three, and the sacred dance of all people in Ebuhleni and other main Temples of Ibandla lamaNazaretha.

Introduction

This book is concerned with Isaiah Shembe, a Black South African Prophet who founded Ibandla lamaNazaretha in 1910; it is concerned with the hymns he composed for himself and his followers to sing in church services and in other contexts; and it is concerned with the sacred dance which is performed using the hymns. Isaiah Shembe founded Ibandla lamaNazaretha near Durban in what is now KwaZulu-Natal, but he himself was born around 1870 in Ntabamhlophe, Estcourt. Ntabamhlophe was the land of the Hlubi clan under Chief Langalibalele Hadebe. Three years after Shembe's birth, in 1873, Langalibalele was attacked and imprisoned by the Natal Government forces. He had been commanded to bring the guns that the young men in his tribe had acquired in the Diamond Diggings for registration in Pietermaritzburg. Langalibalele refused to do so, and instead, armed himself and his men and prepared to flee to Lesotho. The AmaHlubi tribesmen and the Carbineers from Pietermaritzburg met at the Bushman's River Pass (near Giants Castle) and engaged in a fight out of which three Carbineers and two Africans loyal to the government were killed. Langalibalele managed to escape to Lesotho, but was captured there on 11 December 1873 and was brought back to Natal in chains (Pearse, et al: 1973: 4–5). This marked the end of the Hlubi chiefdom, which was then divided among a number of petty chiefs.

Isaiah Shembe was related to the Hlubi royal house on his mother's side as his mother, Sitheya, was a daughter of Langalibalele's induna and uncle Malindi. Some years earlier, according to oral tradition in the church, Sitheya had eaten a strange flower in the mountains when going with other girls to fetch wood. Later that day a "voice" told her that what she had eaten was not a flower but a spirit of God. She was going to give birth to a messenger of God called Shembe. While it may have been strange for Sitheya to hear such a voice, the supernatural was not something unknown to the Hlubi people of Ntabamhlophe. The chief himself was well-known for his rainmaking abilities. But Sitheya became uneasy when a man called Shembe came to ask her to marry his son. The man was Nhliziyo Shembe and the son was Mayekisa, Isaiah Shembe's father. Both Nhliziyo and Mayekisa were the indunas in the Hlubi tribe; Nhliziyo was Mthimkhulu's (Langalibalele's father) induna, and Mayekisa was Langalibalele's induna. Soon after Langalibalele was deposed, Mayekisa left Ntabamhlophe and moved with his family to the Free State where he lived in a farm belonging to a white man.

While Isaiah Shembe could not have witnessed the above events due to his age, he got to know about them through storytelling. His father, Mayekisa, was an important person in the Hlubi chiefdom and witnessing its destruction and

 | DOI 10.1163/9789004320628_002

being forced to leave it was very painful to him. These events then constituted a great part of the stories narrated to the young in the Shembe family. In *Isaiah Shembe's Testimony*, Isaiah Shembe says: "I heard from my father that I was three or four years old when Langalibalele was deposed" (Papini, 1999: 261). Isaiah Shembe's father did not say this in order to refer to his son's age, but Isaiah's age happened to be part of a larger and more significant story: the story of Langalibalele; of the destruction of the Hlubi chiefdom.

It is, perhaps, because he was highly regarded as an induna that Mayekisa's 'exile' from Ntabamhlophe was so painful to him. This is shown by the fact that he did not quite accept his new life in the Free State. As he was living amongst the Sothos, he did not allow intermarriage between his children and the Sotho speaking community. Amos Shembe, Isaiah Shembe's son and third leader of Ibandla lamaNazaretha who founded eBuhleni Village, tells in one of his undated tape-recorded sermons that Mayekisa, his grandfather, instilled this idea to his sons. He tells that when a certain Sotho man wanted to marry his aunt after Mayekisa had passed away, Isaiah Shembe and his brothers chased him away on the basis of his tribe being Sotho, not Zulu (A.K. Shembe, untitled sermon, undated). This is pretty significant for this study because some of Isaiah Shembe's hymns and sacred texts evince a kind of Zulu nationalism that has led most scholars to see him as concerned with Zulu ethnicity while he was interested in broad (South) African issues that impinged on every (South) African. I deal with this issue in more detail in Chapter One.

In this book I am interested in the way in which Isaiah Shembe uses the medium of hymns to imagine the South African situation like the tragedy that befell the Hlubi people and their chief, Langalibalele (even though he does not mention Langalibalele particularly in his hymns); the Zulu king Cetshwayo in 1879 (about which he tells that 'the war between the English and Cetshwayo was fought while we were at Coenraad's. We were uprooted by the Anglo-Boer war) (Papini, 1999: 260); as well as his present historical context. I explore these hymns as spiritual and sacred texts that have an ability also to speak to the 'burning issues' of Isaiah Shembe's time. In other words what I am proposing here is a reading that, while exploring the way in which Shembe used the genre of hymns to deal with socio-political issues, is not reluctant to acknowledge and engage with the spirituality and sacredness of these texts.

This reading is important because even though some of these hymns deal with 'political issues', they are predominantly religious texts used in worship and many times when performed their political content does not take centre stage in the minds of those performing them. For Nazaretha members, the hymns are believed to be "trans-global" texts (Hofmeyr, 2004: 9) that exist here on earth and in heaven. Also, the sacred dance, which forms a significant part of the hymns, is considered a form of worship in its own right and is believed to take place in this world and in heaven, as it is also believed to play a crucial role in one's spiritual journey to heaven. Also, it is common in Ibandla lamaNazaretha that members taking part in the sacred dance claim to be doing so on behalf of their dead relatives, as it is believed that ancestors are able to participate in those dances through the bodies of their living relatives. In return, those in the ancestral realm will reward the living performers by offering them 'blessings'. In Ibandla lamaNazaretha, and through performances like the sacred dance, the physical and spiritual worlds are perceived to be integrated. Thus I examine the sacred dance and the hymns as spiritual and sacred texts whose audience, and sometimes participants, are believed to be not only living people, but also those in the ancestral realm.

In examining these sacred texts and performances I try to respect the "agency" of their creators and their performers. Thus my reading goes beyond the view that Nazaretha performances are rituals of empowerment for the members, a majority of whom are economically, socially and politically marginalised (Brown, 1995), to look at them as significant on their own account. In undertaking the abovementioned task, I examine these hymns and performances in relation to what they are understood to be by the performers, rather than what they may seem to the outsider. Following White's suggestion, I pay particular attention to "their significance to the people who [perform] and [listen] to them" (White, 1989: 37).

My argument is that while the sacred dance (and sometimes the hymns) is supposed to be intended solely as worship, and performers are expected to perform in a unified manner and to dance primarily for the heavenly audience (Shembe/God and the ancestors), this is not always the case. Many dancers compete in the sacred dance and try to differentiate themselves as most adept dancers within particular groups and create their own personal vernaculars as individuals and as groups. This is contrary to what is expected and is ideal: that since the sacred dance was started by Isaiah Shembe as part of worship, the members who perform it are supposed to perform it as it was choreographed in Isaiah Shembe's time, but due to different groups modifying it to create their own personal vernaculars, it has changed somewhat over the years and this worries those senior members (and others not so senior) who want it performed perfectly. But, while there is this gap between what the sacred dance is and what it is supposed to be within the church, never is it understood to be a response to colonialism and apartheid.

Although the church that Isaiah Shembe founded, Ibandla lamaNazaretha, started as a local and ethnically specific church, today it has a strong national following, attracting members from all walks of life across ethnic groups, and has members as far afield as Mozambique and Zimbabwe. The church is rapidly growing in numbers. Thousands and thousands of people are baptised every Sunday in July and in January after the Nhlangakazi (Now Khenana for the Ebuhleni group)[1] pilgrimage. While there are no accurate numbers, the members of Ibandla lamaNazaretha are estimated at a few millions. This is a very significant growth because when Isaiah Shembe passed away, the church was estimated at about 40 000 members (Roberts, 1936). This growth, plus the church's "success in creating a religious presence which is distinctively African", causes Gunner to see it as a "force to be reckoned with in social, religious and political terms" (2002: 1).

But for many years this distinctively African identity has had a negative impact on the broader social perceptions of the church. Until fairly recently, Ibandla lamaNazaretha has been regarded by many to be the church of backward, uneducated and rural people. For instance, Kivnick, in her study of traditional black music and its role in the struggle against apartheid, mentions a conversation she had with her 'very Western' friend, Thandi Mphahlele. She says that Thandi laughingly gossiped about amaNazaretha, saying, "Though they live near the city, they do not live a city life. You will see them when we get there" (1990: 55).

In creating his Ibandla lamaNazaretha, Isaiah Shembe mixed and blended Christian and African forms, many of the latter being downgraded and prohibited in mainstream churches. His theology clashed with that of the nonconformist missionaries, whose intention it was, as the Comaroffs have noted, "to 'civilise' the native by remaking his person and his context; by reconstructing his habit and habitus; by taking back the savage mind from Satan, who had emptied it of all traces of spirituality and reason" (1991: 238). Some of the main issues of conflict were African song and dance, polygamy, and recognition of the ancestors. One of the most significant expressive forms in Ibandla lamaNazaretha is *umgidi* (the sacred dance) in which the performers' dress

1 Due to a number of splits that have taken place in the church over the years since the passing away of J.G. Shembe, Isaiah Shembe's son and successor, there are now about five groups of Ibandla lamaNazaretha and they have all been engaging in conflicts when it comes to the pilgrimage to Nhlangakazi. The biggest group, the eBuhleni group, under the leadership of iNkosi Mduduzi Shembe (UNyazi) has founded a new mountain called Khenana where they go to during the January meeting.

includes loinskins, headties and other attire made from animal hides. The sacred dance itself involves the beating of cowhide drums and the singing of hymns composed by Isaiah Shembe, and is arguably an improvisation on the dances that took place in pre-colonial society, which were labelled 'uncivilised' and 'anti-Christian'.

Isaiah Shembe's hymns were important because the hymns that were in existence in isiZulu prior to Isaiah Shembe and during his time were mainly translations of the English hymns from orthodox churches; something which Bengt Sundkler has lamented:

> One of the most striking – and disconcerting – examples of the White man's dominance even in his spiritual matters over his Zulu co-religionists is this fact that Zulu Christians have not felt led to express their new faith in the composing of songs and hymns of their own, whereas this is quite common in certain Mission Churches in East Africa. (1948: 193)

Isaiah Shembe's contribution therefore was unique in that he created his own original hymns, not ones based on those of orthodox churches. In doing so he drew on pre-colonial African song and the Bible, and used the genre of hymns to articulate his own feelings and ideas. Not only did he make a contribution to the genre of hymns, but he also made a good contribution to South African and African literary history. It is this contribution to South African and African literature that this book seeks to unveil.

The missionaries' endeavours, however, were fruitful only with regards to a fraction of African society, and this led to the division of the Africans between the *kholwa* (labelled *amambuka* (traitors), black Englishmen, *Ama*Respectables and *amazemtiti* (the exempted) on the one hand, and the traditionalists (heathens, pagans) on the other hand. Writing about the ambiguous position of the *Kholwa*, Paul La Hausse maintains that:

> Although many *Kholwa* could trace their ethnic origins to pre-colonial Hlubi, Tlokwa, Sotho, Zulu and Swazi lineage societies outside Natal, having accepted Christianity and the new way of life which went with it they typically found themselves excluded from the traditional societies of which they, or their parents, originally had been part. This was a form of marginality in which many *kholwa* were more than willing to collude since their emerging self-identity hinged on the self-conscious assertion of their collective distance from pre-colonial roots. And yet at the same time they remained without the political and legal rights required to defend their position within the colonial political economy. (1996: 10)

Among the most notable of the *kholwa* was John Langalibalele Dube, founder of the Zulu-English newspaper, *ILanga laseNatal;* first president of the South African Native National Congress (SANNC), forerunner to the African National Congress (ANC); and founder of Ohlange, an industrial school based on Booker T. Washington's Tuskegee Institute (with its strong principle of black self-help and upliftment). The relationship between Shembe and Dube was a complex one: the two men being regarded as friends by some,[2] but constantly engaged in moral and ideological conflicts. Their relationship was entangled in the divide between the heathen and the converts, and the educated and the uneducated alluded to by La Hausse above. Addressing a group of mainly white South Africans, J.L. Dube distanced himself and all the Kholwa from the heathens:

> Go into a native Christian home. It was a humble dwelling, but it had a door which swung on its hinges, and through which a man might walk erect as became his dignity, and there was a window or two to let in the light of heaven, and separate apartments for the sexes, and a bed to sleep upon, and a table to eat from, and chairs to sit upon, and a book or two to read; and last, not least, all livestock was harboured outside. (Laughter and applause.) All humble and plain, but compare it with the hut of a heathen, into which one must crawl like a reptile, to sit on the floor in the darkness along with goats on the one side and calves on the other; with no other furniture than divers evil-smelling things in the hinder portion of the building. Who was it that taught this cleaner and more comfortable life? Who was it that taught the decency and the benefits of wearing clothes? (1911: 116–117).

About J.L. Dube and Isaiah Shembe's relationship Joel Cabrita remarks that it was characterised by "friendly co-operation and mutual respect" and at the same time marked by "rivalry and hostility" (2007: 47). This relationship between Isaiah Shembe and John Dube (as well as other *kholwa* ministers) still forms an important part of Ibandla lamaNazaretha's repertoire in sermons even though it is more centred on 'rivalry and hostility' than 'friendly co-operation' and 'mutual respect'. In one of Isaiah Shembe's praises, this relationship is thus captured:

2 Brown refers to John Dube as "Shembe's friend and biographer". (1999: 212).

Undab'ezavel'obala	The news that came to the fore
Zavel'emehlwen'amadoda	In the eyes of men
Ubuzwe yizazi kwelaseNanda	He was interrogated by the wise men of Inanda
UJan Dube umfokaNgcobo	John Dube of the Ngcobo clan
Lavum'i Bhayibheli,	The Bible consented,
Lavum'itestamente	The Testament consented
Wadana.	And he was disappointed.[3]

A number of scholars have researched and written about Ibandla lamaNazaretha, and their studies have resulted in a number of monographs, theses, journal articles and so on. Due to the work of these scholars there is a body of academic literature on the church. As Oosthuizen noted in the early eighties, "No other independent church (i.e. a church which is not part of the main line historical churches) has attracted more attention from scholars involved in the study of the independent church phenomenon than The Church of the Nazarites" (1981: 1). This is still true, and a number of scholars from disciplines other than religion (like literary studies, ethnomusicology, and performance studies) have done their own studies. These have been mainly white scholars from Western universities.

While I have great respect for these scholars and their achievements, their work has tended to reflect more of their pre-occupations and the demands of academia than of Ibandla lamaNazaretha itself. The reason for this is not hard to find. It is not easy to talk about religion in academic terms, worse still to talk about a religion whose ideas one does not (or cannot) share. In the Introduction to *How Should We Talk about Religion: Perspectives, Contexts, Particularities*, James Boyd White remarks that,

> one's religion's deepest truths and commitments, its fundamental narratives, appear simply irrational, even weird, to those who belong to another tradition, or are themselves simply without religion. This means that in any attempt to study and talk about a religion other than one's own, there is a necessary element of patronization, at least whenever we are studying beliefs we could not imagine ourselves sharing. (2006: 2)

While I do not claim an authentic voice in writing about Ibandla lamaNazaretha, I am, however, writing about beliefs that I predominantly share, and so

3 The praise poem is taken from M. Mpanza, *Ushembe NobuNazaretha*. (n.d.) Inanda: Durban. All translations in this book are mine, unless otherwise stated in the text.

I hope that the "element of patronization" that White alludes to is not applicable in my case.

However, the problem White mentions is not only limited to religion. A.C. Jordan has made a similar claim: that American and European scholars who have studied Africa have come up with superficial books. This is simply because they have "only superficial knowledge and understanding of Africa" (1973: vii). J.G. Shembe, Isaiah Shembe's son and successor, voiced a similar concern in 1968 in one of his July sermons:

> *Nani, uNkulunkulu unikhethile, wanenza naba yinhloko yezizwe eziMnyama. NabaMhlophe uma befuna uNkulunkulu baye beze lapha eKuphakameni. Bafika njalo abafundisi bamaLuthela bezobhala okwenziwayo lapha. Kodwa uma ngibuka sengathi babhala okungaphandle kuphela, okungaphakathi abakuboni. Abaze bawubone lo moya okhona phakathi kwethu. Baye babuke nje amabala angaphandle, bangakuboni okungaphakathi.*
>
> You too, God chose you and made you heads of Black nations. Even the Whites if they want God they come here. Ministers of the Lutheran Church constantly come to write what is being done here. But it seems to me that they write only what is outside, they do not see what is inside. They do not see this spirit which is amongst us. They just look at the outside colours and never see the inside.

In some cases this failure to see the 'inside' is unintentional; it is not because of the patronizing element that White talks about. But it is the demands of Western universities and the fact that these scholars come up against Ibandla lamaNazaretha as a research topic that they have mainly failed to reflect ubuNazaretha in their studies. In Becken's words, even though these scholars try to be unbiased, "they inevitably [look] at the life and history of Ibandla lamaNazaretha through their own glasses. As a result, they [understand] the Church within the framework of their own concepts" (1996: x).

This has resulted in these scholars producing works only meaningful to themselves and their academic colleagues, but almost unrecognisable to the members of the church who are the subjects of those works because those studies are far removed from what amaNazaretha understand to be the case. In Spivak's terms, in trying to represent Ibandla lamaNazaretha, they have ended up "representing themselves as transparent" (1988: 275).

Since they have looked at the church "within the framework of their concepts", their studies have generally disappointed and at times annoyed those members of the church who can read. For example, Minister Vilakazi was very cross with Carol Muller's *Rituals of Fertility and the Sacrifice of Desire* (1999). While he was not impressed with a number of things, what really angered him was that, he claimed, Carol Muller had written that J.G. Shembe was murdered. And Mthembeni Mpanza, who co-authored *Shembe: The Revitalisation of African Society*, read a thesis by one of the European scholars and was so displeased by it that he called me and said: "She is biased! We must write a book and respond!"

These scholars have done etic studies of Ibandla lamaNazaretha and the responses mentioned above are therefore not surprising. In studying institutions like Ibandla lamaNazaretha, one needs rather an emic approach, which is what this book provides. An emic study or system, according to Pike (1999), is more attuned to what is relevant within the institution being studied while an etic one focuses on a "logical plan" that is relevant to the outsiders. Sapir made an observation in the late 1920s which explains the above-mentioned conflict between scholars who have written about Ibandla lamaNazaretha and the members of the church. This is worth quoting at length:

> It is impossible to say what an individual is doing unless we have tacitly accepted the essentially arbitrary modes of interpretation that social tradition is constantly suggesting to us from the very moment of our birth. Let anyone who doubts this try the experiment of making a painstaking report [i.e. an etic one] of the actions of a group of natives engaged in some activity, say religious, to which he has not the cultural key [i.e. a knowledge of the emic system]. If he is a skilful writer, he may succeed in giving a picturesque account of what he sees and hears, or thinks he sees and hears, but the chances of his being able to give a relation of what happens, in terms that would be intelligible and acceptable to the natives themselves, are practically nil. He will be guilty of all manner of distortion; his emphasis will be constantly askew. He will find interesting what the natives take for granted as a casual kind of behaviour worthy of no particular comment, and he will utterly fail to observe the crucial turning points in the course of action that give formal significance to the whole in the minds of those who do possess the key to its understanding (1927, in his *Selected Writings*, 546–547, quoted in Pike, 1999: 30).

Nevertheless, this book does not try to respond to the PhD thesis Mpanza was talking about, as it is not meant to respond to Carol Muller's book (or any other work for that matter), even though it does take her and others to task for some issues raised in their works. What I attempt to do is write a book that remains a respectable contribution to academic scholarship, while being true to the people who provide the material that has made it possible. I try to combine the 'outside' and the 'inside' that J.G. Shembe talks about above. In other words, this study is particularly interested in an 'emic' representation of Ibandla lamaNazaretha, while it does not ignore the 'etic' one. It is this combination of 'emic' and 'etic' perspectives that makes this book unique and a valuable contribution to the research on Ibandla lamaNazaretha.

However, this book's contribution is not limited to this unique contribution to the scholarship on Ibandla lamaNazaretha, but it also makes a significant contribution to the scholarship on African-language literature and (South) African literature in general. It is of special significance for African-language literature because there is a dearth of critical scholarship in this field as there is of creative output. Nhlanhla Maake has remarked that "It can be said with a degree of truth that the literature [in African languages] has not yet, qualitatively and quantitatively, achieved the standards of Afrikaans and English literature, and that both creative *ecriture* and critical writing are unpolitical, and have not established a bond with African literature as a whole" (2000: 127). Also Karen Barber and Graham Furniss make a similar claim, making an example of Zimbabwean literature: "Novels in Shona and Ndebele outnumber Zimbabwean novels in English nine to one, but when it comes to the number of scholars studying them, the ratio is reversed" (2006: 4). Perhaps most relevant for this book is a remark by Innocentia Mhlambi that the 'dominant approaches' in the field,

> Have narrow paradigms that cast African-language literature to the margins, parochially sticking to the writings by the elite, as self-appointed cultural gatekeepers, to the total exclusion of varied and often fascinating, emergent, popular forms from a wide cross-section of society. (2012: 11)

Isaiah Shembe's hymns and the sacred dance in Ibandla lamaNazaretha are examples of the 'emergent popular forms' Mhlambi is talking about. In exploring these popular forms then, I am particularly interested in the way Isaiah Shembe contributed to (South) African literary history. The first two chapters look at the hymns as Isaiah Shembe's creative compositions through which he was able to express his views and ideas, using them to engage with thorny political issues in the case of Chapter One and appropriating the Bible to compose his unique texts in the case of Chapter Two. A point is made about the composition of the hymns: that while many people claim that the hymns came with the messengers of heaven, this is not born out in my reading as

I try to show that Isaiah Shembe was creatively involved in their composition. This is explained in more detail in Chapter One. From Chapter Three onwards the focus is on the sacred dance, but a number of hymns are explored within those chapters.

Conducting this research within Ibandla lamaNazaretha has presented unique challenges for me both in the church and in the academy. While I do believe that my position as 'insider' and 'outsider' comes with a number of possibilities, it creates its own problems and challenges. One of these is the fact that since there has been splits in the church since 1976 when J.G. Shembe,[4] (who led the church after Isaiah Shembe) passed away, my research can only be limited to the group that I belong to: Ebuhleni. While scholars coming from outside may visit the Ebuhleni group as well as the others, I cannot because I am most likely to be identified as a Nazaretha member of another group and be taken to have some hidden agendas. Also, being seen to be attending services in other groups may not sit well with those in Ebuhleni: this could lead to excommunication! However, this limitation only applies to the present activities in these groups, and the possibility of interviewing older members there. As for the older sources, I have as good the access as any. And the fact that Ebuhleni is by far the largest group (much more than treble all the five groups combined), means that my sample has not been badly affected.

Related to this problem is the fact that even within Ebuhleni I may be seen as someone dangerous. One of the senior ministers asked me to come with my own local minister if I wanted to interview him because he needed to be sure that I do not come from the other groups. Another thing is that being the church that has been seen as backward and of the uneducated people, its stance towards educated people is ambiguous. At one point it is welcomed that the church can no longer be accused of being the domain of the backward and uneducated. But educated people are still considered with a bit of distrust. The fact that a number of those who seceded to form what is generally known as the Thembezinhle Temple group after the 2011 split (when MV Shembe, Isaiah Shembe's grandson and second leader of Ebuhleni, passed away) had some kind of tertiary education, and the fact that their leader, Vela

4 For a discussion of the splits in the church see G.C. Oosthuizen, "Leadership Struggle within the Church of the Nazarites-Ibandla lamaNazaretha," *Religion in Southern Africa* 2 (2) July 1981; and J.E. Tishken, "Whose Nazareth Baptist Church?: Prophecy, Power, and Schism in South Africa," *Nova Religio: The Journal of Alternative and Emergent Religions* 9 (4) 2006: 79–97.

Shembe, has a university degree, compounds this problem. For instance, in the meeting in Mzimoya Temple in Msinga (KwaZulu-Natal) I met two members I had known from Maqhaweni Temple in Gauteng. They were very surprised to see that I had not gone to Thembezinhle, because, they maintained, all the educated members had 'strayed' to Thembezinhle to be under iNkosi Vela's leadership. And, there is a line in the praise poem of the new leader, Unyazi Lwezulu (Lighting of Heaven), which captures well the position of being educated in Ibandla lamaNazaretha. It says, "Zajabh' izifundiswa" [The educated were disappointed!].

This book also involves rituals for virgin girls, and as Ibandla lamaNazaretha is a 'gender divided' church, dealing with these rituals and the issues of gender generally has been problematic. While one can safely argue that Ibandla lamaNazaretha is male dominated; my position as a male member of the church did not offer me an unfair advantage. If anything, it was a disadvantage because a man is not allowed in the place where either married women or virgin girls are gathered for their special rituals. The information I have used here is mainly what I have been able to gather over the years through conversations and sermon performances. It is normal in the church that when the all night meetings for married women, (called *u*-14, beginning on the evening of the 13th of every month and ending in the morning of the 15th); for virgin girls (called u-25, beginning on the evening of the 24th of every month and ending on the morning of the 26th); and for men (called u-23, beginning on the evening of the 22nd and ending on the morning of the 24th) happen to coincide with the Sabbath, each group is offered an opportunity to preach on that Sabbath. It is here that a man can hear about some of the things that women talk about in their seclusive meetings. Also, sometimes one of these rituals may be held in one member's home, and if this is the case those who are not allowed to join can at least watch the initiation of the ritual (where all the members go to the gate and pray, before they enter the home singing Hymn No. 173 "Mdedele Angene" [Let Him/Her Enter]) and the sacred dance, and all go away when the dancing has ended. Lastly, having been raised by a woman who was a member of the Church and who regularly attended u-14, and being married to a woman who also attends u-14 regularly means I have gotten to get a sense of what happens in the women's gathering (u-14) even though one is not allowed to talk about what is said there.

Added to that, I have interviewed a number of virgin girls and married women who used to take part in the rituals for virgin girls. Knowing that I am a member of the church has made my female interviewees quite comfortable talking to me about many aspects of the church. It was only in my interview on 14 March 2015 at my office in the University of Zululand, KwaDlangezwa (KwaZulu-Natal, South Africa), that the virgin girls I interviewed were at first reluctant to discuss 'virginity testing' with me. But when I explained to them that I did not want to talk about the details of the actual 'testing', but rather how they felt about it and when and how did they begin doing it, they began to feel comfortable and shared their stories and their views more freely. At the end of the interview, one of them urged me: "Don't forget to tell them that Shembe is God!"

And on the part of the academy, I have also been viewed with a bit of distrust. When I presented my proposal for my MA research on the narratives of near-death experiences in Ibandla lamaNazaretha to the staff of the English Department at the University of KwaZulu-Natal, one of them, who ended up being my supervisor, accused me of trying to 'confirm' my church in undertaking this research. The same happened with the PhD. My credibility as a scholar capable of conducting this research was questioned by the school of Literary Studies, Media and Creative Arts' higher degrees committee. Their concern was that being a member of the church I might not be 'objective' enough when I do my research, especially when I write on the church. So in that way I have been working on an oppressive environment in which I have been conditioned by an attempt not to seem to be confirming my church, and to show that I can be as 'critical' as any outside scholar can be.

It is a positive feature of my subjectivity that I do not or did not come up against the church as a scholar looking for a research topic, but I chose to write about the religious institution that I have known for as long as I can remember, and which continues to be a significant part of my life. Having been born and raised within Ibandla lamaNazaretha by illiterate parents, one of the most prominent books I learnt to read as a child is the *Hymns of the Nazaretha* (Izihlabelelo zamaNazaretha) that I am studying here. The original language, in which the hymnbook is written, IsiZulu, is my mother tongue and the only language that my parents could speak and therefore that was ever spoken at home as I grew up. My knowledge of the Zulu language is far better than that of the English language I am using here, and as such, it has come naturally to me that, although there are translations of the hymns available, I have done my own translations as I noted above regarding the translation of Isaiah Shembe's praise poem.

It was in July 1991 that I was baptised as a member of Ibandla lamaNazaretha in Ebuhleni at the age of sixteen. Although it was the first time I had attended the July meeting, I had attended big congregational meetings sparingly whenever A.K. Shembe and the congregation visited my local temple, Nkonzenjani, in Ntabamhlophe, Estcourt. The first such visit that I remember was in 1985. It was here that I had my first encounter with the 'sacred dance of all people': the sacred dance that takes place in the congregational meeting involving all the different groups of the members, the men, married women and maidens.

Even though I was not forced to get baptized in 1991, I still did it as my mother's son. By this time, even though I associated with the church, and believed and was fascinated by the stories that circulated regarding Shembe and Ibandla lamaNazaretha, I was still not as actively involved or committed as I was to be later on. My own conversion happened in 1994 in the form of a dream. Before this time, I hardly went to church on Saturday/Sabbath, but I used to play soccer with my agemates. However, I was still involved in the Nazaretha faith because at home we did the evening prayer every day and I would alternate with my elder brother in reading the evening prayer from the hymnbook.

Then one Monday night I had a dream. I was at home and I could see some men coming to attack us (or me). I thought as we always prayed, in the name of God/Shembe, those men were not going to be able to enter the gate. They entered. Then I said they would not enter the house I was in. They did. Lastly I said they would not be able to enter my room. But, when the door opened, and somehow I was no longer on my bed but kneeling on the floor, it was not those men who entered but one man I did not recognise. He had a staff on his right hand, ready to stab me with it. He asked, "Usonta kwaShembe wena?" [Are you a member of the Shembe church?] I said "Yes." Then he said, "Yile ndaba awuhambi; yikho ngingakwazi nje." [It's because you never go anywhere; that is why I do not know you.] When I woke up and realised that it was just something in-between a dream and a nightmare, I did not know that my life had changed. On the Sabbath of that week I found myself going to church and a week after that up until today. I felt as if I was searching for that man, or trying to get him to know me.

Before this dream I had hardly went to u-23. But since then I have gone there regularly, rarely missing it and this only if there is something really important. It is in these twenty-three meetings that men learn the sacred dance, and it was during this time that I also learnt it. So I have participated in the sacred dance in twenty-three and in other contexts countless times. Taking part in the sacred dance of all people requires one to be 'complete' and to have a complete dancing uniform. So it was only in 2003 that I started participating in the sacred dance of all people. This was in February in Nkonzenjani when uThingo and the congregation had visited there. I have since participated many times in different temples, but especially in Ebuhleni.

For me, what the sacred dance is can hardly be separated from what it is to any member who participates in it. Except that, I have begun lately to study it as part of the project which has culminated into the writing of this book. I have begun effectively to make notes of things that would otherwise be taken for granted. To an extent that if this were to be read by members of the church, the response would be unlike the ones discernible when some 'foreign' researchers have written on the church, as I have shown some examples above. I believe that while many members may not agree with some of my observations, they would mostly agree with and relate to most of what is written here. However, there is no denying the fact that studying the church and the hymns has meant some kind of reconsideration of my sense of self as a member of the church. As I write this book, I am constantly aware of my subjectivity: I keep checking that I am not clouded by my position as a member of the church while at the same time making sure that I do not fall into the trap of writing about the 'outside' only.

So I believe that my 'closeness' to the church puts me in good stead as a writer of this book since I have been involved in the church ever since I can remember and even though this book is based on the research I conducted mainly between 2006 and 2010 for a PhD, a great deal of it comes from my experience and knowledge garnered over a much longer period of time as I have stated my involvement in the church.

In her *Rituals of Fertility and the Sacrifice of Desire* Carol Muller laments the fact that Nazaretha women cannot write their own stories: "Certainly, it will be better for all when Nazarite women begin to write their own stories and to represent themselves" (1999: 15–16). While this is a noble call on Muller's part, it needs to be understood that the Nazaretha women she talks about are not worse off because they cannot represent themselves "in her own medium": in a scholarly book that she herself has written for her academic audience. They do represent themselves where it matters to them; in oral narratives and in sermons meant for the ears of their fellow Nazaretha members, who understand those stories the same way as they do and share the same beliefs.

That said, this book may be regarded as an attempt at the self-representation that Muller calls for, and tries to look at Ibandla lamaNazaretha through the 'glasses' of one of its own members. I am, however, aware that my position as a member of the church does not make me "a representative consciousness (one representing consciousness adequately)" (Spivak, 1988: 275), and that this work will of necessity be influenced by my subjectivity as a member of the community I am examining. While I attempt to be as 'objective' and self-reflective as possible, I nevertheless believe that if this work reflects greater 'interestedness' in the church as a result of my involvement, this may offer a necessary corrective to the tendency identified by Becken and others mentioned above.

I am also aware of the fact that my audience is mainly non-members of the church. The medium, in which this information is presented, in the English language and in an academic book format, means it will be inaccessible to most members of the church. And the fact that it is published by an overseas publisher makes it even harder to find for those members who are interested in books and can read English. It will also be highly expensive, and almost impossible for many to afford.

Even though there is a body of literature on the church as I mentioned above, there has not been many book-length studies of Isaiah Shembe's hymns and the sacred dance in his Ibandla lamaNazaretha. Oosthuizen's book, *The Theology of a South African Messiah* (1967), looked at the hymns from the perspective of theology and argued that the hymnal needs to be viewed as a catechism of the church. Oosthuizen's book is arguably a colonialist account which sees a collective Zulu mind which is of doubtful capacity: "The Zulu mind, as expressed in the *izihlabelelo*, does not distinguish between physical and spiritual power" (1967: 61). There have been a number of responses to *The Theology*, mainly from scholars in the field of Religion and Theology, and most of them have been critical (See Vilakazi, Mthethwa and Mpanza, 1986; Hexham, 1997).

The other studies that have dealt with Isaiah Shembe and his church are mainly academic articles rather than books, and these include Brown, 1995; Gunner, 1982, 1986, 1988; Muller, 1997; Cabrita, 2009, 2010a, 2010b; and many others. It is so far only Carol Muller's book, *Rituals of Fertility and the Sacrifice of Desire* that has intensively dealt with the hymns and rituals that I explore in this study. While *Rituals of Fertility* is a useful contribution to literature on Ibandla lamaNazaretha, it has a number of flaws that I hope this book will correct. Firstly, it is concerned with only the performances of female members of Ibandla lamaNazaretha, and excludes men's. This makes her underscore some features of the church as particular to women, while in fact they obtain in the case of men as well. For instance, she argues that virgin girls have to 'sacrifice' their sexual desire in order for them to obtain Shembe's protection. As I argue in Chapter Four, this is an overstatement on Muller's part as she seems to suggest that these young women are expected or encouraged to stay virgins forever, but in actuality what is emphasised is sexual abstinence before marriage, and this abstinence is required from both men and women. This book, on the other hand, explores both men's and women's performances and thus presents a more complete picture.

Secondly, as she is dealing with female members' performances, she leans towards a feminist theoretical approach, and this affects her understanding and interpretation of the church and its expressive forms. In other words, in Becken's terms, she "understands the Church through the framework of [her] concepts". For example, she recounts an interesting narrative by a Nazaretha woman and her analysis of this narrative seems to me to imply a "representation of herself as transparent" (Spivak, 1988: 275). In this narrative, a woman tells a story of another woman who once went to u-14 and when she came back, she found that someone had broken into her house and stolen her belongings. She then complained to Shembe, "But *Baba* Shembe, how can I go to praise you, where you said we must go as women, when I come home and all my things are stolen?" (Muller, 1999: 241). When this woman returned from u-14 of the second month from the incident, she found that she could not open the door to her house. She then called the neighbours who helped her break open the door. Inside, they found a man with bags and he told them that he was the one who had stolen the woman's belongings and he had come to steal again. But when he had taken the things and was about to leave, Shembe appeared and locked him inside.

Muller's analysis of this narrative reflects more about her and her intentions than about the woman who told this story and the woman to whom this incident happened. In her Introduction, Muller confesses her feminist connections and her study in Ibandla lamaNazaretha is particularly concerned with gender issues. It is therefore unsurprising that her analysis is articulated as follows: "To the outsider, this story may seem to have many parallels in the experiences of women of faith all over the world ... There is more to this story than immediately meets the eye, however, particularly as one discovers the use of metaphor in the text. The central metaphor here is that of the house, which I propose represents the female body – the womb specifically" (1999: 242).

For the woman who told this story, and all the members of Ibandla lamaNazaretha, the house in this story is not a metaphor for anything. Here, the woman is testifying to Shembe's supernatural powers and his 'omnipresence', as he is believed by the church members to be able to occupy more than one space at the same time. This means he can physically be in one place but through the spirit he can appear in other places where his messianic powers are needed. In sermons (and on many occasions in conversations) the Nazaretha members exchange narratives and testimonies of Shembe's miracles. These narratives and testimonies are central to all members of the church regardless of gender. This story could well be appropriated and retold by all members who have access to it, including men, as its central theme is the power of Shembe. Muller's reading of this narrative is a classic example of the limitations of an etic study.

Thirdly, Muller, as well as Brown in his article, "Orality and Christianity: The Hymns of Isaiah Shembe and the Church of the Nazarites" (1995), suggests that Ibandla lamaNazaretha's sacred texts, the hymns and ritual performances, are responses to colonialism and apartheid. I argue in this book that such a view 'Imposes a Western authority over a non-Western text' and thus offer more power to colonialism and apartheid than they actually had. In other words, this view gives undue credit to the West or the Centre, as all that happens in the periphery is supposed to be initiated in the centre according to it. At the same time this view deprives Shembe and the members of Ibandla lamaNazaretha of agency. Here I propose a reading of the hymns and the sacred dance as important in their own account, not as response. I read them as spiritual texts that speak to Shembe's socio-political context in the case of the hymns, and maintain that the sacred dance happened in spite of the wishes of the missionaries and the state, but Shembe did not initiate the sacred dance just to respond to either the missionaries or the state.

The main idea guiding this study is that religious institutions like Ibandla lamaNazaretha and their expressive forms, such as Isaiah Shembe's hymns with their accompanying sacred dance, need to be understood in terms of an emergent popular culture. Looking at these organisations as response not only curtails their agency, but it also results in their being treated negatively, "as a phenomenon of 'independency' or 'separatism'" (Fabian, 1978: 18), which implies that they exist only because their founders wanted to move away from more orthodox churches – that their overriding purpose is one of response to colonisation and missionisation. In contrast, examining these religious movements and art forms as an emergent popular culture is enabling because it provides a locus in which they can be read as agency.

While it is easy to classify art forms as examples of popular culture, it is not as easy to define what exactly popular art is. The problem emanates from the fact that popular art occupies the shifting space between what Barber terms "traditional" (rural, communally-created and mainly oral forms) and "elite" (individually created, high art) forms and it thus tends to be defined in terms of what it is not; "in terms of absences and deviations from the established categories"(1987: 11). Popular art (like Isaiah Shembe's hymns and the sacred dance) draws from both traditional and elite forms to create new syncretic forms of expression. As Barber argues, "the aesthetic is hard to pin down because it is, precisely, an aesthetic of change, variety and novel conjunctures" (1987: 12).

This study focuses on the postcolonial subjects (Isaiah Shembe and his followers) as agents who, in their encounter with Christianity and the Bible produce "readings often at odds with, or resistant to, the normative discourse of the missionaries" (Brown, 2009: 12), and thus it leans towards Postcolonial Studies. It deals with one of the religious groups that, in the words of Robert Young, "have taken on the political identity of providing alternative value systems to those of the west" (2001: 337). Even though Young's religions that "provide alternative value systems to those of the west" are only Islam and Hinduism, Brown points to the "abundant evidence of other religions, including various forms of indigenised Christianity, expressing 'subaltern concerns' (2008: 3–4). Ibandla lamaNazaretha is one of the religions that Brown is referring to.

Being a complex interdisciplinary theoretical approach that it is, the field of Postcolonial Studies is delineated in Musa Dube (2000) as:

> [involving] texts from different times, places, and cultures and whose boundaries often blur. It propounds a myriad of methods and theories, all of which examine literature and its participation in the building, collaboration, or subversion of global imperial relationships (Dube, 2000: 52–3).

A postcolonial hermeneutical approach, in the words of Jeremy Punt, "includes and gives voice to the voiceless, the muted voices of the colonised, the marginalised, and the oppressed" (2010: 6). The amaNazaretha members, and their leaders from Isaiah Shembe to the present leader Mduduzi Shembe (known to members as uNyazi), who are the subjects of this study are indeed "the colonised, the marginalised and the oppressed", but not "voiceless" and therefore this study does not profess to give them a voice. Instead, it examines the voice of the oppressed, the Nazaretha's voice, and renders it audible to the "oppressor" (both Western and native), who, thanks to the work that has been done on Ibandla lamaNazaretha (and other African Initiated Churches) is not completely unaware of the presence of this voice. I am also mindful of the significance of Brown's call for a 'South (or periphery) centred' approach to Postcolonial Studies: "rather than subjecting inhabitants of the postcolony to scrutiny in terms of postcolonial theory/studies, how can we allow the theory and its assumptions also to be interrogated by the subjects and ideas it seeks to explain?" (2009: 9). While this call is laudable, it is unclear who the "subjects" and their ideas are. In our case for instance, would a non-Nazaretha scholar who happens to be based in (South) Africa be better qualified to carry out this work? Are this scholar's ideas and those of the subject (the Nazaretha members) the same? As I mentioned above, while I am both "the scholar and subject", I cannot claim that I am representative of AmaNazaretha; I am still (in part) motivated and confined by the expectations and requirements of the academy.

That said, while Isaiah Shembe's blending of the Christian forms with the African ones, and his reading of and engagement with the Bible (I deal with this in Chapter Two) would definitely unnerve a number of people in the South (both academic and ordinary people), it is, however, an example of the South centred approach Brown is calling for, and here lies the significance of this book.

What guides and informs this study methodologically is summed up in Landeg White's suggestions on interpreting oral texts and performance genres:

> Ideally, in interpreting oral performance, one would wish to pay the closest attention to the actual meaning of the poems, supported by oral testimony of their significance to the people who performed and listened to them, and supplemented by investigation into the social position of the performers, into the context and contingencies of the performances and into the place of such poetry in the oral literature and general culture of the region as a whole. (1989: 37)

Addressing these areas is a complex but necessary task if one wants adequately to examine Shembe's hymns and the sacred dance in his church. Reading the hymns and performances on their own (outside their contexts) will be limiting because "cultural texts", as Keesing has warned, "no matter how rich – perhaps even because they are so richly allusive – cannot in themselves serve as the basis for ethnographic interpretation" (quoted in Coplan, 1994: 21). Some of Shembe's hymns cannot be understood without knowledge of their historical contexts. An example is hymn 172 from *Izihlabelelo ZamaNazaretha*:

Adedele Aphume	Let them go
We Mashi	Mashi
Akekho Umsengi	The Milker is away
We Mashi.	Mashi.

Reading this text on its own, one can argue that the speaker is deliberating about the milking of cows, and the calves that have to be isolated from their mothers. This sense of isolation and alienation is an important one, but its meaning becomes more painfully clear if one reads this text against another text which is referred to as "The Prayer for Dingana's Day":

> This is a terrible day today young girl of Zululand. The cow needed its milker that day... Old women... shouted to the boys and said to them, let them go my boys, no one is to milk them, their milkers are dead. (Nazareth Baptist Church, 1993)

These in fact are the words Isaiah Shembe said on the commemoration of the battle of Blood River, and they enhance our understanding of the context of the hymn. By reading the 'prayer' one realises that Shembe was in fact referring to the killing of many Zulus by whites, which meant that many young men who were supposed to milk the cows had died. Read on its own, without the Prayer text one would be unable to link the hymn to the event, and therefore one would not be able to offer an accurate interpretation. It is therefore important to heed White's suggestion to examine both the text and its context.

The book is structured as follows: The first two chapters deal with the hymns. Chapter One explores the hymns as sacred texts that speak to Shembe's historical context. It posits that Isaiah Shembe mixed oral and literate forms to create a medium in which he could articulate his experiences as an individual, as a Zulu and as a human being. I look at how his position or voice oscillates between Zulu nationalism, Pan-Africanism and humanism on the one hand, and 'otherworldliness' on the other. I argue that while some of the hymns evince a strong African nationalism, they at the same time exceed and go beyond African nationalism to speak to broader human issues. The hymns (as well as Ibandla lamaNazaretha and its sacred dance) are not simply a response to either colonialism or Christianity: they involve an articulation of identity in this world and in heaven.

Chapter Two looks at how Isaiah Shembe appropriates the Bible in his hymns. This is intended to show that Shembe was consciously involved in the creation of the hymns; that to say the hymns came with the messengers of heaven is not completely true and to further develop the argument made in chapter one that the hymns are not predominantly political, but they are first and foremost 'songs of worship'. The chapter begins by exploring the way in which Isaiah Shembe utilises the Bible to define and imagine his sense of self not only as a Zulu, African or human being but also as a spiritual leader of great prominence who was aware of his powers, both spiritual and political, and ends with Shembe praising God and Jesus Christ.

From Chapter Three onwards I deal with the sacred dance and what it means for Nazaretha members: that it is a form of worship and is considered by members to allow for the integration of this world and heaven. As such, not anyone can take part in it: members have to be ritually clean if they are to take part in the sacred dance because it is not just for themselves. Chapter Three engages with the view that the sacred dance was/is a response to colonialism and apartheid. It argues that such a view is problematic because it imposes a "Western authority over a non-Western text", thus offering colonialism and apartheid more power than they actually had. It further shows how far removed this idea is from what amaNazaretha consider the reason they take part in the dance.

Since the sacred dance, especially the 'sacred dance of all people' (taking place in the religious space where the congregation is gathered with the leader) is for heavenly spirits, people either qualify or do not qualify to take part in it.

One need to be 'complete' in order to qualify to take part in the sacred dance, and this means different things for men and women. Chapter Four examines what it means to be complete for the virgin girls or *amakhosazane*. It looks at the three rituals for virgin girls: virginity testing, *Umgonqo* and *iNtanda* as loci in which the virgin girls celebrate their virginity. Chapter Five looks at the notion of completeness for men by exploring circumcision as both a rite of passage and a way of ritual cleansing for both a man and his ancestors. It also looks at marriage as a way of rectifying or reversing 'incompleteness' for both men and women.

In Chapter Six I look at how different groups create their own particular styles when performing the sacred dance. I argue that, although there are standard ways of performing every song, some groups create their own vernaculars by adding some minor changes to the standard styles of dancing so that even the adept dancer would be unable to dance together with a certain group if he or she has not been 'practising' with them. Here the focus is on the agency of the performers themselves. I argue that although the sacred dance is Isaiah Shembe's creation, it is also to a large extent the work of the performers who keep modifying dancing styles to distinguish themselves from other performers, to perform better than the others so as to attract larger audiences and sometimes to please better the ancestors. Since the dance attire is an important part of the sacred dance and its poetics, I begin this chapter by describing different dance attires for different groups, namely, men, married women and maidens.

CHAPTER 1

Beyond African Nationalism: Isaiah Shembe and His Hymns

Introduction

The hymns of Isaiah Shembe, said to be "religious poetry of great beauty" by Sundkler (1961: 186) and "literary texts of great power and vision" by Duncan Brown (1999: 197), provided a medium for Shembe to articulate his views and sense of self. This genre of hymns provided Isaiah Shembe with a space where he could challenge colonialism and white domination (among other things), at the same time preaching a universal and humanistic gospel. This chapter seeks to locate Isaiah Shembe's hymns within the African and South African literary tradition. I am interested in how Shembe uses his religious poetry to engage with the 'burning issues' of his time. This is important because Zulu literature has been criticised for its eschewing of thorny social issues. I argue that while Shembe's hymns evince a strong African nationalism, they at the same time exceed or go beyond African nationalism to engage more universal issues and speak to the humanity at large. However, this engagement with politics in the hymns does not mean that they are generally about politics. The hymns that engage with the 'burning issues' which I discuss here are not representative of all the hymns Shembe composed; they are only a fraction of the body of his hymns.

One of the prominent features of Isaiah Shembe's hymns is that they tend to combine and mix expressive forms. They 'borrow' from both the traditional izibongo (praise poetry) and the modern western hymns, as much as they combine the oral and the written. What Barber and Furniss have remarked regarding African-language literature is very pertinent to Isaiah Shembe's hymns:

> African-language writing in general offers an unparalleled laboratory in which to ask questions about innovation and creativity;... about the innumerable, protean ways in which orality combines with literacy;... about cultural nationalism and forms of the imagination that exceed cultural nationalism. (2006: 1)

As noted above, my focus here is with "cultural nationalism and [the] forms of the imagination that exceed cultural nationalism." A number of scholars have

 | DOI 10.1163/9789004320628_003

commented and written about Isaiah Shembe's moulding together of the traditional and the modern forms, and the oral and written forms (Brown, 1999; Gunner, 1984). It is, therefore, not my intention to repeat these issues in this chapter.

Isaiah Shembe's hymns were meant to be sung by the members of his Ibandla lamaNazaretha when conducting services and when performing the sacred dance. They are now published in the church's hymnal, which was first published by Johannes Galilee Shembe in 1940. Isaiah Shembe composed 219 out of the 242 hymns in the hymnal that J.G. Shembe published in 1940, and that is still used, with some minor alterations, in the Ebuhleni group of Ibandla lamaNazaretha.[1] The translation of the hymnal has recently been published by Carol Muller (2010).

The Composition of the Hymns

Isaiah Shembe was not educated, so he could not write his own hymns. He had scribes, normally young women members of his church, who would write down the hymns as they "came" to him. I am putting "came" in scare quotes because the belief that is generally accepted by scholars that Isaiah Shembe's hymns came with the messengers of heaven is only partly true, and I have argued elsewhere (Sithole, 2011) that this view deprives Shembe of his creativity and agency. Sundkler has reported that:

> [Isaiah Shembe] would hear a woman's voice, often a girl's voice, singing new and unexpected words. He could not see her, but as he woke up from a dream or walked along the path in Zululand, meditating, he heard that small voice, that clear voice, which gave him a new hymn. He had to write down the new words, while humming and singing the tune which was born with the words. (1976: 186)

This shows the intricate relationship between orality and literacy that Barber and Furniss have noted regarding African-languages literature. But, with regards to the hymns being brought by a 'woman's voice', I am doubtful. While one cannot completely reject this explanation, there are a number of hymns that seem to me to challenge this view as they are related to documented

1 For the Ekuphakameni group, for example, Londa continued to compose his own hymns and the present leader, Vukile, also composes hymns although I can't say much about them.

historical events, and there is no doubt that Shembe created the hymns as reflections to those events. It is this reflection and engagement with current issues in artistic ways that make the hymns compelling and deserving of a literary recognition.

A close and contextual reading of some of the hymns negates the above understanding of the creation of the hymns. Hymn No. 3 is a case in point: it is based on Shembe's prayer before he and his followers took on a journey to Nhlangakazi in 1923. He had been informed by the authorities that he could no longer undertake his pilgrimage to Nhlangakazi without prior permission by the magistrate. When the time had come to go and there was no permit, Shembe decided to defiantly embark on his journey, and before he went, he said a prayer that was to form the basis for this hymn:

Nkosi Nkosi bubusise	Lord, Lord bless
Lobu buNazaretha	This Nazaretha Church
Uchoboze izitha zabo	Crush its enemies
Zingabuvukeli.	That they don't rise against it.
Vuka Vuka wena Nkosi	Wake up, wake up, Oh Lord
Mabulwelwe nguwe	Be the one that fights for it
Uzuhambe phambi kwabo	Travel ahead of it
Zingabuvukeli.	So they don't rise against it.
Noma siya entabeni	Even as we travel to the mountain
Owasikhethela yona	You chose for us
Ethiwa yiNhlangakazi	Called Nhlangakazi
Bungakhubeki.	Let it not falter.

Clearly, this hymn speaks to Shembe's situation at the time of composing it. The "enemies" that are spoken about are the state, the police and the missionaries (with the black believers); all those responsible for his predicament. He was here deliberating about his problem of being prohibited from undertaking a journey he had undertaken for the last five years or so. This then can only have come from his mind, not brought by some spirits. Sundkler's quote above should be understood in terms of the composition of the interview from which it came: A white scholar interviewing a black religious leader (of a church that had for many years been subjected to scrutiny by the state) in a country ruled unfairly by a white government. The statement could have been invoked by Isaiah Shembe and J.G. Shembe to channel people's attention away from the political nature of some of the hymns.

A number of Isaiah Shembe's hymns are said to be "prayers of the servant of sorrow" in their prefaces. These prefaces only appear in some of the later hymns, and I think that hymn No. 3 falls into this category, even though it does not have a preface stating this. The reference to hymn No. 129 says: *"Umthandazo wesikhonzi senhlupheko uShembe wafika ngesifingo sokusa esegumbini lomthandazo eKuphakameni ngomhlaka Julayi 22, 1926".* [The prayer of the servant of sorrow Shembe [which] came at dawn when he was in the place of prayer at eKuphakameni on 22 July 1926.] This suggests that Shembe was praying in the morning and his prayer formed the basis of this hymn. Many members, especially older members, sing hymn No. 129 in their prayers at four in the morning. The reason for this is that it started as Isaiah's prayer at dawn. Unlike "Wake me up Lord, I have been asleep" or "Wake with us, Father of Light" that are directly related to waking up, this one says nothing about the beginning of a new day. In the first stanza of this hymn the addressee is "the enemy":

Ungangilibazisi	Do not delay me
Wena sitha sami	You my enemy
Uma uJehova engibiza	If Jehovah calls me
Mangisuke ngimlandele.	Let me follow Him.

The enemy here is certainly the very same one that the Lord is called upon to protect the church from in hymn No. 3. But it may be referring to an inner conflict in Isaiah Shembe himself, as the second stanza suggests a persona who is feeling pain in his or her heart because of some wrong he/she has committed, and who has now lost hope:

Lihloma lingethwese	Thunder clouds come out of season
Enhliziyweni enecala	In the heart of the penitent
Ithemba lichithiwe	Hope is destroyed
Kumi ivuso lodwa.	Only apprehension remains.

But stanza three suggests that Isaiah was in fact targeting deserters who had been discouraged by the government's endeavours and those of the mission churches (the enemy) to destroy the church:

Akusibona Abangathandi	It is not that they do not like
Ukuza kuwe Nkosi	To come to you, Lord
Balahlekelwe ngamathemba	They have lost hope
Lwaphela uthando lwabo.	And their love has vanished.

This point is validated by what is referred to as "the vaccination controversy" (Hexham and Oosthuizen, 1996), where John Mabuyakhulu tells of the arrival of medical doctors at eKuphakameni to vaccinate AmaNazaretha, against Shembe's wishes. Only one man, Dladla, who was from Ntanda, went with his family to be vaccinated even though Shembe did not approve. Dladla claimed that he did not want to be arrested with his family. The vaccination issue created a heated dispute between Shembe and the authorities, but Shembe was adamant that his people would not be vaccinated. Dladla's action angered him so much that when Shembe was in Mpondoland after the July festival, he sent word to, "Expel this man, who went for vaccination, from the village of God and also from his residence at Ntanda. I do not want to see him, and I do not want his site and his fields, where he was living in the place of God" (Hexham and Oosthuizen, 1996: 146). My point here is that Hymn No. 3, "Lord, Lord bless this Nazaretha Church" can be seen as a prayer for the journey to Nhlangakazi as Hymn No. 129 "Do not Delay Me" is said to be a prayer. However, in these prayers, as well as in other hymns, one realises an expression of Shembe's feelings about his situation and experience and those of other people around him. For him, the government that prevented his and his followers' freedom of movement and choice was an "enemy" and needed to be "crushed". The government that forced people to accept medical help that they did not want (or he did not want) was delaying him. They were a disturbance to him and his mission.

Both Hymn No. 3 and Hymn No. 129 represent Shembe's resistance to the South African state of the 1920s. But what is resisted here is the state's interference with Shembe's mission, not that the creation of the hymns was part of a larger project primarily intended to be used as part of resistance. Joel Tishken writes about this issue and makes a good and valid point that,

> It would be a gross generalisation to presume that every individual in some sort of subordinate role was mired in a constant feeling of hegemonic oppression, and was therefore on a constant quest to find means to resist by any and all methods, public and hidden. (2013: 91)

However, Tishken stretches his argument too far when he claims that Shembe was completely and truly against resistance. He refers to Shembe's statement that, "God has given me certain work to do amongst my people. I therefore realise that God has also placed the Authorities over us, and those who disregard or defy the Government, disregard the Will of God" (2013: 91), and maintains that Shembe meant every word. He tells us that during the interview in which Shembe uttered these words, his interlocutor, McKenzie "explained to

Shembe what happened to the Israelites at Bulhoek two years earlier" and further stated to Shembe that he was convinced Shembe would not suffer a similar fate because "it is shown you are submissive to the Laws and I feel you will continue to do so" (2013: 90). The statement above is Shembe's way of assuring the representative of the state that he was indeed what they wanted him to be.

Tishken considers the possibility of Shembe saying those words to please his interlocutors: "[W]as he cunningly "playing politics", and becoming the agreeable and subordinate black church leader he thought whites and traditional authorities wanted him to be?" (2013: 91). The answer is "no" for Tishken, "Shembe was revealing his genuine political convictions" (2013: 91).

But in the two cases mentioned above, the vaccination issue and the issue of the pilgrimage to Nhlangakazi in 1923, Shembe did defy the authorities. He told his followers to do the opposite of what the authorities wanted, and went so far as to create hymns referring to the authorities as the 'enemy', something very different from what he said in the interview. What Tishken states about the makeup of the interview in 1923 would make one to come to a different conclusion from what he offers, even if one was only working with the official documents and testimonies, disregarding the hymns that came out of these incidences. These hymns, it seems to me, make it very hard to accept Tishken's supposition.

Another interesting hymn worth looking at on the subject of the composition of the hymns is Hymn No. 71. The composition of this hymn also challenges the ideas expressed in Sundkler's interview with J.G. Shembe. This hymn was created after one of the earliest members who joined Ibandla lamaNazaretha as a boy in the time of Isaiah Shembe, Meshack Hadebe, had a vision one night in 1922. In this dream Meshack saw Shembe divided into three forms. The first form was in the middle of the land, the second form, which seemed to shine like the morning star, was up in the north, while the third one was at the edges of heaven in the east (Gunner 2002: 155).

Having witnessed this, the boy heard a great voice saying, "Do you see Shembe? Listen! Before your Father Nyathi was born Shembe was already there, a man of the size he is now – just as you see him in these three partitions of land. I say, when your Father was not yet born Shembe was already there, and he was that very size" (155). The boy was perplexed, thinking that if Shembe was so much older than his father then he should have been very old but he did not look so old. Then the boy felt himself floating on the firmament, "like the book", and perceived the earth "poured out like porridge", the rocks soft as they must have been before solidification. After this he saw the Shembe in the middle walking over the land, treading down the pieces of porridge here and there. Then the voice spoke again, telling Meshack that, "Do you see Shembe? When the world was still just porridge Shembe was already there and was the same size that he is now" (155).

Hymn No. 71 is a direct reference to this dream narrative told by Meshack Hadebe, first to his father Nyathi and then to Isaiah Shembe, and later to the whole congregation. Before this dream happened, hymn No. 71 had not yet been composed and Meshack Hadebe maintains in his testimony that, "Jehovah was preparing the way for that hymn through that vision" (2002: 157). This statement is informed by Hadebe's belief about the composition of the hymns: that they are celestially composed and 'brought' down from heaven to earth. Suffice it to say here that this hymn seems to support such a claim, especially if we are to concede that dreams are a medium through which heavenly spirits communicate with the living. But even so, an interesting twist here is that it is through an ordinary member of the church, a mere boy, that this hymn is transported from heaven to earth. And even if it was this-worldly inspired, the role of the boy and his dream in the creation of hymn No. 71 are tremendously important. What is even more significant is that this shows Shembe creatively involved in the creation of the hymn from a dream that one of his followers had, rather than having it received ready made from some girl's voice.

The premise of hymn No. 71, like that of Meshack Hadebe's vision, is that Shembe existed in spirit long before he was physically conceived. His presence in the universe precedes the creation of the earth, which seems to place him on the par with God. Yet God's precedence and power over Shembe are not disputed. Drawing directly from the vision, Shembe is the first one of God's creations. As Jesus in the Bible claims to be God's first born and only son, Shembe in hymn No. 71 claims to be among many of God's creations, but the first one (or among the very first). Everything else, including the earth, the hills, the rivers, was created after him:

Nkosi yami ubungithanda	My Lord, you loved me
Zingakaqini izintaba	Before the mountains solidified
Kwaphakade wangigcoba	From eternity you anointed me
Ngiwukuqala kwendlela yakho.	I am the beginning of your way.
Ngiwumsebenzi wakho wasendulo	I am your work of long ago
Ingakaqini imimango	Before the hills solidified
Nemithombo yamanzi	And the fountains of water
Ingakampompozi ngamandla.	Were not flowing with strength.

Nemithombo yemifula	And the fountains of rivers
Ingakampompozi ngamandla,	Were not flowing with strength
UJehova wangidala	Jehovah created me
Ngaphambi kwendlela yakhe.	At the start of his journey.
Ukujula kungakabibikho	Before depth existed
Kukade sengizelwe	I was long born
Engakalenzi leli zulu	Before he created this heaven
Kanye nalo mhlaba.	And this earth.
Nelanga lingakakhanyi	Even before the sun shone
Emkhathini waleli zulu.	In the firmament of this heaven
Nenyanga ingakakhanyi	And even before the moon shone
Emkhathini walo mhlaba.	In the firmament of this earth.

Zulu Ethnicity in Isaiah Shembe's Hymns

Isaiah Shembe's grandson, and second leader of the Ebuhleni group, M.V. Shembe, made an important alteration to the hymnal, of which none of his predecessors had recognised the necessity. In the hymn-book that is used in the church today, verse 21 of the Sabbath Prayer reads: *"Ningabi njengokhokho benu, okhokho bethu abazenza lukhuni izinhliziyo zabo, uJehova waze wabajezisa kanje, namhla sesithwele izono zabo."* [Do not be like your forefathers, our forefathers who hardened their hearts, God then punished them like this, now we are carrying the burden of their sins.] Isaiah Shembe had written this verse as: *"Ningabi njengokhokho benu oDingana noSenzangakhona, okhokho bethu abazenza lukhuni izinhliziyo zabo, uJehova waze wabajezisa kanje, namhla sesithwele izono zabo".* [Do not be like your forefathers, Dingana and Senzangakhona, our forefathers who hardened their hearts, God then punished them like this, today we are carrying the burden of their sins.] The reason given by M.V. Shembe for this alteration is that it creates the impression that it was only the Zulu kings who carried the burden of sin while in fact all our forefathers sinned. He said he had seen the impact this verse had on one of the descendants of the Zulu kings, King Goodwill Zwelithini, when the King had visited Ebuhleni.

This reference to "our forefathers, Senzangakhona and Dingana" or "You descendants of Dingana and Senzangakhona" is common in Isaiah Shembe's hymnal. It points to the importance of the Zulu nation for Isaiah Shembe himself and the fact that he was believed and he believed himself, to have been sent to liberate the Zulus. As hymn No. 214 suggests:

Umkhululi wethu	Our Liberator,
Thina nzalo kaDingana	We discendents of Dingana
Simzwile ufikile.	We have heard him.
Umkhululi ufikile	The saviour, he arrived
Umkhululi usefikile	The saviour, he has arrived
WemaZulu sesimzwile.	You Zulus, we have heard him.
Nzalo kaDingana	You descendants of Dingana
Beno Senzangakhona	And Senzangakhona
Phaphamani ufikile.	Wake up, he has arrived.
Umkhululi ufikile	The saviour, he arrived
Umkhululi usefikile	The saviour, he has arrived
WemaZulu sesimzwile.	You Zulus, we have heard him.
Ukudinga kwethu	Our suffering
Thina nzalo kaDingana	We descendants of Dingana
Sekuphelile ufikile.	It has ended, he arrived.
Umkhululi ufikile	The saviour, he arrived
Umkhululi usefikile	The saviour, he has arrived
WemaZulu sesimzwile.	You Zulus, we have heard him.
Ukhumbule Nkosi	Remember, Oh Lord
Umsebenzi wezandla zakho	The work of your own hands
Wenzalo kaDingana.	Of the descendants of Dingane.
Umkhululi ufikile	The saviour, he arrived
Umkhululi usefikile	The saviour, he has arrived
WemaZulu sesimzwile.	You Zulus, we have heard him.
Zibike wena kuye	Tell him your sorrows
Wena nzalo ka Dingana	You descendants of Dingane
Beno Senzangakhona.	And Senzangakhona.
Umkhululi ufikile	The saviour, he arrived
Umkhululi usefikile	The saviour, he has arrived
WemaZulu sesimzwile.	You Zulus, we have heard him.

What emerges strongly from this hymn is that Isaiah Shembe is not just the liberator, but he is the liberator of the Zulu nation. The hymn speaks to the descendants of Dingana and Senzangakhona, the Zulus, about the news that concerns them. The hymn serves as an announcement and a celebration of the great news that God has finally remembered the Zulus and sent them a prophet, and it calls on them to open their eyes so that they will see that through Shembe their wants will be provided for. All they need to do is to tell Shembe their troubles, and he will solve those problems for them through prayer. However, the fact that Shembe singles out the Zulus as in need of a saviour or liberator is a subtle comment on the oppression that the Zulus and other black people were experiencing.

Many scholars who have studied Ibandla lamaNazaretha and Isaiah Shembe emphasise the fact that Isaiah Shembe was concerned with restoring Zulu society to its former state and glory. Hexham states that, "We can safely say that the mission of Isaiah Shembe was to restore the dignity of the Zulu person and the independence of their country… [His] aim was to restore his people to their previous glory and this he believed could be done on the basis of God's presence among the Zulu people in the same way as God had revealed his presence to ancient Israel" (1994: xxvii). In similar vein the argument of Vilakazi, Mthethwa and Mpanza is that in creating Ibandla lamaNazaretha Shembe was trying to forge a new Zulu society basing it on the old, pre-colonial one (1986). About some of the hymns, Mpanza has this to say:

> *La magama uShembe wabe ewaqambela isizwe samaZulu ukuba sithi uma sidumisa uNkulunkulu siwahlabelele, kodwa enomlayezo othile. Isihlabelelo 183 singumyalezo ngezizwe ezifuna izwe lakwaZulu.* (1999: 228)
>
> [These songs were created by Shembe for the Zulu nation to sing when they worship God, but they had a certain message. Hymn 183 is a message about the nations who want to take the land of the Zulu.]

Hymn No. 183 that Mpanza talks about is one of the most powerful and overtly political of Isaiah Shembe's hymns. The hymn is addressed to the Zulu people and it laments the anomaly of being led by outsiders in their native land:

Lalela Zulu	Listen Zulu
Lalela abantu bengiphethe	Listen to people ruling me
Ngezwe lethu.	About (In) our land.)

Here, Isaiah Shembe challenges white domination and the idea of the civilising mission. For him, what the white people brought in (South) Africa is destruction, certainly because it brings sorrow to the people and allows the outsiders to rule the native people. He likens them to the weaver bird (*ihlo-kohloko*), notorious for destroying people's fields:

Siyazizwa izizwe zivungama *Zivungama ngawe* *Njenge nyoni.*	We hear the nations grumbling Grumbling about you Like a bird.
Sish'izinyoni sish'amahlokohloko *Ayicekezel'insimu* *Ka Dingana beno Senzangakhona.*	We mean the birds, the weaver birds They destroyed Dingana's and Senzangakhona's field.
Bayiqedile mamo *Sizwa ngoMnyayiza* *Ka Ndabuko.*	They destroyed it completely We heard from Mnyayiza Son of Ndabuko.

The metaphor of the fields and the weaver birds refers to the South African land that the whites have confiscated and made their own as the weaver birds invade people's fields and feed on what is sowed there as if it is theirs. It also refers to the whole destruction caused by the colonial settlement on South African people. But according to the hymn the fields that are destroyed belong to Dingana and Senzangakhona, even though the white people had influence over all of South Africa and their actions impacted on all the black people.

However, it is my contention in this chapter that even when Shembe used the Zulus as the speaker or addressee in his hymns, his vision went beyond Zulu tribalism. He dealt with much broader issues concerning the whole of Africa. The hymn above could be read alongside Kofi Awoonor's (a poet from Ghana) poem "The Weaver Bird". Not only does this poem deal with similar issues as dealt with in Shembe's hymn, but they also use the same metaphor to refer to the whites' settlement in Africa and the impact of colonialism and missionization to the African people. In Awoonor's poem we are told that the "weaver bird" built its nest in the speaker's house, and because they did not chase it away, it came back "in the guise of the owner/ Preaching salvation to us that owned the house." In both texts the weaver bird, the whites, impact negatively upon the continent and its people. As Shembe claims in his hymn that the weaver bird destroyed Dingana's field, the speaker and his or her people in Awoonor's poem "look for new homes everyday/ For new alters [they] strive to rebuild/ The old shrines defiled by the weaver's excrement" (In Moffet and Mphahlele, 2002: 191).

Hymn No. 183 is preceded by an equally political and interesting hymn:

Wo kusile	Oh it has dawned
Wo kusile Zulu	Oh it has downed Zulu
Wena uthi makahlome!	You say Simakade must arm!
USimakade.	

Prefacing this hymn is a text stating that this is the "song of the Zulu nation when dancing for God (*Nkulunkulu*)" (Shembe, 1940: 139). This is followed by a reference to the biblical text, Psalm 150. While this preface points to the influence of the Bible on Isaiah Shembe's creation of the hymns and his introduction of the sacred dance in his Ibandla lamaNazaretha, what is striking in this hymn is the implied call to God (*Simakade*) to go to war. The reference to the Bible in the preface clearly relates to praising God with "tambourines and dancing" (verse 4), but the idea of God taking up arms is Isaiah Shembe's own, even though it might have emanated from his reading of other texts in the Bible. This idea of God fighting for his (chosen) people is also prevalent in the hymns of the Sabbath prayer where the message seems to be that through God black people in South Africa would be able to win the war against oppression and injustice, and they would end up being the rulers of their own country:

3. *Wasibusisa phezu kwemizi*	He let us rule over the homes
Yezitha zethu	Of our enemies
Ngokuba umusa wakhe	Because his grace
Uhlezi phakade.	Stands forever.
...	
6. *Sabusa phezu kwamaqguma*	We ruled over the hills
Nezintaba zawo	And their mountains
Ngokuba umusa wakhe	Because his grace
Uhlezi phakade.	Stands forever.

It seems that in all instances where the word "enemy" is used in the hymns it either refers to the white rulers of the country, or to both black church leaders and the white missionaries who tried to thwart Isaiah Shembe's religious endeavours. In the above verses Shembe imagines black people living in the spacious and expensive homes in which white people lived. In other words, he imagines an inversion of the entire socio-economic situation in South Africa. As is the case with "*WoKusile*" [Oh It has Dawned], the idea of the enemy in the Sabbath hymn makes one think of a God who is partial towards the marginalized, the ones He loves as He loved the Israelites:

Wasikhulula ngokusithanda kwakhe	He liberated us with his love
Ngokuba umusa wakhe	Because his grace
Uhlezi phakade.	Stands forever.

The only difference between the two hymns is that in the Sabbath hymn the addressees are the Nazaretha members (the opening verse says *Mbongeni uJehova maNazaretha/ Nezi zukulwane zenu.* [Praise Jehovah you Nazaretha/ And your posterity.]), whereas in "*WoKusile*" the addressees are the Zulu people.

African Nationalism in Isaiah Shembe's Hymns

In January 1923 Ndwedwe magistrate Mckenzie wrote: "It must be remembered that [Shembe] is the head of a large following of *mixed natives,* and there is always a danger, whatever Tshembe's present attitude may be, of his organisation, being in the future, *made use of by agitators for political purposes*" (Quoted in Papini, 1999: 250, emphasis in the original). The fact that Shembe was heading a large following of "mixed natives" is important for my argument in this section, because I argue here that Isaiah Shembe was not simply speaking to the Zulus or only concerned about their well-being. There is a sense in which he saw himself as an African speaking to other Africans. Writing about what he calls "Zulu specificity", I think Brown is correct to say that:

> Isaiah Shembe's hymns seem to me themselves to call into question any simplistic co-option of Zulu history in the cause of ethnic separatism, however, since they place Zulu dispossession in a broader Africanist context. The early history of Shembe parallels that of the SANNC, forerunner to the ANC, formed in 1912. Shembe's friend and biographer, John Dube, was a prominent member of the SANNC, and his vision of a nationalism across tribal divisions appears in certain ways to have impinged upon the church of the Nazarites, although without displacing the church's ethnic specificities. (1999: 212)

Whether it was, like Brown states, John Dube's nationalist ideas "across tribal divisions" impinging on Ibandla lamaNazaretha or not, I cannot say. But what is clear from reading the hymns and other texts of Isaiah Shembe is that like Dube, Shembe's nationalist ideology was characterised by a certain kind of instability. Like his educated contemporaries, Isaiah Shembe was torn between a broader Africanist vision and a need to tap into the possibilities offered by Zulu nationalism centred on the figure of King Solomon kaDinuzulu Zulu and the little power over land distribution that he still possessed. Dube's ambiguity when it comes to African nationalism and Zulu ethnicity could be detected very early on in his political career. In his *A Talk upon My Native Land* (1892), for example, his speech shifted from Zulu specificity to pan-African nationalism. In the text it is clear that Dube is bent on turning himself to a Black missionary, and as such he mimics his benefactors' (the non-conformist missionaries) discourse in which Africa is seen as a dark continent and the Africans (those not yet civilised through Western education and the civilising mission) as the savages devoid of reason and soul.

For Dube, the non-kholwa Africans are "sitting in the darkness of sin and superstition, and almost crushed beneath the iron heel of heathen oppression" (45). And he sees his duty as an enlightened person being the 'civilisation' of the heathen. He says that his intention in coming to America was to improve his condition so as to enable himself to do something towards "the enlightenment of a benighted people" (19). This benighted people are at times referred to as Zulus and sometimes as Africans. He asserts, in a way that betrays his ethnic ideology, that "The Zulus are the strongest and most intelligent of the Bantu race" (26) and that "as soon as the heathen Zulus become Christians, they change their way of dressing" (42). Yet towards the end of his speech, he talks of Africans and Ethiopians, not the Zulus:

> Oh! How I long for that day, when the darkness and gloom shall have passed away, because the "Sun of Righteousness has risen with healing in His hand." This shall be the dawning of a brighter day for the people of Africa ... Then shall Africa take her place as a nation among nations ... May the day speedily come when Ethiopia shall stretch out her hands unto God (47).

Isaiah Shembe's hymns are also characterised by this oscillation between Zulu ethnicity and African nationalism that permeates Dube's formulation above. However, it is important to note that, it was mainly in the 1920s, after his ousting as the President of the SANNC that Dube became more involved in regional, Zulu ethnic politics that led to the formation of Inkatha kaZulu in 1924. And it is during the same period that the relationship between Isaiah Shembe and the Zulu king Solomon became more remarkable. Inkatha KaZulu came into being due to the kholwa's endeavours to align themselves with the Zulu royal house, with Solomon kaDinizulu. Nicholas Cope associates the formation of Inkatha with the issue of land in South Africa in the wake of the 1913 Land Act:

> If there was one overriding issue which prompted the Natal kholwa to redefine their policy directions in the early 1920s, thus embarking on negotiations with the most influential of the region's tribal authorities, the Zulu 'king', it was the land issue. (1993: 97)

This interest in King Solomon was not only limited to the educated kholwa like Dube and his associates. Religious leaders, including Shembe, also tried to align themselves with the Zulu royal house. As it has been mentioned by many scholars writing on him, Shembe was interested in buying land for the poor and orphans all around Natal and Zululand, and as will be seen in Chapter Four, he did encounter challenges due to the 1913 Land Act. So it may be that he tried to create links with King Solomon for the same reasons as those of the kholwa. What is known for certain though is that Shembe married his daughter Zondi to Solomon in 1926, and composed a hymn, Hymn No. 116, that was clearly directed to Solomon:

Uyabizwa Nkosi Solomoni	You are called, King Solomon
Mntaka Dinizulu	Child of Dinizulu
Nalu udumo lukaJehova	The glory of Jehovah
Lusekuphakameni.	Is at eKuphakameni.

However, Shembe makes it clear that in calling Solomon, he does not exclude other non-Zulu people. While the Zulus are called upon to come to eKuphakameni with their king, the call is not just for them. Other tribes too, like the Bhaca and Mpondo, are called; as are all the other nations.

Yizani maZulu	Come you Zulus
Niyabizwa eKuphakameni	You are called in eKuphakameni
Udumo lukaJehova	The glory of Jehovah
LusekuPhakameni.	Is at eKuphakameni
Yizanini maBhaca,	Come you Bhacas
Yizanini maMpondo,	Come you Mpondos
Udumo lukaJehova	The glory of Jehovah
Lus' eKuphakameni.	Is at eKuphakameni.
Yizanini zizwe nonke	Come all you nations
Niyabizwa eKuphakameni	You are called in eKuphakameni
Udumo lukaJehova	The glory of Jehovah
Lus' eKuphakameni.	Is at eKuphakameni.

Another factor that seems to explain Brown's 'Zulu specificity' is the tendency amongst Black South Africans to refer to an African as *umZulu* for a Zulu person and as *umSotho* for a Sotho person. In other words for Dube and Shembe, as well as other Black Africans, due to this tendency they see no ambiguity in referring to the same people as Zulus and as Africans at the same time. This is further exemplified in many people calling *umqombothi* (African beer) *utshwala besiZulu* (Zulu beer) if they are Zulu, and *joala baseSotho* (Sotho beer) if they are Sotho.[2]

In the Introduction I mentioned that Shembe's growing up as an exile amongst the Sothos played a significant role in the moulding of his identity and inculcating in him Zulu ethnic nationalism and partiality towards Zuluness in a variety of ways. Not only was this strengthened by his father's agony caused by his exile from Ntabamhlophe and his need to keep his family purely Zulu by prohibiting intermarriage with Sotho people, this was also compounded by the fact that even though the Shembes were proud Zulus among the Sothos, their living together led to Isaiah Shembe's identity as a Zulu being doubted by some people. Oosthuizen states that some people believed that Shembe was of Sotho or Tswana descent, not Zulu (1981). This is clearly the result of his being brought up in the Free State amongst the Sothos, and his ability to speak Sotho fluently.

My argument here is that many scholars have overemphasised Shembe's concern for Zuluness, and thus downplay his broader pan-Africanist nationalism. The hymns I discuss in this section show that Shembe's work and concern went beyond Zulu specificity. Hymn No. 46, for instance, warns Africans about their oppression at the hands of colonialism: that it enslaves them and makes them a laughing stock to other nations:

Phakama Afrika	Wake up Africa
Funa uMsindisi	Seek your Saviour
Kuseyisikhathi esihle	It is still good time
Ziyakushiy' izizwe.	Nations leave you behind.

2 This point was driven home to me back in 1997 at Wits where we had an open day and the department of African Languages had prepared '*umqombothi*' to signify its representation of African culture. Interestingly, the woman who had brewed *umqombothi* was the only white member of staff at the time (I have forgotten her name). Being Zulu myself, I understood the beer she had brewed to be '*utshwala besiZulu*' (Zulu beer), so I was shocked when the then head of the department, Prof. Nhlanhla Maake drank the beer and said, "*Renoa joala baseSotho*" (We are drinking Sotho beer).

Phakama Afrika	Wake up Africa
Funa uMsindisi	Seek your Saviour
Namhla uyisihlekiso	Today you are a laughing stock
Sazo zonk' izizwe.	Of all the nations.
Phakama Afrika	Wake up Africa
Funa uMsindisi	Seek your Saviour
Namhla siyizigqili	Today we are slaves
Nezigqilikazi.	And female slaves.
Phakama Afrika	Wake up Africa
Funa uMsindisi	Seek your Saviour
Namhla siyizigqwashu	Today we are door-mats
Zokwesula izinyawo zezizwe.	For wiping other nation's feet.
Phakama Afrika	Wake up Africa
Funa uMsindisi	Seek your Saviour
Namhla amadodakazi akho	Today your daughters
Ayizigqili zezizwe.	Are slaves of other nations.

This hymn tries to conscientise Africans about their situation, and proposes that it is a strong religious leader like Shembe who can help liberate them. It seems to me that one of the things that attracted Isaiah Shembe to the concept of the Zulu nation was the work that Shaka had done in forging a strong nationalism, and his vision of bringing all the black nations under one leadership. J.G. Shembe, Isaiah Shembe's son and successor, said this in his tape-recorded sermon in eKuphakameni in 1968:

> *Abanye abantu baye bathi uShaka kwakuwuSathane. Sonke nje sikhule kushiwo njalo ezikoleni kuthiwa wuSathane uShaka. Kodwa uShembe ufike wathi uShaka kwakuyingelosi kaNkulunkulu. Wayethunywe eZulwini ukuba azogeza abantu abamnyama ezonweni zabo. Wayengazi-ke ukuthi kwenziwa kanjani lokho, wayekwenza ngomkhonto yena. Wayebageza ngomkhonto. Ezobenza futhi bathandane. Badle ngakhezo lunye. Ngiye ngifise sengathi uShaka engabuye avuke, aphinde akwenze futhi lokho. Kulokhu kwenyanyana kwabantu okungaka! Nalokhu kuzondana okungaka! Kodwa uShaka wabashiya abantu bakwaZulu bethandana kumuntu munye.*
>
> [Some people say Shaka was Satan. When we all grew up it was said in schools that Shaka was Satan. But Shembe said Shaka was an Angel of

> God. He was sent from heaven to cleanse black people from their sins. He did not know how to do that so he did it by the spear. He cleansed them by the spear. He also came to make them love one another. Eat with one spoon. Sometimes I wish that Shaka could be resurrected and repeat what he did. In this mutual disgust of people! In this hatred people have for one another! But Shaka left the Zulus loving each other as one person.]

While Shaka used force and violence in his attempt to create and expand his kingdom, an able religious leader would use spiritual power to attract people peacefully. Shembe loathed violence greatly, and one of the reasons why he disliked white colonialists was the pain and violence they inflicted on black people in the colonial wars, especially the battle of Blood River and the Anglo-Zulu war.

In the same way as the above hymn, hymn No. 17 "*Oshaywayo Akalahlwa*" (The one who is Beaten is never Forsaken) talks to the Africans and urges them to open their eyes to see their predicament. While this hymn shows that Shembe did not see himself as just a Zulu prophet (if he saw himself as a prophet), but as one sent to all black people especially, it also points to his shifting state of reference to African people, at times calling them Zulus or South Africans or referring to them as Africans:

Oshaywayo akalahlwa	The one who is beaten is never forsaken
Makangazideli	Let him/her not lose hope
Phaphamani phaphamani	Wake up, wake up
Nina ma-Afrika.	You Africans.
Imbombo zokhothamo	The archways of the doorway
Zithobisa wena	Make you stoop
Phaphamani phaphamani	Wake up wake up
Nina ma-Afrika.	You Africans.

It is worth noting that this hymn was actually not addressed to all Africans but to amaNazaretha. According to oral tradition in the church, some white people came to Shembe and offered to take him overseas where they would teach him about religion and theology. According to this story Shembe refused, stating that God is not studied in books (*UNkulunkulu akafundelwa*). Perhaps it was after that incident that Shembe said about himself: "If you had taught him in your schools you would have taken pride in him. But that God may demonstrate his wisdom, he sent Shembe, a child, so that he may speak like the wise and educated" (Quoted in Gunner, 1986: 182).

Isaiah Shembe's Hymns in 'this' and the 'other' World

However, Shembe's ministry was not restricted to only black people or Africans. The problems African people were faced with troubled Shembe a great deal, but his vision also extended to universal peace and harmony. In hymn No. 153 he makes it clear that his church is not meant to be only for black people:

Nanti ilizwi elomemo	Here is the word of invitation
Liyamema bonke abantu	It invites all people
Alikhethi noma munye	It does not exclude even one
Liyamema bonke abantu.	It invites all people.
Abansundu nabamhlophe	The brown ones and the white ones
Libamema kwana njalo	It invites them always
Alikhethi noma munye	It does not exclude even one
Liyamema bonke abantu.	It invites all the people.
Zimpumputhe nani zinyonga	You blind people and you cripples
Sabelani niya bizwa.	Respond you are called
Lolu memo ngolwe zulu	This invitation is of heaven
Ziya menywa zonke izizwe	All the nations are invited.
Alikhethi noma munye	It does not exclude even one
Liya mema bonke abantu.	It invites all the people.

It is apparent from this hymn that Shembe did not intend to exclude anybody from his church regardless of their colour. It does not matter if the person is black or white, but all are invited to join the church because the church prepares people for the way to heaven and heaven does not discriminate. Interestingly, Thulani Kunene had a near-death experience in which he was spiritually transported to 'heaven' and he found the Nazaretha in 'heaven' walking to the temple and singing this hymn.[3] According to Kunene's account, despite the fact that the Nazaretha on the other side sang this hymn which suggests no existence of discrimination in heaven, he himself was prohibited from joining the Nazaretha. But of course the basis of that discrimination was not race but was rather denominational as he was "told" by his late grandmother (who herself had not been a member of Ibandla lamaNazaretha on earth) that he could not join the people in the white gowns because he

3 For a discussion of near-death experiences in the Nazaretha Church see Sithole (2005).

did not have the "symbol" of *ubuNazaretha* (sense of being Nazaretha). In effect this means he could not enter because he was not a member of Ibandla lamaNazaretha. When he asked for that "symbol" from his grandmother, she told him that he had left that "symbol" on earth and had to come back to earth to find it (Kunene, untitled, undated sermon).

In another hymn, No. 178 "*Ziningi izizwe*" (There are Many Nations) Shembe questions racial and ethnic difference while at the same time lamenting their existence. He says that the only difference among the nations is language:

Ziningi izizwe	There are many nations
Phansi kwelanga	Under the sun
Zehlukana ngentetho	They are separated by language
Kumazwe ngamazwe.	In all places.

He meditates about what might have caused this separation of nations, seemingly wondering if it was God's creation or the creation of people:

Ziningi izizwe	There are many nations
Phansi kwelanga	Under the sun
Zehlukaniswe ngubani	Who separated them
Kumazwe ngamazwe?	In all the places?]

But what is more important is his attempt at uniting all the nations in his church as he asks,

Lizwi lini	What word
Elingahlanganisa	Can bring together
Lezo zizwe	Those nations
Wozani maShaka nizwile.	Come, you Shakas you have heard.]

Clearly, Shembe's universal vision was generally limited by his knowledge that his audience was predominantly black people. Even though he wanted his church to include all the nations under the sun, his followers were mainly restricted to black people. That is why when he involves his addressee, the language returns to nationalism not universality as he calls on the Shakas [Zulus] and the AmaBhaca. It is made clear, however, that these nations are mentioned because "they have heard", not because the call is restricted to them. Isaiah Shembe offers a resolution that one can expect from a religious man like him: that God is the only one who has an answer:

NguThixo yedwa	It is God alone
Ongahlanganisa lezo zizwe	Who can unite those nations
Wozani maBhaca	Come Bhacas
Nilizwile izwi lakhe.	You have heard his word.

Another interesting feature of Isaiah Shembe's hymns is that not only do they speak to universal issues. They are also perceived to exist in this world and in heaven. An example is hymn No. 214 (Umkhululi wethu/Our Liberator) mentioned above. According to Muntuwezizwe Buthelezi's testimony in Oosthuizen and Hexham (1999), this hymn was composed by Isaiah Shembe in Msinga. Isaiah Shembe had sent Muntuwezizwe and Phelalasekhaya Maphumulo to go to the Mountain eNtshoze to pray for people on the other side of eNtshoze. Shembe told them that when they get to the mountain they should shout: "All those who are suffering, come and see Shembe and you will be saved" (1999: 179). The two men did as they were told and many sick people were healed. When they came back they informed Shembe about what they had done, and Shembe was very pleased with them and "blessed them". He then sent Phelalasekhaya, who was his scribe, to go fetch his writing material. When Phela came back, Shembe told him to "sit down facing the east and write what I say". And thus came hymn No. 214:

Our Liberator has come
We the offspring of Dingane
We have heard him
The Liberator of the Zulus has come.[4]

Thereafter Shembe went to the house and called all the people to come and listen to him. He said: "I sent young men to the top of the mountain eNtshoze to save God's suffering people there. When they came there, they saved those people, who were still living on earth. However, I wanted to save also those people who had already died. And these people came with this hymn, to thank their salvation with this hymn. Now these people, who died in war, have been

4 No Zulu version is offered in Hexham and Oosthuizen's book, and this stanza is different from the one in the hymnbook. The reason for this may be that the informant was just telling the story and inserted the hymn as he remembered it. But this English version can be translated as follows: *Umkhululi wethu, usefikile/ Thina nzalo kaDingane/ Sesimzwile/ Umkhululi wamaZulu ufikile.*

liberated. God has dug them a hole and buried them there in the mountain and they praised God with this hymn" (1999: 180).

In a tape-recorded sermon, MaDlomo Mchunu (1990) tells of a time when Isaiah Shembe was travelling in the mountains of Ndwedwe on his way to Nhlangakazi. She says that Shembe saw a young woman working in the fields. He said to her: "*Ngiyakuthanda mntanethu*" [I love you, *mntanethu*.[5]] The girl responded that she did not love Shembe. This happened three times and then Shembe left the girl and carried on with his journey. When Shembe had left, the girl was hit by lightning and passed away. Shembe told his followers that the girl had appeared to him in spirit and was singing a hymn which is No. 209 in the hymn book:

Duma besabe	[Thunder and let them be scared
Abasemhlabeni	Those who are on earth
AbaseZulwini	For those in heaven
Balifezile idinga.	Have done their due.
Webantu bomhlaba	You people of the earth
Nesaba ngani	Why are you afraid
Lifezeni idinga	You must do your due
Uyanishiya umhlaba.	The world is leaving you behind.]

While the story told by MaDlomo regarding the origination of this hymn echoes Thulani Kunene's case about these hymns existing in this and the other world, the call here too is not nationalist but universal and religious. It is all the people of the earth, not the Zulus or Africans, who are addressed here and are accused of not doing what is required. The punishment for these earthly people seems to be death by lightning and as a result they need to be scared of thunder and lightning. It may even be suggested here that potentially destructive natural forces like thunder and lightning happen because the people of the earth do not hear the word of God. In this hymn, then, Shembe uses natural forces that affect all human beings to show that he is not only concerned with the Zulus and Africans. All the people of the earth are contrasted with those of heaven, who are said to be doing what they should. However, it is not specified exactly what is it that earthly people are not doing right and those in heaven do right.

---

5 Like *mntakwethu*, *mntanethu* literally means child of my home but is used figuratively to refer to a lover.

Before I conclude this chapter, I want to emphasise the fact that while it is important to note Shembe's engagement with politics in some of the hymns discussed here, this is not to say that the Nazaretha Church should be seen simply as a political movement. The politics of South Africa in the early 1900s affected and concerned Shembe so much that he had to deliberate and deal with them through song and performance; through the language well-known to him. But, perhaps what is more important is that he provided his own people (black people in South Africa, especially the Zulus) with an alternative world view to that of the West. While in orthodox churches black people needed to jettison their African ways – the houses they lived in, the kind of dress they were used to, and their customs – Isaiah Shembe offered them a place where they could worship God without changing their identities as much as they were compelled to do in missionary churches. My point here is that even though there are these hymns that respond to certain political issues that concerned Shembe, the hymns are not generally about politics as the Nazaretha church itself is not essentially about politics. They are hymns or songs of worship designed to be performed in religious services, and deal with the spiritual needs of Shembe himself and his followers.

Conclusion

It is true that even today the Nazaretha Church is predominantly a Zulu Church because its membership, although there are some people who belong to other ethnic groups in South Africa and beyond, the Zulus far exceed the others in number and the church's foundational texts, especially the hymn-book, is still not available in any African language other than isiZulu. My contention in this chapter is that such was not Isaiah Shembe's design. It happened as a result of the seclusion of the races that happened in the country at the time. It seems to me that had apartheid not been introduced in South Africa, there would be more members of the church from other tribes in South Africa as McKenzie's report claimed Shembe was a leader of 'mixed natives'. It is known that there were a few Indian members of the Church in the time of Isaiah Shembe and early in Johannes' ministry. Esther Roberts states that during Isaiah Shembe's funeral, "Some of the Indian followers had brought wreaths and there were sheaves of flowers from the florists" (1936: 26) and in one of his undated sermons J.G. Shembe talks about an Indian member of the church called Aaron, who had donated 200 pounds towards the building of a house in eKuphakameni. But these Indian members disappeared after the tightening of Apartheid laws in the fifties or sixties. That said, I conclude by suggesting that Isaiah Shembe's hymns are indeed literary texts and should be read alongside the poems of great Zulu poets like B.W. Vilakazi as they present a similar kind of vision and concern for the plight of black people in South Africa and beyond.

CHAPTER 2

The Bible, the Hymns, and Shembe's Sense of Self

Introduction

Ibandla lamaNazaretha marked hundred years of existence in 2010 and it can be argued that those have been years of engagement with colonialism, cultural imperialism and the Bible. Isaiah Shembe, who founded Ibandla lamaNazaretha in 1910, was an avid reader of the Bible, and his tremendous knowledge of the Bible is amazing because he was not educated in missionary schools. One of the earliest scholars to study Isaiah Shembe and his church, Esther Roberts, writes that 'Shembe, later, became a remarkable scholar. He used to reply to many of the questions asked him with apt quotations from the Scriptures' (Roberts 1936, 49). West's point that while Shembe "seized" and "reconstituted" the Bible, it "also [took] hold of him, drawing him and his female followers to its narrative [and here I think not just his female followers]" (2007: 498) is validated by the fact that the Bible still plays a significant role in the life of the church today. In this chapter I look at how Shembe "seizes" the Bible and uses it in his hymns (*izihlabelelo*) to negotiate his own identity in relation to colonialism, pre-colonial African life and missionization. I argue that in the Bible Shembe found, in Duncan Brown's terms, "a mode of spiritual power and personal articulation" (2006: 40–41), which allowed him to imagine himself as a Black Messiah while at the same time celebrating the life of Jesus Christ and rejoicing in being "saved" by him. This engagement with the Bible shows that Shembe was actively involved in creating the hymns, which also supports the claim made in the previous chapter that to say the hymns came with the spirits is not completely true. Shembe deserves the credit for his creativity.

As West has pointed out, there is a dearth of scholarship on Africa's engagement with the Bible. An important task demanding attention from African Biblical scholars, West argues, is a "comprehensive account of the transaction that constitutes the history of the encounters between Africa and the Bible" (2003: 65). This is the case because, West goes on to say, "while the accounts we have of the encounters between Africa and Christianity are well documented, the encounters between Africa and the Bible are partial and fragmentary" (65). In the similar vein Roland Boer laments the absence of the Bible in colonial and postcolonial studies, even though there is "perpetual, if not overwhelming, presence of the Bible in colonialism and postcolonialism themselves" (2001: 7). And Duncan Brown, coming from the point of view of literary

 | DOI 10.1163/9789004320628_004

scholarship, rather than theology and religion, has pointed to the central role the Bible plays in the lives of Africans. Drawing on the assertion made by Terence Ranger that, "any scholar who aspires today to 'think black' about many of the people in eastern Zimbabwe has to learn also to think Methodist" (1994: 309), Brown extends that assertion by saying that "any scholar who aspires to 'think in black' about the African (sub) continent has to learn also to think biblically" (2008: 81–82).

West has proposed a refocus of biblical scholarship on the impact Africa has had on the Bible, rather than the impact the Bible has had on Africa. Drawing on Kwame Bediako's statement that, "Further developments in African Christianity will test the depth of the impact that the Bible has made upon Africa" (1994: 252), West suggests an inversion of this comment:

> But, what if we make Africa the subject and the Bible the object? We would then have the following formulation: *Further developments in African Christianity will test the depth of the impact that Africa has made upon the Bible.* (2000: 29, italics in the original)

The engagement with and transaction between Isaiah Shembe and the Bible that is explored here is epitomized in the "conversation" between Gerald West and a member of the church in which West had spoken in the launch of *The Man of Heaven and the Beautiful Ones of God* (Gunner 2002) about how Isaiah Shembe was "a remarkable re-memberer of the Bible" (West, 2006: 179). The member of the church rebuked Gerald for his statement, stating that, "We do not interpret the Bible, the Bible interprets us" (179). This interpretation and counter-interpretation, the church's action upon the Bible and their being acted upon by it, or, this "mutual engagement" (Peel, 2003: 1) constitute the relationship between Isaiah Shembe (and his church) and the Bible that this chapter focuses on.

Isaiah Shembe and the Notion of the Black Messiah

There is no doubt that Shembe spent some time in his life reflecting on his own identity not just as an African, Zulu or human being, but also as a religious figure of great prominence. It is also apparent that in his endeavours to understand and articulate his own self he found the Bible to be very useful. That he was aware of his (healing) abilities and wisdom is clear from his self-delineation in his assertion that, "[i]f you had educated him in your schools you would have taken pride in him. But that God may demonstrate his wisdom, he sent Shembe, a child, so that he may speak like the wise and the educated" (Gunner, 1986: 182). Nellie Wells, "Special Representative" of *The Natal Mercury* and Isaiah Shembe's ardent admirer who wrote a transcript for a proposed film on Shembe, reports that,

> Everywhere chapels, churches and schools were emptied as Shembe approached and the people crowded to listen with great joy. Immorality so prevalent among Christians who were living under false economic conditions was driven to shame, mental snobbery was pricked like a bubble, and a simple folk wearing skins or next to nothing accepted the gospel with great joy and were baptised, then the missionaries waged warfare, because, as they said, Shembe was undoing much if not most of what they had done. (Quoted in Mpanza, 1999: 56)

The popularity that Shembe commanded and the conflict with the missionaries, the educated elites, and the State which resulted from such popularity made it important for Shembe to deal with the question of his identity. On a number of occasions he was interrogated with regards to his identity and praxis. In 1921 he was invited to give his life story to then assistant Magistrate C.N.C. Barrett and in 1923 he was interviewed by Magistrate Charles McKenzie in Ndwedwe Court (Papini, 1999: 254). He was also interviewed in 1929 by Carl Faye (see Papini, 1999) and in April 1931 by the Native Economic Commission. Clearly, in these interviews he told his interrogators what they would like to hear, as I have stated regarding the 1923 interview. To return again to Shembe's words in the 1923 interview:

> God has given me certain work to do amongst my people. I therefore realise that God has also placed the authorities over us, and those who disregard or defy the Government, disregard the will of God. (Quoted in Papini, 1999: 255)

While this is clearly a reference to Romans 13, it also echoes Jesus' words in Luke 20 verse 25, "Give unto Caesar what is Caesar's and to God what is God's." However, as stated in the previous chapter, this is not what Shembe encouraged and taught his followers to do. I stated elsewhere (see Sithole, 2010), following on James Scott's formulation, that in the Nazaretha Church there is a marked difference between the "public transcript" and the "hidden transcript." According to these concepts, the above statement in the interview would belong to the "public transcript" while there are a number of other texts (hymns and sermons) that would constitute a "hidden transcript" in which

Shembe addresses his followers away from the ears of the authorities. In these texts he teaches defiance, rather than submission.

The kind of wisdom and powers that Shembe was believed and believed himself to have commanded are close to those which Jesus was believed to have commanded, and Shembe was aware of this fact. Thus, in hymn 34 he appropriates the story of Jesus's birth and uses it to claim that what Jesus was for the Israelites is what Shembe is for the Zulus or even Africans:

Kwafika izazi	The wise men came
Ziphuma empumalanga	They came from the East
Zathi uphi lowo	They said where is that one
Oyinkosi yabaJuda.	Who is the Lord of the Jews.
Chorus:	
Kunjalo-ke namhlanje	It is like that today
Emagqumeni as'Ohlange	In the hills of Ohlange
Nawe-ke Betlehema	And you Bethlehem
Muzi wakwaJuda	Village of Judah
Awusiye omncinyane	You are not the smaller one
Kunababusi bakwaJuda.	Than the rulers of Judah.
Chorus:	
Lanyakaza iJerusalema	Jerusalem was shaken
Bathi niyayizwa lendaba	They said do you hear this news
Evele phakathi kwethu	That happened amongst us
Efike nezazi	It came with the wise men
Sibutheleni abafundisi	Call for us the priests
Bahlole imibhalo.	To examine the scriptures.
Chorus:	
Bafike bathi yebo	They came and said yes
Kulotshiwe kanjalo	It is written so
Nawe Kuphakama	And you Kuphakama
Magquma as'Ohlange.	Hills of Ohlange.
Chorus:	
Awusiye omncinyane	You are not the smaller one
Kunababusi bakwaJuda	Than the rulers of Judah
Kuyakuvela kuwe	From you shall come forth
AbaProfithi	Prophets

Abayakusindisa	Who will save
Umuziwas'Ohlange.	The village of Ohlange.

Chorus.

One of the reasons why Shembe was such an avid reader of the Bible as stated above was so that he could use it to defend himself against the people (black church leaders, the missionaries and the state) who seemed troubled by his work. That is why Esther Roberts says that he outwitted a number of missionaries by his knowledge of the Bible. He called on the educated and knowledgeable people to examine the scripture and hoped that they would realize – by identifying the similarities between him and other prophets – that he himself was a prophet and was sent by God. Thus he begins the above hymn at the time when the wise men were going to see and salute the young Jesus. Shembe emphasises that the wise men came with the question, "Where is that one who is the king of the Jews?" This challenges his enemies to enquire about who and what he is, instead of simply dismissing him as "the madman, son of Mayekisa" (Papini, 1999: 251). Rather than following the story of Jesus as it is told in the Bible, at this point he inserts the chorus which makes a statement about himself and places this narrative in the context of South Africa, using a location occupied by only black people (*Ohlange*) to emphasize the fact that he was sent to "save" black people in South Africa.

What Isaiah Shembe does with the Bible here is what West calls "re-membering" the Bible. West argues that ordinary people (as opposed to trained biblical scholars) have their own tools for "reading" the Bible. Their 'reading' of the Bible is "more akin to 'rewriting' than reading in any scholarly sense" (2003: 78). They reinterpret the Bible (sometimes in the way antagonistic to that of the missionaries) and give it new meaning relevant to them and their contexts. As West goes on to argue, while the ordinary African interpreters of the Bible do not rewrite the Bible as such,

> they are [also] not as transfixed and fixated by the text as their textually trained pastors and theologians ... The Bible they work with is always an already 're-membered' "text" – a text, both written and oral, that has been dismembered, taken apart, and then re-membered (2003: 78).

The text that is commonly used or appropriated in the church to confirm Isaiah Shembe's messianic position is that of Deuteronomy 18:18. While this text was used by Isaiah Shembe himself (as can be seen in his writings) and church members even today use it, an example of its use by Amos Shembe will suffice here. In an undated cassette, Amos (known to members as iNyangaYeZulu /Moon of Heaven) preached a sermon in which he dismissed Jesus as white and calls for a black prophet for black people. He told the story of a woman who wanted her children to go to church. The children asked who was to be worshipped and the mother told them it was Jesus. When they asked who Jesus was, and were told that he was 'white', the children were very angered and disappointed.

> *"Kanti mama sihlupheka kangaka nje sikhonz' umlungu?" Wadumala umam 'esephethe incwadi eya esontweni… Zathi "Siyabuza?… Kant' uJesu wumlungu?… Abelungu basihlupha kangaka nje sikhonza bona?… Kwakwenze njani? Kwakonakeleni e-Afrika mama? Kwakwenze njani uNkulunkulu engavezi umuntu?" Ngiyoniveze… ves 18 Deuteronomy 18… wa… zibuza ingane ukuthi akamvezanga ngani uNkulunkulu uma umuntu omnyama kuyisizwe ngempela kusho ukuthi siqalekisiwe thina mama?… Bafundele phela ngoba nazi ingane zathi akufundwe lapho.* ***(Ngiyakubavezela umprofethi kubafowabo. Abe njengabo. Ngiyakubeka amazwi ami emlonyeni wakhe. Uyakukhuluma konke akutshelwa yimina. Uyakuthi ongawalaleliyo amazwi.)*** *Eya! Ngiyakubavezela… Abantu!… Umprofethi… Abantu!… Onjengabo… Abantu!… Hhayi ilokhu u Sheti… iNdiya mina alifani nami. Hhayi uFerguson! Hhayi uFerguson umlungu.no.no.no! Ngiyoveza umuntu kwabakubo. Akushiwo ukuthi kwabakubo?… Ehhe! Kwabakubo onjengabo abantu…*
>
> ("Is it true, mother, that we worship a white man as we suffer like this?" The woman was disappointed as she held her books on her way to church… They [the children] said, "We are asking! Is Jesus a white man? The whites abuse us like this but we worship them? What happened? What went wrong in Africa mother? Why didn't God raise a person?"… I will raise for you… verse 18 Deutoronomy 18… he… the children [were] asking, "Why didn't God raise a person? If black people are a nation it means we are cursed, mother".… Do read for them because the children said we should read there[1]… **(I will raise the prophet among your brothers. He will be like them. I will put my words into his mouth. He will speak to them what I tell him and if anyone does not listen to the words)** I will

1 In the Nazaretha Church there is a tradition of reading the Bible where a person preaching a sermon will not read the Bible for himself, but will ask another person in the congregation. While one person reads from the bible, the preacher would reiterate what is read, sometimes changing some words and emphasizing whatever he feels like emphasizing. Here, I have used the parentheses and bold to show the voice of the person reading for Amos Shembe.

raise for them ... the people ... the prophet ... the people ... from their race ... the people ... he will be like them ... the people. Not the ... not Shetty ... the Indian does not look like me ... Not Ferguson ... Not Ferguson he is white ... No! No! No! I will raise a person from his race ... Is it not said that from his race? Yes! From his race who is like them ...)

The above text does not suggest who the messiah for the black people is, but the audience need not be told. They see the "chosen" one sitting in front of them. While Amos Shembe states clearly and openly his relationship to Jesus, that he was white and, therefore, represented the whites, he states in a subtle way Shembe's position and his relationship to God. He does this through singing verse two of hymn No. 239:

Ufikile abakhuluma ngaye	He has arrived, the one they spoke about
Aba profithi	The Prophets
Babazani wemadoda	Praise, you men
Babazani zizwe nonke	Praise, you nations.

The singing of this hymn serves two purposes here, a common tendency in Nazaretha sermon performance. It is firstly a way of engaging with the audience, allowing them to be active participants in the performance. Secondly, it is a subtle way of making a point: that Shembe (and here he has his father, Isaiah Shembe in mind, even though he was himself believed to be a messiah) is the prophet the children confronted their mother about. It means God has actually done what the children were crying that He had not done.

Now back to the hymns. How exactly does Isaiah Shembe "re-member" the story of Jesus's birth in his hymns? Shembe does this by appropriating a written story and making it a predominantly oral one by renewing it "in a sung context" (Watson, 2009: 330) and thus allowing it to be received communally. This rendering of the text in oral form also "Africanises" it because, as Ruth Finnegan has noted, "Africa is celebrated above all for the treasure of her voiced and auditory arts, and as the home of oral literature, orature and orality, and the genesis and inspiration of the voiced traditions of the great diaspora" (2007: 1). The text itself is not 'borrowed' as it is from the Bible. Isaiah Shembe omits certain parts and emphasizes others as he sees appropriate for his own purpose. That the story of Jesus's birth was important to Isaiah Shembe is exemplified by the fact that there are two hymns based on this story. Another hymn telling the story of Jesus' birth is No. 152 "*Jerusalema Betlehema*" (Jerusalem Bethlehem). Unlike hymn No. 34 where the speaker simply narrates the story, here in the first stanza Isaiah Shembe uses two crucial locales in the story of Jesus's birth,

Jerusalem and Bethlehem, as the addressees. But here too the wise men take the position as the second most important characters in the story. Shembe did not see Jesus as important in and of himself, but what was important was what he did and what he stood for. That is why the name Jesus is not mentioned in this stanza. What is emphasised is the fact that he is the Saviour (*uMsindisi*):

Jerusalema Betlehema	Jerusalem Bethlehem
Izazi zisitshelile	The wise men told us
Umsindisi uselezelwe	The Saviour is born
Kwelase Betlehema.	In the land of Bethlehem.

What Jesus does is important because of the people for whom it is done. The significance of the Saviour is dependent or reliant on the people who are saved, and I think that is why Shembe downplays or omits the name of Jesus in his re-membering of the biblical story of Jesus's birth. The text on which both hymn No. 34 and hymn No. 152 are based is Matthew 2. Interestingly, the name of Jesus, which Shembe avoids completely in hymn No. 34 and only mentions in the very last line of hymn No. 152, is the very first one in Matthew 2:

> *UJesu se e zelwe eBetlehema la se Judia, emihleni kaHerodi iNkosi, kwafika eJerusalema izazi zivela empumalanga, zithi, "U pi lowo o zelwe e inkosi yaba Juda na? Sabona inkanyezi yakhe sise mpumalanga, size kukhuleka kuye."*
>
> [When Jesus had been born in Bethlehem of Judea, in the time of King Herod, the wise men came to Jerusalem from the East, they said, "Where is the one born king of the Jews? We saw his star while we were in the East, we have come to salute him."]

The way in which Isaiah Shembe re-members this text (Matthew 2) in each of the two hymns mentioned above is different. Hymn No. 152 seems to be simply a re-telling of the narrative, albeit with certain omissions and alterations of some parts of the text. Hymn No. 34 in contrast is unapologetically claiming the story of Jesus for the amaNazaretha, for the Africans. In hymn No. 34, Isaiah Shembe inserts the chorus that claims that what happened in Jerusalem has happened in Ohlange too. For instance, stanza 3 talks about the stirring of the people in Jerusalem because of the news that the king of the Jews had been born, and a call is made that the ministers should examine the scripture to ascertain if what was happening was in accordance with what had happened or had been prophesied before. This call is Isaiah Shembe's own and is not part of Matthew 2. Through it Shembe is arguing that he and his work should be judged and examined in terms of what the scripture says. This is probably in response to what Elizabeth Gunner refers to as the 'police surveillance' and to the "Makholwas" (Believers), for whom Shembe's appeal was "very alarming and threatening" (1988: 215).

But what is even more telling is the fact that although the call to examine the scripture is with regards to Jesus' birth and Jerusalem, in Shembe's text, the ministers' examination shows that eKuphakameni (not Bethlehem), in the hills of Ohlange (not of Judah), is not smaller than the rulers of Judah, as the biblical text says about Jerusalem. Here Shembe is claiming that the black people of Africa are God's chosen people as the Israelites were. He says in another of his hymns (No. 101):

Akusiyo iJerusalema kuphela	It is not Jerusalem alone
Owayithandayo.	That you loved.

As stated earlier, hymn No. 152 does not deviate a great deal from the biblical text on which it is based. Here Shembe does not make a statement about ubuNazaretha, at least not openly. It seems to me that even though hymn No. 34 comes before hymn No. 152 in the hymn-book, it is the latter that was composed first. In "Jerusalem Bethlehem" Shembe repeats the Matthew 2 text, although with a great deal of selection and very little alteration of the way in which the text is presented. I think when he composed this hymn, Shembe was still coming to terms with his own identity and spirituality, and this text appealed to him so much that he wanted it to be part of his church's repertoire. He then worked on the story itself, selecting some parts and leaving out others without bringing in as many of his own ideas as he does in hymn No. 34. This is not to say that this hymn is without creativity on Shembe's part. While the act of selecting itself is a creative process, Shembe presents the story in his own way. As mentioned above, the addressees of this hymn are "Jerusalem and Bethlehem." It is to these two that the persona narrates the story. And while the beginning of hymn No. 34 is based on the biblical text itself, "the wise men came", in hymn No. 152 the same idea is presented, but here "the wise men told us" that the saviour is born.

The Story of Creation in the Hymns

The biblical story of creation is another of Shembe's favourite texts as can be seen by the way in which he appropriates this story in his hymns and teachings.

In the hymn-book there are a number of references to his congregation as the progeny of Adam and Eve. Teaching about diligence in the "Morning Prayer" he says, particularly to the ministers:

> *Uma wena-ke uyisizukulwane sika Adam noEva, okwathiwa kuye ensimini yaseEdeni lima ulinde, ubonakala uthabatha isimo sobunja, uyazethuka wena ngokungathandi ukusebenza.* (*Izihlabelelo zamaNazaretha* 1940: 6)
>
> [If you are the progeny of Adam and Eve, to whom it was said in the garden of Eden, that you should plough and wait, but you are seen to be following a dog's example, you insult yourself by not wanting to work.]

And in hymn No. 21 stanza 4:

Thina sonkana siyinzalo yomuntu wakho	We all are the progeny of your man
U Adam no Eva	Adam and Eve
Owabenzakuqala	The ones you created first
WeNkosi yeSabatha usishiyelani.	You Lord of the Sabbath why do you desert us

However, while this reference to Adam and Eve as the progenitors of all the people brings forth Shembe's universal voice, as a human being among human beings, what seems to be given more attention is the 'sin' story of the serpent, Eve and Adam, and the punishment from God that resulted from the 'sin'. Hymn No. 114 "*Wangidala Nkulunkulu*" [You Created Me, God] espouses the idea of the human as the sinner and presents God as the all graceful and loving one.

Wangidala Nkulunkulu	You created me, God
Thixo Nkosi yamakhosi	Lord, King of kings
Wangibeka kuleyo nsimu	You placed me in that garden
Ngokungithanda okungaka.	With so much love for me.
Insimu eyayingadingi lutho	The garden that wanted of nothing
Insimu eyayinezithelo zayo	The garden that had its fruits
Wangiyalela ukuzidla zonke	You urged me to eat them all
Ngokungithanda okungaka.	With so much love for me.

Emzuzwini nesikhathi	But in time [and minutes]
Ngakhohliseka Nkosi yami	I was misled my Lord
Ngaze ngawudla lowo muthi	I ate that plant/medicine
Baphela bonk'ubuhle bami.	And all my beauty was finished.
Ngingabuyiselwa ngani na?	How can I be returned
Ebuhleni enganginabo	To the beauty I once had
Ngingakayephuli imithetho	Before I broke the laws
Ngokungithanda okungaka.	With so much love for me.
Ngiyadinga Nkosi yami	I do need, my Lord
Insipho yokungigeza	The soap that can wash me
Ngibuyele ngokushesha	So I will return quickly
Ebuhleni enganginabo.	To the beauty I once had.

From the text of Genesis 3 Shembe appropriates the idea of 'sin' (or breaking the law) and uses it in this hymn to warn his followers against committing sin and also to encourage them to repent. The story of Adam and Eve's sin is appropriated here to speak to Shembe's present (and perhaps future) audience. Noticeable is the omission of all the characters in the biblical story and the way in which the blame is placed on no one other than the persona him/herself. This technique, coupled with the fact that the persona uses the first person, makes this hymn to speak powerfully to anyone who sings or reads it.

While the punishment for Adam (and Eve) is exile from Eden in the biblical text, here the sinner loses his or her beauty. This may suggest that a human soul has inherent beauty that can only become damaged if a person sins. The hymn ends (on a positive note, I suggest) with the search for the lost beauty. What is positive about this is that, since a human being is essentially a beautiful soul, it is, or it may be, possible to reclaim one's beauty. In the hymn the persona asks God (or him- or herself, perhaps) how the lost beauty can be reclaimed. This still leaves this person as someone who lacks knowledge, but the positive aspect is that he or she is searching for the answers. It is in the last stanza that the voice of the speaker is articulate and fearless, telling God what can bring back his beauty and demanding from Him to be given the soap that can bring back the lost beauty. The speaker here demands to be taken back to Eden!

Hymn No. 33 "*Kwezwakala ilizwi*" (The Voice was Heard) is based on the same text as hymn No. 114 and deals with the same issue but in a different way. Here the focus of the blame is on Adam, from whom it is constantly demanded in the chorus: "*Sewenzeni weAdam/Sewonakele umhlaba*" [What have you done now, Adam/ The world has been spoiled.] This is a direct reference (although with omission of much of the text) to Genesis 3 verse 17: "*Wati ku Adamu, Ngokuba u lalele izwi lomkakho, udhlile umuti engakuyala ngawo ukuti, U nga u dhli, wonakele umhlaba ngenxa yakho; uyakuzidhla izithelo zawo, uhlupeke zonke izinsuku zokupila kwako.*" [He said to Adam, because you listened to your wife's word, you ate the plant I warned you not to eat, the world has been spoiled because of you; you will eat its (the world's) fruits, and suffer all days of your life.] Adam here is representative of all (and only) men, and therefore Shembe makes a statement that men are stronger and have more responsibility than women, an issue which I discuss in more detail below. Interestingly, in the biblical text's (Genesis 3) characters' order of appearance, we encounter Adam after we have already met the serpent and Adam's wife. The serpent is omitted completely from Shembe's hymn, and the woman is only mentioned in the last chorus:

Kwezwakala ilizwi *Ekushoneni kwelanga* *Ensimini yase-Eden* *Ekushoneni kwelanga.*	The voice was heard At the setting of the sun In the garden of Eden At the setting of the sun.
Chorus:	
Sewenzeni we-Adamu *Sewonakele umhlaba.*	What have you done, Adam The world has been spoilt.
Izwi lezi nyamazane *Ezazihlala e-Eden* *Lithi maye webaba* *Namhla soshonaphi?*	The voice of wild animals That used to live in Eden It says, oh my father Where are we to go today?
Chorus:	
Sahlukana nobaba *Sewonakele umhlaba* *Sisize Jehova umkhiphe u-Adam* *Wakhishwa-ke u-Adam ensimini* *yase-Eden.*	We were separated from our father The world has been spoilt Help us, Jehovah, expel Adam Adam was then expelled from Eden
Chorus:	
Wakhala-ke u-Adam *Esekhishwa esangweni* *Wathi inhliziyo yami inosizi* *Ngokwephula imithetho.*	Adam then cried When he was forced out of the gate He said my heart is filled with sorrow Because of breaking the laws.

Chorus:	
Ngoniswe ngulomfazi	I was misled by this woman
Owanginika yena.	You gave me.

Nightfall or sunset is associated with darkness which itself is associated with evil. Even though the mention of the setting of the sun in the first stanza alludes to Genesis 3 verse 8a, "*Bezwa izwi likaJehova uTixo ehamba ensimini ntambama*" (They heard the voice of the Lord Jehovah walking in the field in the afternoon), Shembe seems to be making his own statement about the sin that Adam committed: that it creates chaos and the whole of life is turned upside down because of it. To do this Shembe emphasises the time in which God spoke to Adam about what they had done, and instead of the afternoon which is stated in the Bible Shembe chooses sunset. Here prominence is given to the time (sunset) at which the event took place rather than the event itself (the voice [of God] which was heard) and the place where it took place (the garden of Eden). Shembe emphasises the time issue by repeating the same line twice in a stanza made up of only four lines. In doing so he tries to reinforce the impact of the sin on the life of the sinner and the lives of other beings close to him or her.

In addition to placing the blame on Adam as a man, this hymn also underscores the sense of alienation and exile Adam is subjected to. While Shembe omitted the serpent from the original biblical text, he has inserted his 'own' animals that are perhaps easier to sympathise with than the serpent because they are victims rather than perpetrators. This he does so that the responsibility for the sin is not directed away from Adam to the serpent. Instead, Shembe uses animals that had nothing to do with Adam and Eve's sin, and these are the ones who suffer the most because of the sin. However, the place of these animals in the whole text (Shembe's hymn this time) is unclear. At first, they complain about expulsion from the garden of Eden, but later, they are the ones who beg God to remove Adam from Eden. The last chorus, in which Adam places the blame on the woman (and by implication God, who gave her to him) references Genesis 3 verse 12 which reads: "*Wati u-Adamu, Umfazi owanginika yena ukuba abe nami, wangipa umuti nga u dhla.*" [Adam said, the woman you gave to me to live with gave me the fruit and I ate it.]

Shembe's position about where the blame should be placed on this issue – that it is Adam, the man who is to blame – accords with his take on the issue of adultery in the "*Umthetho*/ The law" text (Gunner, 2002: 70–71). In this text Shembe unequivocally positions the man as the one responsible for preventing adultery and to whom blame needs to be apportioned should adultery take place: "I have placed the weight of the law on adultery on the man's shoulders, as it is he who ought to use most control in that matter because a woman is but a child in bodily strength compared to a man." I think that this part of 'the law' echoes an African cultural (and patriarchal) idea that a man is the father of his children as well as his wife, or wives.[2] It is in the second paragraph of 'the law' that Shembe begins to reference the biblical text related to the story of creation: "But in the case of woman, woman was created from man therefore she lacks the strength to hold herself back if she is assailed by a man's weakness because she herself is formed from man. If a man lures her through the tricks of love she will succumb quickly because man is the father of woman" (71). West argues that this text alludes "to 1 Timothy even though the citation that follows the next sentence refers to Genesis" (2006: 172). In 're-membering' this text, as West goes on to argue, Shembe,

> draws on elements of this text [he is talking about 1 Tim 2:12–15], recasting them for his own purposes. In this case, he retains the interest in the male-female relationship, the first-person form of address, and the argumentative style. He shifts the focus, however, from issues of male and female roles to issues of marriage, desire and adultery. What allows Shembe to make this shift is the dependency of 1 Tim 2:13–15 on Gen 2:21–25 and Gen 3:1–6. (172)

However, there is a problem with Shembe's formulation (or his re-membering of the biblical text) even though it is interesting that he shifts the blame for adultery from a woman to a man, something which is against the grain of the traditional Christian church's reading of 1 Timothy (Bal 1986, quoted in West 2006). Shembe's formulation leaves women no space for action; they are allowed only a passive role in this formulation. As West argues, "it is the woman who is 'assailed (*-ehlelwa*) by a man's weakness'. The repetition of this verb repeats the point. The men (and temptation) are the active subjects, while the woman is the passive unless activated by the man" (2006: 174). What is interesting about this role of women as passive is its implication for the reading of Carol Muller's virgin girls as central to Shembe's church: "The apparently very passive view of women evident within Shembe's teaching on this subject raises questions of how we reconcile such an understanding with Carol Muller's location of women at the centre of Shembe's enterprise. Though constructed differently from Paul's women, Shembe's women too are trapped between a patriarchal Bible and patriarchal culture" (West, 2006: 179).

---

2 It is common for a woman in traditional African societies to refer to her husband as "Father".

In this statement West raises an important question which I touched on about the problem of Muller concentrating on women and thus emphasising certain aspects as particular to women while in fact they obtain in the case of both women and men. I think here the answer lies in the manner in which Shembe organised his church, separating women from men at certain times. This made it possible for him to focus his attention on a single gender group and make them feel they are responsible and at the centre of the church's well-being. My suggestion is that in reading Shembe's texts, we need to be aware of the fact that Shembe was simply speaking to a particular group of people who were his prime focus at the time, and the writing down of the texts only took place later.

Jesus in Isaiah Shembe's Hymns

However, Isaiah Shembe's imagined relationship with Jesus was more complex than simply viewing him as an equal who was for the Jews what he himself was for the Zulus/Blacks. In hymn No. 82, Shembe praises Jesus' perseverance in the face of adversity, and the fact that Jesus did not resort to violence of any kind when his enemies abused him.

Mangibe njengawe Nkosi	Let me be like you, Lord
Ekukhonzeni kwakho	In your worshipping
Awesabanga lutho	You feared nothing
Noma bekuhlupha.	Even when they ill-treated you.
Mangibe njengawe Nkosi	Let me be like you, Lord
Noma bekuhlupha	Even when they ill-treated you
Nasekufeni kwakho	Even in your death
Awushongo lutho.	You said nothing.

That "Lord" refers to Jesus is not immediately clear in the hymn. The word *Nkosi* that is used in this hymn could also refer to God, as in hymn No. 71 "*Nkosi yami ubungithanda*" [My Lord/God you Loved Me], and it can even refer to a chief/king. As suggested above, the use of "Lord" instead of Jesus here is likely to reflect respect, since in Zulu and other Nguni languages and cultures the first name of the respected person or being is avoided in speech. This avoidance makes it hard to tell who this *iNkosi* is. It requires one to be familiar with the story of Jesus' life, especially his crucifixion, in order to be able to tell that it is Jesus who is referred to here. In this hymn Shembe sees Jesus as a righteous man and wants to follow his example. There are at least two reasons given in the hymn for claiming Jesus' righteousness, and both of them had a bearing on Shembe's life. The first one is that Jesus was treated badly but he never gave up. He was persistent in his ministry even though it went against the will of those who wielded power both in the state and in religious institutions. Shembe himself encountered a similar predicament of being opposed by the state and the church. Also, it is said that Jesus did not retaliate to his tormentors in a violent manner, but instead he kept quiet until the end of his life. This may explain Shembe's stance of a non-violent resistance to the colonial government that mistreated him and all the black people.

That Jesus died for all the people's sins Shembe accepts and celebrates in Hymn No. 132:

Bamenywa ngowayelenga emthini	They are invited by he who hung on a tree
Esiphambanweni	On the cross
Emthini wokudelwa	On the tree of the forsaken
Umhlaba wazamazama	The earth quaked
Wayevuma ezami izono	He was confessing my own sins
Emthini wokudelwa	On the tree of the forsaken
.....	
Mina ngaphunyuzwa	As for me, I was relieved
Ngowayelenga emthini	By the one who hung on a tree
Senizwile wozani.	Now that you have heard, come.
Ezami zagqitshwa kanye naye	[My sins] were buried with him
Ethuneni, senizwile, wozani.	In the grave, you have heard, come.

Conclusion

Isaiah Shembe's appropriation or engagement with the Bible depends on what he intends to accomplish with a particular hymn he is composing. With the hymns on the birth of Jesus, he tries to negotiate his identity as a powerful healer and religious leader who is constantly violated by the state, the missionaries, and the Black educated elites. While this may seem to be pointing to a claim to be a Black Christ, it is in fact meant to iterate that his predicaments are the same as those faced by Jesus. This becomes clearer in the later hymns (at least according to the order of presentation in the hymnal) where he praises Jesus and wishes to be like him, and when he rejoices in the knowledge that Jesus died for his sins. He thus calls on the people to join him in worshipping Jesus. As stated earlier, it is this worship, not only of Jesus, but of God especially, which is the most prominent aspect and function of the hymns, rather than the 'politics' that is dealt with in the previous chapter. And also, this engagement with the Bible and its deliberate usage for particular purposes support the claim made in the previous chapter that the hymns need to be read more as Isaiah Shembe's creative texts, rather than as having been brought to him by heavenly spirits. These texts then become interesting and powerful religious poetry that contributes not only to the literature in IsiZulu but to (South) African literature more broadly.

CHAPTER 3

The Sacred Dance and the Question of Resistance

Introduction

The growing membership of Ibandla lamaNazaretha mentioned in the Introduction happens in tandem with the increasing popularity of the sacred dance both in terms of performers and spectators. Today, a number of dance regiments or groups have been established to make it possible for all the participants to get the opportunity to dance. In large meetings in July and January that take place in Ebuhleni, there are now about ten regiments (*izigcawu*) for men that are made up of people ranging in number from approximately one hundred to three hundred each (during weekdays these become smaller as many people are at work). Married women make up about twenty-five regiments while *amakhosazane* (maidens) make five regiments. This growing popularity of the sacred dance, post-apartheid, challenges scholars who posit that the sacred dance, as well as other Nazaretha expressive forms, was a response to the racial state. One of these, Muller, maintains that "Isaiah Shembe built a religious empire whose cultural truth facilitated a notion of power in opposition to the repressive and debilitating force of the state. For Isaiah's membership, power was induced as a creative force, enabling women and men to foster notions of hope, and thereby to survive the devastation and violation of their communities" (1999: 20). In a similar vein Brown has argued that, "The performance of the hymns constituted a ritual of empowerment for Shembe's followers, almost all of whom had been politically and economically marginalised" (1999: 211).

In her paper "Figures of Colonial Resistance" (1989), Jenny Sharpe deals with this important issue of articulating resistance to colonialism. "Are the colonised indeed passive actors of a Western script?" she asks. In response to her question she suggests tentatively that, "It might well be argued that studies expounding the domination of dominant discourses merely add to their totalizing effects, for they show colonizers to have the power that even they were incapable of enforcing" (1989: 138). However, she also warns, in a way more relevant for my argument here, that "the correction of such readings with the simple presentation of native voices can equally impose a Western authority upon non-Western texts" (138). My contention here is along those lines: that in trying to find resistance to colonialism by simply equating events like the sacred dance with resistance or response to colonialism, without examining if

 | DOI 10.1163/9789004320628_005

these performances are indeed connected to colonialism in the way they are said to be, such postulations end up offering undue power to colonialism itself. In other words, they "impose a Western authority upon non-Western texts". At the same time, their tendency deprives people of their agency as actors in their own history since all they do can only be reactive.

So much has been said about the importance of context in social sciences. Bauman and Briggs maintain that, "Attempts to identify the meaning of texts, performances, or entire genres in terms of purely symbolic, context-free content disregard the multiplicity of indexical connections that enable verbal art to transform, not simply reflect, social life" (1990: 69). I am not arguing against a consideration of context in ethnographic studies. What I am strongly against are formulations like the ones stated above that tend to restrict their investigations to the surfaces, not going deep enough to find out exactly why people do what they do. Or to demonstrate, beyond reasonable doubt, that such connections as they are making do exist.

In other words, my worry is that their methodology, which allows them to study the historical context on its own and then use their findings to explain events that take place in other contexts, offers them an easy way out. If they know that people engaged in a particular event are oppressed, then it goes without saying that their participation in that event is in response to their circumstances. Such ideas should be used as hypotheses that need to be tested and confirmed, not just be taken as 'the truth' or what actually happens. What is needed, and this book is trying to do, is an analysis of the motivations for people to act the way they do, or to do what they do.

The demonstrations and strikes that were the order of the day during the years of apartheid decreased significantly after the end of apartheid. So, one would expect the same to happen to the sacred dance if its overriding function had been as response to the socio-economic and political problems of the people who performed it. And while I do acknowledge that the economic conditions of many South Africans still remain unchanged, it would be opportunistic to say that these performances are now a response to those economic challenges.

What I am trying to demonstrate in this chapter in particular, and in this study in general, is that there are particular motivations for people to take part in the sacred dance performances, and it is through searching for and exploring these motivations that we can begin to understand the role and meaning of these performances for the people involved. Here I look at oral narratives of dreams and miracles about the importance of *umgidi* (sacred dance) in this world and in 'heaven'. Oral testimony relating to the sacred dance shows that in the imagination of many members of Ibandla lamaNazaretha who take part in the dance, God, Shembe and the ancestors are the main audience. I argue that, while the sacred dance is meant to be a form of worship, and members take part in order to appease their ancestors as well as Shembe, it is also (in actuality) a form of entertainment, and provides performers with the space in which they can define their individual and collective identities. As a result, the presence of the living audience has an impact on the way in which performers perform. But, never is the sacred dance seen as a means of resistance to the state!

It is worth noting, however, that in dealing with the narratives I present below, I am not interested in their "truth claims" (Brown, 1999: 199). Instead, I treat these narratives as sources that have the capacity to reveal the forms of consciousness that would otherwise be hidden (Bozzoli, 1991). These narratives will help us understand what the sacred dance is, or what it is understood to be in Ibandla lamaNazaretha.

The Sacred Dance as a Miraculous Practice

In one of the testimonies in Hexham and Oosthuizen (1996: 110), Qambelabantu Ngidi tells of his arrival at eKuphakameni. Like many people, he came to eKuphakameni because he was sick. I suspect that (from listening to and reading other stories and testimonies) he had tried a number of traditional and Western doctors without success. But what is interesting for this chapter is what he saw when he had got to eKuphakameni:

> When I arrived there, I looked at the dancing. There I saw in the midst of the dancers my late brother coming up. I saw him in daylight. I was not asleep. Then I remembered what people had said that there is Malay magic in this place. Now my brother was there before my eyes and laughed at me. I pinched myself to see if I was still alive. Then I ran away from the dancing ground, and I ran as far as Durban. On another day, I met one of my brothers from home and told him what I had seen at eKuphakameni. My brother was perplexed and said: "Hau, they had fetched this brother from McCord Hospital, where he had been a patient, to bring him home. They had pulled the seats in the car flat and laid him on them. When they were at Vokwe, he said to them: "Tell me, when we shall come to the fork, where the way branches off to eKuphakameni." However, when they got there, they forgot to tell him. When they had already passed that place, he said the same request again ... Then he said to them, "When I shall be better, I shall go there to the hills of eKuphakameni." They were astonished, how he could speak of his recovery, since he was so sick. This was my brother, whom I had seen at eKuphakameni, who had said these

> words. He had come home and passed there away. Then I began to see the events at eKuphakameni in another way. (Hexham and Oosthuizen, 1996: 110)

In another story, an Indian man travelled to eKuphakameni in the 1940s to tell the congregation that Isaiah Shembe had come to him in a dream. Shembe told the man to come to eKuphakameni to tell amaNazaretha that they were no longer dancing the dance of heaven. He said men were dancing to attract women, not to worship God. The Indian man told AmaNazaretha that when Shembe came to him while in India, sending him to South Africa, he (the Indian man) told Shembe that he had no money to go to South Africa. Shembe then told him to go fish in the sea, and that the first fish he would catch would have enough money inside it for him to travel to South Africa and back. When he went to fish the following day, he caught a fish and as promised he found the money inside the fish, and he used it to come to eKuphakameni. His story was recorded by the then secretary and archivist of the church, Petros Dhlomo, but was lost in the fire after the split in the church in 1977 (Minister Khumalo, Interview, 10 January 2009). While this story echoes a biblical narrative in Matthew 17:24–27 where the temple-tax collectors find Jesus with Peter in Capernaum (Jesus urges Peter to go and cast a line in the lake. He tells him that if he opens the mouth of the first fish he catches he will find a silver coin and give it to the tax collectors for both of them), it says a lot about the significance of the sacred dance in the church: that it is primarily a form of worship, even though sometimes the performers use it differently.

Both these stories are representative of the narrative culture that characterises Ibandla lamaNazaretha. They are part of the church's cultural capital that circulates in sermons, tape and video records, and in conversations. These two in particular testify to the importance of the sacred dance as a ritual practised in the church by and for both the living and the dead. As stated earlier, the sacred dance is imagined to bridge the gap between the physical and the spiritual worlds.

In Ibandla lamaNazaretha the sacred dance is not just taken to be a physical act that an onlooker would perceive it to be. It is considered to be a form of worship, and even the audiences themselves, by watching the sacred dance, are involved in worship. Thus when amaNazaretha go to watch the sacred dance, they wear their prayer gowns (*iminazaretha*) and are urged to sit down when they watch. And when the performance is finishing for the day, the virgin girls' leader, MaSangweni[1], or Shembe himself, blesses the dancers and when this happens, all the dancers and the audience kneel to accept the blessing by

1 MaSangweni has since passed away and MaDuma is the one who does this.

uttering "amen", even though the person giving the blessing would be facing those who had been dancing.

Both watching and participating in the sacred dance are believed to have healing powers. J.G. Shembe is reported to have sent people who had come to him sick to watch the sacred dance. One man by the name of Mbambo was very infuriated when he was told to go and watch the sacred dance when he had come to eKuphakameni because he was sick. He kept complaining that "I'm so sick but he (J.G. Shembe) says I should sit here?" But when the dance was completed and Shembe said "*Inkosi inibusise*" (God bless you) Mbambo claims he felt as though a burden was being lifted from his shoulders and his illness ended (Bheki Mchunu, Interview, 15 Nov. 2008). In a similar story, a white girl from England had a dream in which Shembe told her to come to eKuphakameni to be healed. The family left England for South Africa when they had been told that the man who came to their daughter in a dream could be in Africa. In Cape Town they continued their enquiry and they heard about the presence of Shembe in Durban. When they arrived at eKuphakameni J.G. Shembe told the girl to take part in the sacred dance with virgin girls:

> She danced for a while. Shembe said, "*Hawu*, have you ever seen a white person dance? Bring her back here." And so the Lord Shembe said to the parents, "Take her away, she is healed." And so they took the girl to Durban and booked a place in one of the hotels. They wanted to see the truth of what the God's prophet had said without even praying for, or laying hands on, the girl. (Muller, 1999: 160)

The girl's menstrual problem came to an end after three months. Her parents went to eKuphakameni to find out how much they could pay for the help they had received, but Shembe told them that "God's gift is not to be bought by money". He told them to go back to their country and tell other white people there that the saviour had arrived and he was at eKuphakameni. When they were overseas the white couple sent gifts to Shembe in the form of a flag, a watch and a bell. In the letter accompanying the gifts, they wrote: "Remember us when the bell rings, the clock will tell the time for the beginning of the service. May the Lord remember us when he calls the people into church. With the flag I am saying that Africa has triumphed ... The nations of the world have been waiting for the Lord. Now they have heard that he is at eKuphakameni" (Muller, 1999: 160).

Predictably, in her interpretation of this narrative, Muller emphasises the fact that it was the dance of the virgin girls which the white girl was urged to join: "A provocative narrative, Mrs Ntuli's telling of this Nazarite cultural treasure powerfully links together Isaiah Shembe's ability to heal *with the ritual purity of the dancing bodies of virgin girls*. He did not even lay hands on her. All she had to do was participate in the sacred dance of virgin girls, and wait for her body to heal" (160, emphasis added). As Mbambo's story, and many others, show, it is not so much the purity of the bodies of virgin girls that is emphasised in this story, but the sacred dance itself. In other words, a sick person could have been a man and he would have been told to join the sacred dance of men, or simply to watch it.

There are stories told in the church in which a person merely watches the sacred dance without having been instructed to do so and is healed in the process. An example is that of a woman who used to live near George Koch Hostel. This woman is said to have gone to watch the Nazaretha men doing 'practice' there and as she watched, she claimed she saw lightning coming out of the *amashoba*[2] as the men were dancing. When she left, she realised that her bleeding sickness had stopped. She went the following weekend to tell the dancers what had happened (Bhekinkosi Mhlongo, Interview, 16 Dec. 2008).

Two of Isaiah Shembe's hymns, Hymn No. 124 "*Ngiyahamba weGuqabadele*" [I am Travelling, oh *Guqabadele*] and Hymn No. 135 "*Baba Ngikulolu hambo*" [Father I am in this Journey], talk about a journey to heaven, and touch on perhaps the most important function of *umgidi* in the imagination of the Nazaretha members. *Umgidi* is viewed as playing an important role in the journey to heaven. The heavenly spirits who come to fetch the soul of a dying person come beating the drums and singing dance hymns. Bongani Mthethwa (1996: 8) tells the story of a member of Ibandla lamaNazaretha who had died and encountered demons on his way to heaven. The demons said the man belonged to them:

> But, it was pointed out to the demons that the good deeds of that man far outweighed his sins. Then the angels, who were dressed in full *ukusina* regalia, arrived, singing and playing the drums, to rescue this man's spirit from the demons. When the demons heard the sounds of the approaching drums, they vanished in great fear!

One of the common teachings of the overnight meetings of *u*-14, *u*-23 and *u*-25 is that a person needs to be able to dance, sing dance songs and 'play' the sacred dance instruments like beating the drum and blowing the *imbomu* (kudu horn trumpet) because sometimes these spirits are believed to ask the

2 *Ishoba* (singular). A stick decorated with the skin from the tail of a cow, leaving the furred end of the tail at the point of the stick.

person they have come to fetch to do either of these things as a test of whether that person is worthy of travelling with the spirits from heaven. Hymn No. 124 points to the obstacles one encounters on the journey to heaven. The journey to heaven is a dangerous one, and anyone taking it should dedicate him- or herself to serving God; and in return God will stretch out His arms and protect the person from the dangers to be encountered on the way. If the person is proven to be a true Nazaretha, having dedicated him- or herself to singing and dancing for Jehovah here on earth, then that person will do the same on the way to heaven, thus pleasing those who have come to fetch him/her, and it is the same singing and dancing which will open the gates to heaven for that person:

Basinda ngokuphephisa	It is only by chance that they escape
Abahamba engozini	Those who travel in danger
Baphunyuzwa wukuzidela	Respite for them is through dedication
Balithande elizayo.	And loving the world to come.
Chorus:	
Ngiyahamba weGuqabadele	I am travelling, Oh *Guqabadele*
Ngalolu hambo lwakho	In this journey of yours
Yelula isandla sakho	Spread out your hand
Ulubusise uhambo lwami.	And bless my journey.
Ngesifingo sokusa	At the dawn of the morning
Ngiyongena eKuphakameni	I will enter eKuphakameni
Amasango ayovuleka	The gates will open
Ngokungena kwami.	Upon my entrance.
Chorus:	
Ngohlabelela ngentokozo	I will sing with happiness
Emzini oyingcwele	In the holy village
Bajabule abahlangabezi bami	Those fetching my soul will rejoice
Ngokungena kwami.	Upon my entrance.
Chorus:	
Ngomsinela obongekayo	I will dance for the praiseworthy one
Ngingasenanhloni	Having no shyness
Phakamani masango	Rise up you gates
Phakamani singene.	Rise up so we can enter.

In a similar vein, the greater part of hymn No. 135 talks about the difficulty of the way to heaven. In the first part of the hymn the words "sorrow", "tears", "death", and "fear" abound. The journey is said to be of sorrow and tears, and the speaker begs God, the Beautiful One, to keep him or her company in 'this' wilderness which is a journey to heaven. The speaker is overwhelmed by fear and wishes God may give him/her strength to stand the suffering one encounters in the valley of sorrow. It is in this valley that those who did not do well on earth will stay and suffer till judgement day which itself is likely to bring more sorrow and suffering:

Ukwesaba kungembethe	Fear has engulfed me
Kepha ngawe mangingesabi	But with you let me not fear
Thela kimi umoya wamandla	Pour me the spirit of strength
Ngiyakwedlula esigodini sosizi.	So I will pass the valley of sorrow.
Lapho abaningi bemisiwe	Where multitudes are stopped
Esigodini sosizi lokufa	In the valley of sorrow of death
Balindele umhla wokuphela	They await judgement day
Ukukhala nokugedla amazinyo.	The crying and the disappointment.

The hymn concludes on a positive note where the triumphant ones enter heaven. These ones become heirs of heaven and enter the gates dancing. This dance is both a celebration of victory over the earth and its whims and is proof that this person worshipped God on earth and is worthy to enter heaven:

Izindlamafa zonke zimenyiwe	All the heirs are invited
Ziyongena ngokusina emasangweni	They will enter the gates dancing
Makabongwe uJehova	May Jehovah be praised
Inkosi enamandla.	The Lord with strength.

One member of the church mentioned above, Bheki Mchunu, believes that the sacred dance happens on earth and in heaven at the same time. It is Shembe who mediates between these two worlds. In elaboration of his statement he narrated to me two stories. The first one happened in eKuphakameni in the time of J.G. Shembe. It was the July festival and the church members were going to dance. As a rule they waited for the word that they had to go. Before this word, which says, "*Lithi izwi leNkosi, ayiphume imigidi*" [The word of the iNkosi says the dance regiments may go to dance], the dancing cannot start. So this day they waited and waited and there was no announcement that the dancing should start. Later, when the word did come that the dancing should start, some dancers heard the drums and singing underground as if leading the way to *esigcawini* (the dancing ground). Mchunu concludes from this narrative that Shembe, in not giving the word that the dancing should begin, knew that the heavenly spirits were not ready yet.

In another story, J.G. Shembe was watching the sacred dance of the virgin girls. After some time, he sent someone to tell one girl that "God bless her, she may stop dancing". The girl, like everyone else who saw what happened, was astonished by what Shembe had done. In the following service, Shembe asked the congregation if they knew why he had urged that girl to stop dancing. The congregation said they did not, and he said her dancing was too close to that of heaven. She was dancing with heavenly spirits and if he had let her continue, she could have died. This story echoes the story of Mthethwa's aunt, MaTembe Nzuza. Mthethwa says she had reproached her for taking part in both the morning and afternoon sacred dance performances while her health was not good due to her old age; "She replied that she had actually hoped to die during that *ukusina* event. She claimed that while she was dancing she had reached the gates of heaven, and was sorely disappointed at having been returned to the earth" (Mthethwa, 1996: 8).

While all these miraculous stories relating to the sacred dance are important in understanding what the sacred dance is in Ibandla lamaNazaretha, and they inform people's decisions about taking part in the sacred dance and the way they dance the sacred dance, an examination of the sacred dance as practised shows that there are other motivations for Nazaretha members to take part in the sacred dance and there are other factors that influence the way they perform. In his study of gender and performance in Swahili, Ntarangwi points to the discrepancy between what is stated as ideal and what actually happens in practice: "That lived experiences and practices form the crux of a culture, and not the expressed ideals that are constantly negotiated through practice, is now a truism in the social sciences" (2003: 105). The ideal with respect to the sacred dance is that since it is not just for the performers but for their dead relatives as well, and also because it is meant to integrate this earth and heaven, the sacred dance is supposed to be performed similarly by everyone and everywhere. But what actually happens is not always what is ideally expected. As Ntarangwi goes on to say: "it is by looking at Swahili life as practised rather than as stated that I have been able to understand the social contradictions and contingencies reflected in Swahili musical expression" (2003: 105). I argue the same for the Nazaretha and the sacred dance. The rest of this chapter looks at the discrepancy between what *umgidi* should be and how it is practised.

The Sacred Dance as a Ticket to 'Hell'

Ideally, since the sacred dance is meant to be solely for worshipping God, it has to be performed in the same way every time. In other words, if members dance for the same song, they should do the same thing, so that even someone who comes from a far-away area would be able to participate if he or she knew how to dance for that particular song. To achieve this similarity, it is important that the dance is kept unchanged. It should be done the way Isaiah Shembe taught it. However, there are many people and groups who improvise on the standard dance styles to create their own vernaculars, so that anyone who does not 'practise' with them would be unable to dance with them. In most cases it is the younger members, mostly young men, but young women as well, who meet on some days to teach each other the sacred dance, and it is they who tend to improvise on the standard dance style. Many older members of the church are against this improvisation, although one can tell from the story of the Indian man (mentioned above) that this tendency to improvise the sacred dance started many years ago. Many older members in higher positions in the church criticise this 'alteration' of the sacred dance. The title for this section comes from the speech given by one of the most influential intellectual leaders of the church, Evangelist M. Mpanza,[3] in the workshop organised by the Nazaretha Tertiary Student's Association (NATESA) on the Pietermaritzburg campus of the University of KwaZulu-Natal on the 14th September 2008:

> *Ukusina kwethu lapha ku 23 naku 14 naku 25 akunginamisi mina. Because siyasina nje. The way okusinwa ngayo ayingitshengisi ukuthi sifundisiwe ukuthi ukusina kuyini. You have to be taught firstly about i-religious significance yokusina. That's why ukusina kwethu... Mvangeli baningi abantu abayongena esihogweni ngokusina. Kunabantu abayongena esihongweni bengeniswa wukusina. Bahambe baye emgidini besina zonke izinsuku bese bengena esihogweni bengenela lokho kusina kwabo. Because they have no idea ukuthi ukusina kuyini. Ukusina bacabanga ukuthi yinto eyenzelwa abantu. Immediately uthatha ukusina ukuthi yinto yakho okufanele ubukwe ngabantu, you are gone. That's why kukhona... lento eniyenzayo, ikakhulukazi intsha... ukube kusekhona ubaba iLanga, thina saphila ngaphansi kwababa iLanga. Ukusina akushintshwa. Njengamanje njena sekuthiwa kukhona isikotshi. Lapho uthola ukuthi ngisho*

3 Mpanza has since left Ebuhleni to form his own New Nazareth Baptist Church. He was still a member of Ebuhleni when this event took place.

> *ukuhlabelela akusahlatshelelwa ngale ndlela lena uma kuthiwa kuhlatshelelwa isikotshi. Isigubhu asisa... ayikho leyonto. Ukusina kukodwa, akudingi ukuthi kuthiwe kukhona ukusina kwensizwa kukhona ukusina kwabantu abadala. Ukusina kunesitep esisodwa. Uma sisina kufanele sikwenze ukusina kube yinto yasezulwini. Uma siko23 sifundisane ukusina.*
>
> Our dancing here in u-23, u-14 and u-25 meetings does not make me happy. Because we just dance. The way the dance happens does not show me that we were taught what the sacred dance is. You have to be taught firstly about the religious significance of the sacred dance. That is why our dancing... Evangelist, there are many people who will go to hell because of the sacred dance. There are people who will enter hell as a result of the dance. They go to the dance and dance every day and enter hell because of that dance. Because they have no idea what the sacred dance is. They think the sacred dance is something that is done for people. As soon as you take the sacred dance to be something you can use to attract people's attention, you are gone. That is why there is... this thing you do, especially the youth... if ILanga [J.G. Shembe] was still alive... we lived under the leadership of Father iLanga. The sacred dance is never changed. Nowadays it is said that there is the dance of the scotch. Where you find that even the singing it is no longer the way if they sing for the scotch. The drums are no longer... that is not it. The sacred dance is the same, it should not be that there is the sacred dance for young men and the other for older men. There is one step of the dance. If we dance we should make the dance to be the dance of heaven. If we are in 23 meetings, we should teach each other to dance. (Mpanza, Speech, September 2009, PMB)

Mpanza's talk incorporates many of the issues concerning the sacred dance that were discussed in the previous section. An important issue which is raised here that I have not touched on in the previous section is that of the conflicting ideologies of young and old members of the church and the struggle for the definition of personal identities and the identity of the church as such.[4] An interesting shift in his formulation is that, instead of transporting a person to heaven, if performed incorrectly, the sacred dance will send or will cause a person to go to hell. Also, he maintains that the sacred dance should be treated as something that is of heaven, meaning that it belongs to the spirits of heaven.

4 I look at this issue in more detail in the following chapter.

If the living beings do it, they do it on behalf of their dead relatives, so they should be aware of that fact.

But what comes out even more strongly from this speech is that the way the sacred dance is performed is not as Mpanza and many others think it should be performed. Another senior member of the church present at the workshop, Evangelist Mngwengwe, also voiced his concern about the present state of the sacred dance. His main point too was that the dance styles should be the same because Shembe taught his followers the same style. To expand on his point he told of the dream an *umkhokheli* (leader of women) had about the sacred dance. In his story, as in that of an Indian man, men are accused of using the sacred dance to attract women:

> *Ake nginixoxele lo mzekelo maNazaretha. Uthi omunye uNkosikazi, usengumkhokheli manje, owale kwaZulu, kodwa ngokuzalwa owaseMkhambathini. Uthi inkosikazi yasezweni lakubo kwaZulu ivuke nesibonakaliso. Kwalalwa ngesikhathi nje esejwayelekile, kwaze kwashaya o- 9/10 le nkosikazi ingavuki. Ithe uma seyivuka le nkosikazi, ithi le nkosikazi ibikade ihambile ihambe neNkosi iNyanga yeZulu. Ithi iNyanga yeZulu "Woza lapha mntanami ngizokukhombisa ongakwazi ngikukhombise nokwaziyo. Okwaziyo yilokhu kusina osekusinwa amaNazaretha inhlayisuthi isinela ukuqonywa. Yikona-ke engizokukhombisa kona ngoba yikona oye ukubone. Inhlayisuthi incintisana ngo... isigcawu sisinye inkundla iyinye ulayini nolayini usine okunye okungasinwa hhabanye, kodwa isihlabelelo sibe sifana." Uthi lomama iNyanga yeZulu ithe basinela ukuqonywa. Wathi "Woza ngikukhombise!" Uthi ngempela wazibona esehamba, kwakusasinelwa esigcawini esingenzansi kungakayiwa phezulu. Uthi bathi uma befika lapho wathi "Yima-ke lapha mntanami ungabe usaqhubeka kakhulu. Bheka ngasesangweni." Uthi zaqhamuka izimoto kwaqhamuka amabhasi. Babe wukwehla nje, ibe wukwehla nje inhlalisuthi isine. Ibe wukwehla nje ikhiphe ulayini. Nabanye besasina laba baqhamuke abanye. Uthi ukusina kwakwehlukile kodwa isihlabelelo sasisisodwa. Uthi yathi iNyanga yeZulu, "Mntanami buka ukuthi lokhu kusina kuyefana na?" Uthi yayiphethe ipeni. Ilokhu idweba nje. Ihambe isigcawu nesigcawu ifike kulabo abasinayo ibabuke ibabuke besine ithi uma isiqedile ukudweba iqhubekele kwabanye. Uthi yaziqeda zonke izigcawu uthi ithe isuka yayililahla phansi lelobhuku, yathi lelibhuku lingcolile aliyi kuShembe.*

> Let me tell you a tale, you Nazaretha. A certain woman, she is a woman leader now, she lives in Zululand but she was born at Mkhambathini. She says a woman of their area in Zululand woke up with a dream. They

> went to bed at the normal time and nine/ten struck while this woman had not woken up. When she had woken up she said she had gone with *Inyanga Yezulu* (The Moon of Heaven, referring to Amos Shembe, the third leader). *INyanga Yezulu* says, "Come here you child so I will show you what you know and I will show you what you do not know. What you do know is this dance that is performed by the AmaNazaretha, the men, who dance in order to attract women. It is it that I will show you because you are used to seeing it. The *inhlalisuthi* (men) competing about… in one regiment each and every line dances its own dance different from that of others but the hymn is the same." This woman says *Inyanga Yezulu* said they dance so as to attract women. He said, "Come let me show you!" She says indeed she saw herself walking, by then the dances took place in the dancing ground below [meaning in the area where the main entrance to eBuhleni is], not high up [this is where *isigcawu*, dancing ground, is now]. She says when they arrived at the gate, he said stop here my child, do not go on any further. Look at the gate. "She says the cars appeared, buses appeared. As soon as they got off, as soon as the men alighted, they danced. As soon as they alighted they made a line. As the ones are still dancing, the others came and started dancing. She says the dancing was different but the hymn was the same. She says the *INyanga Yezulu* said, "Look my child, see if this dance is the same or not?" She says he was carrying a pen. Always putting crosses. He went to every regiment, watching them as they dance and after making a cross, moved to another regiment. She says he went to all the regiments and then she says he threw away that book. He said "This book is dirty; it will not go to Shembe." (Mngwengwe, Speech, September 2008, PMB)

One of the challenges facing the church today is trying to restore the sacred dance to what it used to be or to what it should be. UThingo, the father of the present leader, UNyazi Lwezulu, is reported to have told ministers to 'correct' the sacred dance so that he will also take part in it.[5] The problem though is that there are not many people who know how exactly the sacred dance was performed during the time of Isaiah Shembe. The oldest men still dancing today used to dance in the 1940s, and while they claim that the real dance is what they perform, this is questionable when one considers that the accusation that men were dancing to attract women, not what Shembe had taught, started in the 1940s and is exemplified in the story of the Indian man.

---

5 I heard this from a man called Phungula who used to live in Gauteng, at George Koch Hostel.

A question asked by one member of the audience in the workshop was "Who is responsible for teaching the sacred dance?", and there was no helpful answer. According to Mpanza, there should be a leader who will be able to go around all the regiments inspecting how they dance and stopping those who dance the 'wrong' way. He said the then present leader of all men, Minister Mathunjwa, was a quiet person by nature and does not confront people who abuse the sacred dance. But even if Mathunjwa was a different person and did confront dancers, it is still questionable to what extent his dance style is the one taught by Isaiah Shembe himself.

For my purposes what is important about this issue of the sacred dance being not what it should be is not the fact that dancers may 'go to hell', as Mpanza stated in his speech, but the implication of this issue with regards to the agency of the members as the creators of their own dance styles. The sacred dance in the Nazaretha Church is one of the forms of expression that is used in the constitution of selfhood. The problem stated above, of there being no one who can help teach the sacred dance as it was taught by Isaiah Shembe, worries only some of the Nazaretha members. There are many sacred dance performers who spend time improvising the sacred dance styles so that they create their own vernaculars. The idea behind these improvisations is both the perfection of the sacred dance, performing it in the best possible way, and the creation of difference through competition.

Competition involves declared competitions where different groups openly compete with each other in dancing for a given dance hymn, and it also involves undeclared competition where different groups or regiments and different lines in each regiment (as stated in Mngwengwe's story) compete with each other in the sacred dance of all people. Both these senses of competition include a definition of the self, which involves, "'a poetics of social action' (Herzfeld, 1985), an attention to the performance itself, in which it is the way things are done, rather than things themselves, which are foregrounded" (Erlmann, 1996: 226).

Competition in the Sacred Dance and Sacred Dance Competitions

Up until 2013 when the new leader, UNyazi, put an end to male leaders, before every sacred dance performance, the all-male leader, Minister Mathunjwa, (mentioned by Mpanza above) used to spend time advising dancers about the importance of the sacred dance for the members' ancestors and their guardian angels, and warning them against 'changing' the sacred dance from what Isaiah Shembe made it to be. Put differently, he used to warn them against abusing the sacred dance. But it was not all the members who were interested in hearing what the minister had to say. Some saw Mathunjwa's talks as a waste of time. Many did not join in his admonishing, but preferred to spread around the dancing ground, waiting for Mathunjwa to let the others go so that the dancing can begin. In the final dance of the 2008 January meeting on the 28th, this is what Mathunjwa said to the dancers:

> *Njengoba silapha nje phambi kukaNkulunkulu kumele ukuthi uma sekushaywa ifodo, nelakho liphume ebuhleni. Lingaphumi ebubini. Ngoba phela njoba silapha nje, kukhona nakho okunguSathane kulokhu kukuxabanisa. Njalo nje uyathuka abantu... Uyababonake abantu abangawazi umthetho? Uyababona labantu abaphuma bebheka le? Abawazi umthetho. Abazothi bebuya bebe begwabula abanye...*
>
> [As we are here in front of God, it is necessary that when the photo (of heaven) is taken, yours should appear on the good side. Not on the bad side. Because as we are here Satan is also present, causing us to quarrel. Always you find people... Do you see people who do not know the law?[6] Do you see these people who are going in the other direction? They do not know the law. They are the ones who will come back to push others.]

As Minister Mathunjwa was speaking, one of those who did not attend to his admonitions shouted: "*Zidedele zibulalane!*" ("Let them be so they will kill each other!") This remark reminds one of Viet Erlmann's chapter entitled, "Attacking with Song: The Aesthetics of Power and Competition" (1996: 224) where he deals with *isicathamiya* competitions. He traces these competitions to the idea of civilised advancement through "friendly rivalry" (226), where he argues that *isicathamiya* competitions need to be understood in terms of the economic situation of the majority of black people. The Africans in Natal and other parts of South Africa that Erlmann is talking about were at this time contending with difficult economic challenges that it was impossible for them to be involved in economic competition. This brought to them a need to garner "symbolic capital", and it is out of this that choral competitions emerged as compensatory strategies (226).

While this notion does inform the ideology behind *isicathamiya* competitions today, regional conflicts are perhaps the more powerful basis through which *isicathamiya* competitions can be explained. Drawing on the work of Jonathan Clegg, Erlmann states that *isicathamiya* competitions need to be

6 He was referring to those who did not come to listen to him.

seen as a form ritually expressing the regional conflicts in Natal, especially in the Msinga district where Clegg did his study. This conflict came after the destruction of the Zulu kingdom in 1879 when the system of age regiments lost its function "to counteract 'horizontal' opposition and territorial conflict" (1996: 226). The precolonial territorial conflicts, exacerbated by the shortage of land, could no longer be contained by the age regiment system and therefore they spilled over into conflicts where families and clans were pitted against each other.

A form of expression called *umgangela* (an inter-district competition of playful stick fighting) was developed as a mechanism to defuse these conflicts. The strict rules governing these *imgangela* events included the prohibition of stabbing and the use of other lethal weapons. However, in Msinga there were new territorial boundaries that had been set in place. This meant that people who used to belong to different districts might find themselves competing for jobs and grazing rights on the same white-owned farm. Consequently, there were many instances of conflict in these districts and institutions like *umgangela* could lead to serious confrontation. Thus, Erlmann maintains:

> It was in yet another attempt to mitigate these conflicts, that *ingoma* dance competitions arose (Clegg, 1982: 9). Stick fighting and *ingoma* were, of course, the creation of migrant workers. And it was migrant workers who transported these ritualised conflicts into the cities and transformed them to expressions of competition between rural territorial units for urban resources ... *isicathamiya* competitions, as I have indeed said, have to be seen as possibly the most recent form through which migrants give ritual expression to these conflicts. (1996: 228)

Both these senses of understanding about the origins of *isicathamiya* competitions may help explain sacred dance competitions in Ibandla lamaNazaretha. Firstly, there are many people who are now amaNazaretha who used to be engaged in conflicts between regions and between opposing political parties in their communities.[7] The reference to people having been involved in regional conflicts is common in Nazaretha sermons. UThingo, the late father of Unyazi (Inkosi Mduduzi Shembe) the present leader of the church in Ebuhleni,

7 I heard the story of two men I know who had been fighting on opposite sides. When they saw each other on opposing sides they were both so amazed and one of them promised that he would not close his eyes when praying because he was afraid that the other might kill him then.

touched on this topic in his sermon on 28 October 2008 at Judea Temple near Gingindlovu:

> *La manje sekuvikw'impi la. EBuhleni ngo Julayi ngasizwa wukuthi ngingene endlini kaBabomkhulu. Ngambiz'uBhombela, "Babomkhulu awuchithe nanguSathane usefikile la. Umi futhi ngezinzwane akabekile nezithende phansi." Ngaya futhi nakwekaBaba iLanga. "Baba nay' inhlekelele bo! Ngiphebezeleni." Ngaya nakweye Nyanga yeZulu ngafike ngasho into efanayo. Sayibona yehla lento. Siyayibong' iNkosi yaseKuphakameni! (Ibandla: Ameni! Uyingcwele! Ameni!) Senifun' ukulwelani manje ngoba niphuma ezimpini. UNkulunkulu kaShembe wasithanda wasikhipha kukho konke lokho. Abanye benu angabe abasekho manje. Nami angabe angisekho. Kodwa manje niyonelani kanje lento. Yini nifunukulwa manje?*
>
> [Here we are now trying to stop the war. In eBuhleni in July what helped me was to enter into Babamkhulu's room: "Babamkhulu please destroy this Satan, for he has come here. He is standing on tiptoe. His heels are not touching the ground." I entered Father *iLanga's* room (Galilee) and I said: "Father there is chaos here. Stop it for me." I went to Father *iNyanga YeZulu's* room and said the same thing. Then we saw this thing diminishing. We thank the Lord of eKuphakameni.
>
> (Congregation: Amen! You are Holy! Amen!)
>
> Why do you want to fight now because you are from the wars? Shembe's God loved us and removed us from all that. Some of you would have left this world by now, and me too I would have gone. Why are you spoiling this thing like this now? Why do you want to fight?]

While it is true that many amaNazaretha members have a history of territorial fighting, it does not seem to me that these conflicts are an important explanatory factor of competition in the sacred dance. Erlmann and Clegg's argument is not convincing even with regards to *isicathamiya*, because competition existed even in pre-colonial Africa and was manifested in many forms. *Ukuqhatha* and stick fighting (which Erlmann incorrectly claims is the creation of migrant workers) existed before colonialism and were rituals aimed at teaching young men self-defence and were performed by young men and men as forms of entertainment. Also, men would try to excel in stick fighting or in fighting in general in order to attract women because it was considered valuable knowledge. Even in the time of Shaka, people who excelled in battle were popular with women, and competing for the attention of women involved both fighting and dancing, among other things. Some men would compete in dance so as to attract women as the most adept dancers. They would also fight playfully (this is called *umgangela,* if it is between different districts, and it is called *ukuthabela* if it is between two men who may come from the same area), displaying their abilities in fighting, and they might fight seriously over a woman[8]. This links well with competition in the Nazaretha sacred dance and the idea that men dance in order to attract women.

Another more relevant form of competition is found in weddings. Nazaretha weddings, as well as African weddings in general, are characterised by dance competitions between the groom's and the bride's parties. This is playful competition created to add fun and interest in the dancing. But in Ibandla lamaNazaretha, perhaps because the sacred dance is important in both the initial wedding (taking place in Temples of big congregational meetings where the leader of the church is present) and the final wedding that normally takes place at the home of the groom, this competition extends to even the bride and the groom. While this is a kind of undeclared competition where there are no judges and written judging criteria, the question of whether the groom beat the bride or vice versa in the dance is the one that is often asked. This, however, becomes more interesting news if the bride beat the groom.

Even though I have argued in this chapter that the sacred dance is not always practised as it was ideally meant to be – a practice that is meant solely for worshipping God and is performed with the heavenly audience in mind – but that sometimes people perform in order to articulate their own personal identities, the third type of competition was designed in order to rectify the problem of the sacred dance being used for purposes other than worshipping God and honouring the ancestors.[9] These are declared competitions where all the participants are aware of the fact that they are competing; they are given the hymn to be used in the competition so that they can practise beforehand and there are prizes to be won in the competition. These competitions were first organised by NABACHU,[10] which was started in 1990 at the behest of the then leader, Amos Shembe. The purpose of forming this

8 There are many stories of women who married their men because they were good fighters. My own maternal grandmother is reported to have had an abusive boyfriend who beat her and anyone who courted her. She used to tell her children (and others) how she felt sorry for a poor man who was about to be beaten by her former boyfriend. But when my grandfather beat the bully, he won the love of my grandmother.

9 Personal communication with Evangelist Mkhize, President and founder of the Nazaretha youth organisation generally known as NABACHU [YO FO SHE] (Short for Nazareth Baptist Church Youth for Shembe).

10 See footnote 19 above.

organisation was "to strengthen and revive the culture of respect and of *ubuNazaretha* (the sense of being Nazaretha) to the youth of the church" (Evangelist Mkhize, Interview, 20 April 2009). Put differently, the formation of NABACHU was an attempt to get the children of amaNazaretha interested in the church as they were seen to be falling away: "If they were tired [of the church] while we were still alive, what was going to happen to *ubuNazaretha* when we were gone?". To tackle this problem, the organisers of this body tried to find ways to interest the young. They sought to bring together aspects of the church that were likely to interest the youth, and they also looked around them for help. A programme aired on UKhozi FM every Sunday, "*UNkulunkulu nomuntomusha*" [God and the Youth], became a role model for NABACHU, and slogans used in "*UNkulunkulu nomuntomusha*" were copied and used by NABACHU. One of these, which became like the trademark of *UNkulunkulu nomuntomusha*, went like this:

Leader: *Kumnand'ukuba lapha!*
Group: It's nice to be here!
Leader: It's nice to be here!
Group: *Kumnand'ukuba lapha!*

When addressing the youth, especially members of NABACHU, the leaders of this organisation often used this slogan as it was used in "*UNkulunkulu nomuntomusha*" with a little addition at the end which went like:

Leader: *Ameni-ke!* [Amen, then]
Group: Amen!

Within the church the sacred dance was on top of the list of things that could be used to interest the young. Thus sacred dance competitions were started with the aim of attracting the youth as well as standardising the sacred dance. As Mkhize maintains, competitions "are not merely competitions, they were started in order to bring about the correct way of dancing the sacred dance". This meant bringing an end to dancers having different styles of dancing. To achieve all this, the competition organisers used older knowledgeable people as judges, and designed their scoring grids in such a way that the competitions promoted the "correct" way of dancing. The features that were looked for by the judges included:

1. Connectedness between group and leader. Here they are looking at how the leader is able to communicate with the rest of the group and at whether or not the group hears and understands the leader.[11]
2. Steps for dancing the hymn. This looks at whether or not the group follows all the correct steps for that particular hymn and also how well they go about moving from one step to the next.
3. The positioning of the shields. Here a group receives points for holding up and lowering their shields at the correct points of the hymn. The judges also look at whether the group hold their shields in the same way i.e. if the shields are raised, are they raised by all the dancers at the same time?
4. The positioning of *ishoba.*[12] What is marked in *ishoba* is the same as with the shield.
5. The rhythm/stamping of feet. At times when dancing one is expected to touch the ground softly and at other times to stamp hard on the ground. Points are given for doing this at the right places.
6. Facial expression. This is perhaps the most interesting feature and it encourages dancers to relate their performance to the meaning of the hymn. The facial expression of the dancer has to correspond with what the hymn is saying, so that, says Mkhize, if the hymn says "the sun has arisen and set/ While I have done nothing good", the dancer is not supposed to be smiling because what is said in the song is not good.[13]

While it is true that the marking criteria (and therefore the competitions) can promote the 'correct' performance of the sacred dance, they also promote dancing the sacred dance not with God and the ancestors in mind. As the dancers prepare for and dance in the competition, what they think about is how to impress the judges (and the whole audience) and win trophies.

---

11 The leader is the one who uses the flute to tell the rest of the group what to do.

12 This is the short stick used for dancing. It is decorated with the skin from the tail of the cow, with its furred end. This fur is called *ishoba* and gives its name to the stick. If it is not decorated like this it is simply called *induku* (stick) and if the stick has a knob at its point it is called *iqabanga.*

13 I think the idea for this may have been borrowed from *isicathamiya* as it is here that performers tend to demonstrate what their songs say, and their facial expressions are in line with what they are singing.

NABACHU's sister organisation, NATESA (Nazaretha Tertiary Students' Association), also organises functions in which sacred dance competitions feature as part of the programmes. In the workshop held in September 2008 mentioned above, the main parts of the programme were a talk by Minister Mvubu about the practice and importance of overnight meetings of *u*-23, *u*-14 and *u*-25, and the sacred dance competition in which representatives from seven campuses took part, of which three (University of KwaZulu-Natal, Pietermaritzburg; Durban University of Technology, Durban and Pietermaritzburg campuses) were represented by both male and female dancers. The score sheets used by the judges to allocate points were the same for both the young women's and the young men's competitions, except for the headings stating "*Inhlalisuthi*" for young men and "*Intabayepheza*" for young women. The criteria used for evaluating the dancers (see below) were markedly different from the ones used by NABANCHU:

TABLE 1 *Criteria for judging religious dance* (Umgidi)[a]
Intabayepheza [*Virgin Girls*]

To be judged	Marks	UKZN DBN	DUT PMB	UKZN EDGW	UKZN PMB	DUT DBN	UNIZUL	MUT
Uniform	10							
Line Co-ordination	15							
Steps Followed	15							
Singing	10							
TOTAL	50							

a I am grateful to Ndumiso Zuma, chairperson of NATESA in PMB campus (2008/2009), for giving me this 'score' sheet.

Even though points 1, 3 and 4 in NABACHU's competitions could be classified as "line co-ordination" in the NATESA one, and the one about steps followed is the same for both, I think the inclusion of uniform in NATESA's and its exclusion in NABACHU's score sheets (even though it is allocated lower marks than 'line co-ordination' and 'steps followed') emphasises different purpose on the part of the designers. The question of dress is an important one for NATESA members, whose tertiary education culture imposes on them certain dress codes.[14] As stated in the Introduction, amaNazaretha have until fairly recently been regarded as backward and uneducated, and both these bodies of Nazaretha youth engage with these criticisms (consciously and unconsciously) in their respective activities. Most Nazaretha members in tertiary institutions (and those who did not reach that level of education) I have spoken to were marginalised while they were still at school as Nazaretha children. They were ridiculed as people who worshipped a human being and whose leader was believed to have created artificial wings and attempted to fly. They are also aware of the fact that they are seen to be backward and try to present themselves otherwise. While in the original score sheets of NATESA photos of a man and a virgin girl wearing *umgidi* attire were inserted, the designers were not expecting those when they included "uniform". They were thinking of more 'modern' and acceptable kind of dress (in the context of the University).

This leads to my argument with regards to this 'declared' competition in the sacred dance. While it is hard to explain where the first types of 'undeclared' competition are coming from, this one is more clear-cut because as these are declared, one can gain clues from things like criteria used for judging and the identities of the bodies that organised the competitions as well as the participants. The idea of sacred dance competitions offers organisers a chance to develop interest in the Church because the sacred dance is popular with the youth (as a means of entertainment, not worship) and the idea of 'friendly' competition and the prospect of winning add more attraction to the dance. These competitions are also linked to the need for the youth of the church to articulate their own identity as members of the Nazaretha Church. The sacred dance competition on the Pietermaritzburg campus allowed Nazaretha students to leave the closed doors of the lecture theatre where the talks were taking place and occupy an open space on the university lawns where all could see them. As they were beating the drums, blowing the kudu-horn trumpets and dancing, they were declaring that they were Nazaretha members and they were proud of it.

---

14 There are a number of Nazaretha girls who succumb to peer pressure and start wearing trousers when they are in tertiary institutions even though these are prohibited in the Church and they had not been wearing them before.

Conclusion

In this chapter I have been concerned with showing that, according to the members of the Nazaretha Church, there are acceptable and unacceptable ways of performing the sacred dance. I have attempted to show that while the sacred dance is ideally meant to remain unchanged and to be uniformly performed at all times, this tends not to be the case in reality. I argued that even though this is an ideal generally accepted by many older members and members in higher positions, in reality there are many other motivations for people to take part in the sacred dance and there are many other factors that influence the performance of the sacred dance. It is through competitions, both declared and undeclared, that one actually encounters the sacred dance being used for purposes other than worshipping God and appeasing the ancestors. In exploring the ideals about what the sacred dance is and how it should be performed, and the motivation for people to take part in the sacred dance – which may or may not be to worship God and appease the ancestors – I have been trying to challenge the view that the Nazaretha expressive forms, including the sacred dance, were intended to challenge the state or were a response to colonialism. The reason why these scholars hold this view is that they "[understand] the church within the framework of their own concepts" (Becken, 1996: x). And because of this, in Spivak's terms now, in representing amaNazaretha, these scholars "represent themselves as transparent" (1988: 275).

CHAPTER 4

Virginity, Sexual Abstinence and the Maidens' Rituals

Introduction

Since its inception, Ibandla lamaNazaretha's followers were mainly women and girls. Many, if not most, of these women and girls were joining the church against the wishes of their husbands and fathers. Joel Cabrita points to the dialogic relationship between Isaiah Shembe and the headmen, the chiefs, and the state regarding women who deserted their homes to follow Shembe: "Chief Msebenzie of the Lower Umzimkhulu complained in 1915 to the Magistrate that since 1913 Shembe has drawn 'women and children, (who) have gone away with these preachers to Ixopo and Durban for two and sometimes three months at a time, without the permission of their husbands and fathers'" (2007: 114). There are many other accounts of conflict between women who wanted to follow Shembe and their men who tried to stop them. In one case, Chief Mthengeni of Eshowe District appeared in court for assaulting a Nazaretha preacher. In his defence, Mthengeni claimed that, the Nazaretha "induce our womenfolk to their kraal and they co-habit with them ... we object to our women going to them but they persist" (Cabrita, 2007: 115). Despite these objections from men and chiefs, women continued to follow Shembe. The members of Ibandla lamaNazaretha are reported to have been 95% female in a report of 1921.[1]

While Ibandla lamaNazaretha has certainly never been an egalitarian community in terms of gender and other social categories, women followers of Shembe, especially virgin girls, have always played a significant role in the life of the church. The significant space that virgin girls occupy in Ibandla lamaNazaretha is exemplified in the number of special rituals for them alone. I wish to focus on two rituals, *iNtanda* and *umgonqo*, which are linked to and continuous with each other. The first one, *iNtanda*, commences on the seventh of July with virgin girls leaving eBuhleni for *iNtanda*, and ends on the eighth when the girls return to eBuhleni to march around the home carrying long sticks (*izintingo*) they cut from *Ntanda*. Before they leave for *Ntanda*, the girls

1 Cabrita 2007: 114. See also SAB (NTS 1431, 24/214 Sergt Craddock to District officer, South African Police, 10 September 1921).

 | DOI 10.1163/9789004320628_006

hold a service which involves the reading of the Jephtah story. *Umgonqo* ideally begins on the eve of the 25th of July and ends on the 25th of September. On the 25th of July and on the 25th of September *amakhosazane* (virgin girls) go to the river (*ezibukweni*). Crucial for both these rituals is that the maidens need to be virgins for them to be qualified to take part in them. So below, I look at virginity testing in Ibandla lamaNazaretha before I examine in more detail the two abovementioned rituals.

Virginity Testing in Ibandla LamaNazaretha

Isaiah Shembe placed a great deal of significance on virginity and saw the role of virgin girls as crucial in the life of the Nazaretha community. In the words he said at Msinga (Machunwini) in 1933 he called upon parents to inspect their daughters for virginity so that they "may be worthy to stand before God" (Papini and Hexham, 2002: 119). He went on to recommend that, "in all the large temples, there should be twenty-four maidens who are virgins, and in medium-sized temples there should be twelve maidens and in small temples there should be six maidens who are virgins" (119). This recommendation is quite telling, in that it seems to suggest that virgin girls are the most important component of the temple, for without a particular number of virgin girls, a temple cannot exist. There is no such stipulation with regards to men, boys and young men, and married women.

However, this stipulation about the number of virgin girls is no longer adhered to or observed, to an extent that one hardly hears about it in sermons and other contexts. But what has recently been introduced (or reintroduced) is a more public kind of virginity testing that takes place in large congregational meetings; in July especially, normally from the second to the third of July. This is due to the fact that on the first of July is the commencement of the July meeting which is referred to as *ukungenisa umdedele* – literally meaning to let mdedele in – and the testing process has to take place immediately after that so as to allow the maidens to go to iNtanda having been tested for virginity. The testing process usually takes about two days or more, due to the large numbers of virgin girls being tested.

This reintroduction of virginity testing in Ibandla lamaNazaretha coincides with its revival in the larger community, especially in KwaZulu-Natal. Tessa Marcus remarks that virginity testing was "reinvented by older isiZulu speaking women who bear a disproportionate share of the burden of AIDS, caring for gravely ill adult children and coping with the economic crises that sudden mortality creates" (2009: 536).

As a response to the AIDS pandemic especially in KwaZulu-Natal, Marcus concludes that the ritual has little or no help at all: it does not safeguard virginity and it hardly has any clear relation to AIDS. One student interviewed argued that virginity testing is useless because a girl who passed the test "can lose her virginity any time after that certificate (given to show that she took the test)" (2009: 540), and another respondent voiced his/her doubt about the impact of virginity testing on the spread of AIDS, saying, "you get an (ornamental) hood for your behaviour and nothing else" (540).

I do not intend to enter into debates about the role of virginity testing in alleviating the spread of HIV/AIDS, or whether or not virginity testing can "contribute to altering patriarchal power relations in Zulu communities" as Nomagugu Ngobese and Kathryn Kendal have suggested (see Lambard, 1999: 551). Suffice to say here that I think the two scholars who have written articles on this topic, Murcus and Lambard, and are critical of virginity testing, seem to be looking at this, in Becken's terms, "through their own glasses" and they understand the ritual "within the framework of their own concepts" (1996: x). Thus it seems the research interviewees mentioned in their chapters are either not participants in the ritual or in the case of Lambard, those few who were unhappy with it. It is quite telling that when Lambard comments on what he calls the invasive nature of the ritual, he mentions a girl of thirteen who remarked that "she was shocked by the 'checking' procedure and would not participate again" (1999: 549). At least, this tells us that the many who do participate again do so on their own will, and like the girl mentioned here they know that they can choose not to participate again if that is what they want, and if they do lose their virginity as soon as they get their certificates (as someone suggested above), they will not have to participate again.

So if indeed in KwaZulu-Natal virginity testing has been revived as a way of dealing with HIV/AIDS, the reason for its reintroduction in Ibandla lamaNazaretha is quite different. Its significance is still in line with Isaiah Shembe's words in Umsinga where he said that maidens need to be tested in order to be 'worthy to stand before Jehovah.' On the side of the 'invasiveness' of virginity testing, one of my informants[2] concurred that it is quite unsettling to have to show your privates to someone else, even though she is a woman and the people around who see you are also women.

But it is important to note that, in Ibandla lamaNazaretha, as in the Zulu speaking community that does virginity testing, maidens are not forced to

2 This informant requested that I do not use her name. The interview took place on April 2013, in Pietermaritzburg.

take part in virginity testing.[3] The above mentioned informant has been taking part in this ritual for years; she started when she was still a student at the University of KwaZulu-Natal where she studied Dental Therapy, and now takes leave from work just to take part in virginity testing and the *iNtanda* ritual. So the question is why does she, as well as thousands other girls, do it? The three *amakhosazane* I interviewed at the University of Zululand emphasised that there was no push from their parents, as it seemed like there was no coercion on the side of the church as well (Interview with Slindile Malinga, Phindile Dube and Nqobile Buthelezi, University of Zululand, 17 August 2013). While it is required that maidens who take part in all the virgin girls' rituals must be virgins, there is no requirement for a virginity test certificate to take part in the *iNtanda* ritual and in the sacred dances that take place afterwards, even though it is encouraged that the girls who take part in these rituals should start by going for virginity testing.

The *inkosazane* I mentioned earlier is a twenty-five year old woman, and she takes part on the virginity testing on her own accord as her parents are not members of the church and so are not interested in the church's proceedings. The girls from the University of Zululand also are more or less in the same situations. While Phindile Dube's parents are members of Ibandla lamaNazaretha, she started virginity testing in 2004 in her community in Mtubatuba where she got interested when she saw other girls doing it. It was only in 2009 that she realised that it was done in the church as well and started doing it. She has participated every year since then. The second girl, Slindile Malinga, is the only Nazaretha in her family (it was her grandmother who was a Nazaretha member), her parents are Roman Catholics. Nqobile Buthelezi's mother is a Nazaretha, but she does not live with her, she lives with her aunt and uncle, who are not members of the church. So she is only grateful that they let her go to church and to the church's rituals including virginity testing.

It is Nompilo Mdletshe,[4] a 17 year old who lives in a flat in Mpangeni, who had a somewhat different situation with regards to taking part in the testing. She is the only member of the church in her home, so when she did go to eBuhleni for the first time in 2011, she did not quite like to go for the test. But the woman who lives with them in the flat who had taken her to eBuhleni insisted that she must go. She went there on the first day and before her was a girl who was no longer a virgin (she learnt later that she had been two months pregnant) and she was yelled at, beaten and chased away (the testing ladies

---

3 It is only recently, year 2013, that maidens who are getting married as virgins get tested for virginity before they are allowed to go to the temple for the wedding.

4 I interviewed her in a Flat in Empangeni on 16 December 2013.

said she was showing them filth). This scared her so much that she decided to leave without being tested but the woman who was staying with her insisted that she must do the test, or else give up *inansook* (warn by virgin girls to cover their heads) and wear a *doek* and stay with old women and girls that have children or have lost their virginity. She went the second day and felt so good about it that she claims whenever she goes to eBuhleni in July again, she will do it. Asked why she would do it again, she said: "Because it is the rule that before you can go to *iNtanda* you must be tested. And it feels good to have that red dot on your forehead and to hold the certificate."

The most important reason for the maidens to take part in the ritual of virginity testing is, in the words of Slindile Malinga, "to show that you really are *inkosazane* and you deserve to dress the way *inkosazane* dresses." This is very important because nowadays there are many girls who have lost their virginity but they still dress like virgin girls and treat themselves as virgin girls because they have no children. The church has been subjected to a number of scandals where a man would be engaged to a woman who is supposed to be a virgin girl, only to find that she was lying about it. In one such case which was written about in a local newspaper, the man had paid the lobola and other requirements like *umembeso*, and they had done the first part of the wedding called *ukuhlanganisa* which takes place in the large Temples where the church's congregational meeting takes place, but before the final wedding at the groom's home, the girl gave birth to someone else's child. Situations like this tarnish the name of the virgin girls, and those who are still virgins, and therefore 'complete', need to prove that and virginity testing is the only way they can go about it.

The *iNtanda* Ritual

The ritual now referred to as *iNtanda* or *oThingweni*[5] (long stick) appears to have started after Shembe encountered obstacles acquiring the land which is now called *Ntanda*. This ritual is intricately linked to the politics of South Africa at the turn of the century, especially the Native Land Act of 1913. The Native Land Act was the Union Government's response to the demands of the White South African farmers (and those in gold mining) who needed cheap Black labour. The Act separated more the 80 percent of good arable land for 'Whites' and prohibited Black South Africans from buying land in those 'White' areas. It was also intended to put to an end what was generally known

5 Because it is where virgin girls get their long sticks (*izintingo*).

as 'squatting'. This was a system in which Blacks could live in and plant the land owned by a 'White' farmer, and in return pay them in cash or part of the produce (Cope, 1993). The *iNtanda* story represents Isaiah Shembe's spiritual battle with an unjust government and its laws of segregation.

One of my interviewees, MaNtanzi Mhlongo, tells that Shembe was promised by a Frenchman that he would sell him the farm. When the Frenchman spoke to other white people, they told him that he should not sell his farm to a black person. When Shembe came with the money to pay for the farm, the Frenchman was not present. Shembe found a black man who worked for the Frenchman who told him that he should not leave the money because he [the worker] overheard the whites saying that the farm should not be sold to a black person. Shembe was saddened by this and went back to his congregation. He requested that the girls go to the farm to pray that the church should acquire it. He told the *amakhosazane* (maidens, sometimes referred to as *intaba yepheza*) to make grass coils and sleep on them instead of using sitting mats. The Frenchman then sold the farm to Shembe and, as a way of thanking God, Shembe made a vow that virgin girls would go to worship at *Ntanda* every July seventh. In this way, Shembe was offering his girls to God even though they were not to be a burnt offering like Jephtah's daughter. (MaNtanzi Mhlongo, Interview, 14 August 2009).

In terms of the actual practice of this ritual, the girls go to *Ntanda* on the seventh of July where they cut the long sticks and go to sleep. They wake up early in the morning and go to bathe in the river. At nine they hold a morning service and then the leader, referred to as *Mphathi* or *Anti* (aunt), advises them on how to behave as *amakhosazane*, emphasising the fact that *iNtanda* is for virgin girls only. One of the younger girls is urged to read the story of how the land which is now *iNtanda* was acquired and also the story of Jephtah and his daughter. The *iNtanda* story goes as follows, and covers in detail what MaNtanzi Mhlongo above summarised.[6]

> *Indaba Yomlando waseNtanda*
> *Inkosi yaseZulwini yakhuluma noNkulunkulu. Wathi akazi ukuthi uzobabekaphi abafelokazi nezintandane. UNkulunkulu wathi, "Ngiyezwa mntanami". Emveni kwalokho, kwafika umFrench wathembisa ukudayisela uShembe indawo. INkosi yaseKuphakameni yajabula kakhulu. Wathi,*

6 It was impossible for me as a male member of the church to get hold of the original text for the ritual, so I have used the text from Muller (1999) and translated it back to isiZulu. I am aware that the original text from which Muller translated may not be exactly like this, but I suppose the main ideas are the same.

"Ngempela Baba uhlale ungizwa." Wabe esehamba umFrench, eseyithathile inxenye yemali. Abamhlophe bambuza bathi, "Kungani umnikeza umhlaba? Kade kwashiwo ukuthi umhlaba akumele uthengwe ngumuntu omnyama." Babesho lokhu bengazi ukuthi bakhuluma ngoNkulunkulu. UmFrench wase eya kuShembe nemali ayeseyithathile kuyo iNkosi yaseKuphakameni. Wathi, "Umthetho eMgungundlovu uyangiphikisa". INkosi yaseKuphakameni yathi, "Ungangiqambeli amanga ngoba uzobona ukuthi ngingumphrofithi."

Wadumala kakhulu. UNkulunkulu wakhuluma kuye wathi, "Usungikhohliwe na? Udumaleleni?"

UShembe akamphendulanga umFrench. Wathi uzothumela izingane ziyohlakula ukhula emasimini akhe umFrench. Eyokuqala inkosazane yafika. Yaphotha izinkatha ezanele amakhosazane ayekhona lapho. UNkulunkulu wathi, "Zinike amakhosazane ahlale phezu kwazo uma ethandaza." Umphrofithi uShembe wabe esekhipha elinye izwi, ethi inkosazane eyaziyo ukuthi ayiphelele emthethweni kaNkulunkulu akumele iphathe inkatha.

Emveni kwalokho kwabe sekufika isihlabelelo esaqanjwa mayelana naleso senzo. Leso yisihlabelelo 84. Wathi amakhosazane kumele ahlale ezinkatheni hhayi emacansini. Uma sebesukuma kumele bathathe izinkatha zabo bazikhweze endaweni ekhethekile, eyaziwa yibo bodwa. Uma sebebuya, bayothatha izinkatha zabo kuleyondawo abazibeke kuyo. Umphrofithi njengoba ayekhuluma wayazi ukuthi kukhona inkosazane engafanele ukwenza lokhu, ukuthatha inkatha. Ngesikhathi amakhosazane esebuya, kwaba khona inkosazane eyayilokhu ifuna eyayo inkatha, ingasazi ukuthi iyibekephi.

Kanti izingelosi zaseZulwini zasezifikile zayithatha zayoyilahla. Ngoba ngesikhathi zithandazela amakhosazane, lena enye inkosazane ayitholakalanga ezulwini. Izingelosi zasuka zaqonda kumFrench owayedayisele uBaba indawo. Zambuza ukuthi uyazi yini ukuthi ulwisana nobani njengoba engasafuni ukudayisa indawo. Zathi zihamba kwase kushayisana amazinyo kumFrench. Wathi, "Ngizoyibuyisa imali. Ngizohamba ngiyoyifuna." Ngosuku olulandelayo wahamba waze wayofika eKuphakameni, eyobona uShembe. Wathi, "Ngikhulume iphutha kumprofithi ngendawo, iNkosi ngizoyinika indawo." Ngakho iNkosi yaseKuphakameni yatshela amakhosazane ayethandazile, yathi, "UJehova unizwelile. Ngakho nina zingane kumele nibonge lendawo kuNkulunkulu njalo ngomhlaka 7 Julayi. Kumele nibonge lendawo kuNkulunkulu. Inkosazane kumele iphinde inikele ngamarandi amane. Amakhosazane aphelele kuphela okumele ahambe. Igama lalendawo kuSensabathandwa."

[Historical Narrative of Ntanda]
The king of heaven spoke to God. He said he did not know where he could put the widows and orphans. God said, "I understand, my child." Thereafter a Frenchman arrived and offered land to Shembe. The King of *eKuphakameni* was so happy. He said, "Yes indeed, my father, you always hear me." Then the Frenchman went away, having taken half of the money. The white men asked the Frenchman, "Why do you sell him land. It has been said that a black man cannot buy land." They said this not knowing that they were talking about God. Then the Frenchman went back to Shembe with the money he had received from the King of *eKuphakameni*. He said, "The law is against me in Pietermaritzburg." The King of *eKuphakameni* said, "Do not lie to me, for you will see that I am the prophet."

[Shembe] was very sad. Then God spoke to him, saying, "Have you forgotten me? Why are you so sad?"

Shembe did not respond to the Frenchman. He said he would send the children to weed the fields of the Frenchman. The first maiden arrived and twined together enough grass coils for all the girls present. God said, "Give them to the maidens so they will sit on them while praying." Then the prophet Shembe issued another rule, saying that the maiden who knows she is not perfect in terms of God's principles should not take this grass coil.

Thereafter, a hymn came which was created in accordance with these happenings. This is hymn number 84. Shembe said that these maidens should sit on the grass coils [*izinkatha*] not on the sitting mats. When they stand up, they should take their grass coil and place it in a special space known only to them. When they come back, they will take the grass coil from that special place. As he was speaking, the Lord of *eKuphakameni* knew that there was one maiden who was not supposed to be taking the grass coil. So when the maidens returned, there was one maiden who kept looking for her grass coil, not knowing where she had put it. The messengers of heaven had come and thrown it away because when they had prayed for the girls one of them was not there. The angels then went straight to the Frenchman who had sold the land to my Father. They asked if he knew whom he was going against as he would not sell the land. When they left, the Frenchman's teeth began to chatter. Then he said, "I will return the money. I will go and fetch it." The following day the Frenchman walked until he came to *eKuphakameni*, to see Prophet Shembe. He said, "I lied to the Prophet about the land. I will give it to the king." Thus the King of *eKuphakameni* decreed to the maidens who had prayed, saying, "Jehovah has responded on your behalf. Thus, you,

> the young children, must give thanks to God on the 7th of July. You must thank God for the land. A maiden must then pay four rand, this is for those who are yet to be born, the coming generations. Only those maidens who are morally upright may go. The name of the Temple is *Sensabathandwa*."

This is an important and complex text that sheds some useful light on the Nazaretha consciousness and their belief about God, Shembe and the role of virgin girls. About this text Muller writes that, "At first glance this letter from the prophet Isaiah Shembe might seem to be no more than a confused set of messages transcribed rather poorly into written form" (1999: 194). She goes on to state that, "I suggest that it is a document that outlines a complex discourse on the [re-]creation of ritualized performance as a mechanism for the enactment and transformation of historical moment in time, a moment when Isaiah wished to purchase land for the widows and orphans, the poor, and dispossessed" (1999: 194). While Muller's statement may be valid, it needs to be emphasised that this text was written by one of Shembe's followers (perhaps even after Isaiah Shembe had passed away),[7] not Isaiah Shembe himself. As such, this is an edited transcription of an originally oral text that Shembe must have narrated to his followers. This means the text is an attempt to represent Isaiah Shembe's actions and belief on a number of issues: the importance of caring for the orphans and widows; the role of virgin girls (and their purity) in communicating with God; and the need to challenge injustice on the spiritual and physical levels. However, the text ends up offering us something in between Shembe's and his followers' consciousness. This is worth noting because, as Murray (1999) has argued, in dealing with the Zionist churches like Ibandla lamaNazaretha (he is writing about Solomon Lion and his church) we need to make a distinction between the attitudes of the leaders and those of their followers.

For a maiden to be complete[8] she has to be a virgin, and it is as a virgin that she is allowed to take part in the sacred dance and other important rituals for maidens. If she takes part but is not a virgin she annoys God, the Angels, and her own ancestors. The belief in Ibandla lamaNazaretha is that even though

---

7 In his time Isaiah Shembe was referred to as *iNceku kaNkulunkulu* (messenger of God). The tendency to say Shembe is God started later, after Isaiah had passed away.

8 Other scholars use 'perfect' for *ukuphelela* but I use 'complete' which is a literal translation. This is because a maiden may be a virgin, but fail to attend all the 25th meetings, all the sacred dance ceremonies, and the holy communion. That maiden would be 'complete' (because she is a virgin) but not 'perfect' because she does not take part in all the required rituals.

living people may not see that a maiden is no longer a virgin; those in heaven (God, the Angels and the ancestors) can see it. Thus the above text tells that the maiden who had lost her virginity but still took part in the *Ntanda* ritual could not find her grass coil because the Angels had taken it and thrown it away. However, that it is the Angels who had taken the maiden's grass coil and thrown it away appears to be the narrator's voice and idea, not Isaiah Shembe's. This is because this idea reflects more of the Nazaretha members' consciousness and belief than that of Isaiah Shembe.[9] The same is true about the fact that the maiden who had lost her virginity was not found in heaven. The above text oscillates between earth and heaven, with God speaking to Shembe and the Angels talking to the Frenchman. This reveals the Nazaretha perception mentioned in the Introduction with regards to the sacred dance that the spiritual and physical worlds can be integrated. The same happens with this text and *iNtanda* ritual.

After the service in which the above text is read, on the 8th, the girls travel back from *Ntanda* to *eBuhleni*. But this is not how it happened in the time of Isaiah Shembe. *Mphathi* (leader of virgin girls) MaDuma told me in an interview that in Isaiah Shembe's time the maidens used to go to *eNtanda* on the 7th of July, spend the whole of the following day there worshipping, and only came back on the 9th:

> *Ngalolu suku, lwesibili, sasiba nenkonzo ekuseni, sibe nenkonzo emini sibe nenkonzo ntambama. Njengoba sesihamba ngomhlaka 7 sibuye ngomhlaka 8 akushintshwanga amakhosazane. Kwashintshwa yiNkosi iLanga. Wakushintsha ngoba leya ndawo ibanda kakhulu, inamanzi. Wathi kumele sihambe usuku olulodwa kuphela bese sibuya ngolwesibili. Manje njengoba sesilala kanye, siyafika khona sithandaze bese siyalala. Ekuseni ngonayini siya emthandazweni. Uma umthandazo usuphelile siyabuya. Ngalesi sikhathi sisenesikhathi esiningi, sasiba nanesikhathi sokugida. Yize sasingayigqoki imvunulo kodwa sasidumisa uNkulunkulu ngokusina nangenkonzo.*
>
> During this day, the second day, we would go for the service in the morning and the service in the afternoon and in the evening. That we're now going on the 7th and coming back on the 8th was not changed by

9 The consciousness and belief of *amaNazaretha* are not always the same as those of the leaders of the Church, from Isaiah Shembe onwards. For instance, in the past few years there has been a subtle debate in sermons between *uThingo* and Nazaretha members, especially ministers, about who Shembe is. *UThingo* was maintaining that he is not God, and members claimed that he was because only God can perform the miracles that he performs.

> *amakhosazana*. It was J.G., *iNkosi iLanga*, who changed it. He changed it because that place is very cold, it has water (i.e. small rivers which make it wet). He said we should go and spend only one night, and then come back the following day. So now that we are going for only one day, we just get there and then we pray and then sleep. So in the morning, at nine, we go to the service. When the service is finished, then we come back. That time when there was plenty of time, we would even have time to dance. Even if we won't be wearing the *umgidi* attire, we would praise God by dancing and by the service. (Interview with Mphathi MaDuma, 8 July 2008)[10]

For the final *uthingo* ritual the girls leave their long sticks just outside *eBuhleni*, and go to their *amadokodo* (makeshift accommodation) to wash and put on clean dresses called *amahiye*. They go outside *eBuhleni*, to collect their sticks. Then they are divided into groups (or regiments) of about one to two hundred (In July 2014, the sticks that were left by the virgin girls after this ceremony were counted and added to more than 12 500 (Bheki Mchunu, Interview, 14 July 2015). In these groups, up until 2008, they marched from the entrance to *eBuhleni* to the present dance area for girls, near *uNyazi's* (Then belonging to his father, *UThingo*) house. From 2009 onwards, this ceremony has been taking place inside the new Temple next to where the leader's new homestead, named Ebuhleni obusha [New Ebuhleni] has been built. As they march, they sing "*Qubula Nkosi*" (Lift O Chief),[11] one of the hymns not included in the hymn-book. This is sung in the call and response style resembling that of *isigekle* songs. It goes as follows:

Lead Singer:[12]	*EHlobane*
Group:	*Qubula Nkosi*
Lead Singer:	*Qubula Nkosi*
Group:	*OkaMpande samshiy' eHlobane*
Lead Singer:	*EHlobane*

10 I conducted this interview with Joel Cabrita, who was at the time a Post-doctoral Fellow, working on Ibandla lamaNazaretha.

11 Muller translates this as "Perfom a War Dance". She is correct to say that the hymn is difficult to translate because it uses a deep form of isiZulu. But this is the only line that is unclear; others are simply incorrect in Muller's text. Here I have used "lift" which is meant by the word "*qubula*", instead of Muller's "perform a war dance".

12 Due to the large number of girls participating in the ritual, the lead singer uses a loud speaker to ensure that all the girls in the regiment ready to go and make a circle (creating an image of a rondavel) can hear the song.

Group:	*Impi*
Lead Singer:	O! *Impi*
Group:	*Zinyane lendlovu*
Lead Singer:	*Elendlovu*
Group:	*Samshiy' eHlobane.*

[Lead Singer:	At Hlobane
Group:	Lift O Chief
Lead Singer:	Lift O Chief
Group:	The son of Mpande, we left him at Hlobane
Lead Singer:	At Hlobane
Group:	The war
Lead Singer:	O the war
Group:	Baby elephant
Lead Singer:	(Calf) Of elephant
Group:	We left him at Hlobane.

About this hymn Muller asserts that it "was not a song arbitrarily selected by the girls, but one that invoked the words of the ancestors themselves" (1999: 195). This assertion is correct in that this song is a standard one for the *Ntanda* ritual. There is no other song/hymn sung in this ritual other than "*Qubula Nkosi*", even though there are many that may 'invoke the words of the ancestors'. The older members of the church, and even virgin girls' leaders,[13] do not know why this song came to be used in the ritual. The meaning of the song is unclear, but according to Muller the song was a praise to King Cetshwayo "who was believed to cause thunder, lightning, and rain immediately after it was sung" (1999: 195).

But this hymn, even though Shembe seems deliberately to obfuscate its meaning, is a prayer for King Cetshwayo rather than his praise. In it Shembe remembers Cetshwayo and laments his death. In the first line, "*Nkosi*" refers to God, who is requested (or commanded) to "lift" Cetshwayo. It is Cetshwayo's spirit that God is asked to lift. This relates to the tradition among the Zulus of slaughtering a cow for a dead person. The first such ceremony is called cleansing (*ihlambo*), and cleanses the homestead and its inhabitants, while the second, called *ukubuyisa* (to bring back) or *ukukhuphula* (to raise), is particularly important for the spirit of the late person as it is meant to remove it from the

13 Cabrita and I asked one of the oldest and most senior leaders of the virgin girls, MaDuma, and she did not know.

place of darkness and sorrow, to the place of light and happiness higher up. Here Shembe calls for such a removal of Cetshwayo's spirit from the valley of sorrow to the place of rest and tranquillity.

When performing an *ukukhuphula* ritual for a dead person, it is important to know where the person died and where he or she was buried, because that is from where the spirit will be fetched: that is, those who are performing the ritual go to the person's grave to communicate with him or her. Thus it is important for Shembe to state that Cetshwayo was buried at Hlobane.[14] This is where his spirit is supposed to be lingering, waiting to be fetched. Clearly though, it is because of his fight against white domination in the Anglo-Zulu war of 1879 that Cetshwayo is remembered and revered by Shembe. This is so because after stating that Cetshwayo died in Hlobane, the line that follows says "*impi*" (the war) and then the last one salutes the king as the calf of an elephant. But it is the word *impi* that is controversial and may be the reason why this hymn was omitted from the hymn book. It may refer to the fact that Cetshwayo was caught in battle, or more radically it may be Shembe's call to the present king, Solomon, to go to war to avenge Cetshwayo's death.

A less radical version of this hymn appears in the hymn-book as hymn No. 111. This hymn confirms my earlier suggestion that in fact "*Nkosi*" in the hymn performed by the virgin girls refers to God, and if that is the case then the word "*Qubula*" is unlikely to mean "perform the war dance"[15] as suggested in Muller's book. In hymn No. 111 Shembe asks God to remember his Zulu nation. Here God is referred to as "*Nkulunkulu*" (which is less ambiguous than *Nkosi* which may mean chief/king) and instead of God being requested to "lift" Cetshwayo, he is asked to remember him as well as all the Zulus:

Sikhumbule Nkulunkulu	Remember us, O! God
Thixo wethu	Our Lord
Ngoba uyasithanda wena	Because you love us
Nkulunkulu wethu.	Our God.
Oka Mpande samshiya eHlobane	Mpande's son, we left him at Hlobane
Mkhumbule Thixo wethu	Remember him, our Lord
Ngokumthanda.	With love.

---

14 This may be the place where he died.

15 Also, "*isiqubulo*" is a noun which may be translated as "war dance", but if you want to denote the act of performing the war dance you do not create the verb "*qubula*" but you say "*ukusho*" or "*ukuhaya isiqubulo*".

Ungasilibali isizwe sakho	Do not forget your nation
Nkulunkulu wethu	Our God
Owasidala ngomsa wakho	Which you created with your grace
Ngokusithanda.	With your love.
Sikhumbule isizwe sakho	Remember your nation
Nkulunkulu wethu	Our God
Indlu kaSenzangakhona	The progeny of Senzangakhona
Nkulunkulu wethu.	Our God.

But all this does not explain why Shembe standardised this hymn as the only one for the *Ntanda* ritual. Perhaps the reason lies in the link with the war which is mentioned in the hymn the girls sing and the fact that the story of Jephtah's daughter is based on Jephtah fighting and winning the war with the aid of God.

Now I return to the virgin girls' performance. As they march, the leaders (*abaphathi*) run around the area in pairs, occasionally jumping up and moving backwards from each other, exclaiming "*Nang' umntwana*!" (Here is the child!) as they do. In the dance area each regiment makes an imaginary rondavel by forming themselves into a circle, raise their sticks up, and then move forward and then backwards. Muller says this is "build[ing] a house for Shembe" (1999: 190).[16] After that the group/regiment marches on to the 'inside area' where Shembe's house is. Since there are normally thousands of girls taking part, many girls remain in the temple because they cannot fit into the area. When most groups had come in, in the July 2008 ceremony, they sang hymn No. 69:

Ilizwi leNkosi	The word of the *iNkosi*
Selifikile phezu kwethu	Has come to us
Nathi masilamukele	Let us accept it
Ngenhliziyo ezimhlophe.	With open (white) hands.
Bongani webangane	Give thanks my friends
Ngalezo ziqhamo	For all those rewards
UJehova inkosi yethu	That Jehovah, our Lord
Aziletha phezu kwethu.	Has given to us.
Nithini webantu	What do you say people
Ngalezo zibusiso	About those blessings
Esinazo thina	Which we have
Nabantwana bethu?	And our children

16 I comment on this and the whole ritual below.

After the hymn they prayed, and UThingo said the last prayer which is called *ukuvala* (to close) or *ukubusisa* (to bless). Then he addressed the girls who had gathered in the open area in his living quarters (where his house, the huts of his ancestors, the house for the girls who help him, and those for other people living with him are all situated). But the loudspeaker allowed even those who were not inside the living quarters to hear his address. I recorded the speech in the video camera I used for research. It went as follows:

> *Ewu! Siyabonga bantwana bethu uma kuya ngoba le nto enhle kangaka yesizwe esinsundu nisayigcinile. Abamnakanga uBabamkhulu ozala obaba ngesikhathi ekhuluma ethi intombazane nomfana abahlangani, baze bashade, kulotsholwe kushadwe bese beyahlangana. Ngoba sivikela isifo esingeke silapheke esizayo. Ngoba kwakuyisikhathi eside kakhulu, akekho owakholwa ukuthi le ndoda kukhona into eyikhulumayo. Bambukela phansi. Abantu baye bambukele phansi umuntu uma engafundile… ISilo-ke samaZulu sanibonga, sathi awu Baba ngiyabonga. Sesizwile ukuthi njengoba kufike lesi sifo esibhuqabhuqa isizwe nje, cha eNazaretha sithembile ukuthi isizwe sakithi ngeke siphele. Sithembele kinina Ntaba yepheza. Siyazicelela-ke ukuthi abaphathi benu laba nisize nibahloniphe bantwana bethu uma beniyala ngezinto ezithile eziqondene nokuphatha. Nibalalele nibahloniphe. Niyokhula nakhe isizwe esibusisekile. INkosi inibusise.*
>
> [*Ewu!* We thank you our children if you are still keeping this beautiful thing of our brown nation. They took no notice of *Babamkhulu* (Isaiah Shembe) who is the father of my fathers when he said that a girl and a boy should not come together (have sex) until they get married, until the *lobolo* is paid and they get married then they have sex. "Because we are preventing a disease that is coming which will not be curable." Because it was a long time ago, no one believed that this man was making any sense. They looked down upon him. People look down upon a person who is uneducated… The Zulu king thanked you, saying, "*Awu*! Father, I thank you. We have heard that as there is now this disease which kills the nation, here in Nazaretha we have hope that our nation is not going to end. Our hope is in you *Ntaba yepheza*. We request that you listen to your leaders if they advise you on certain matters relating to behaviour. You should listen to them and respect them. You will grow up and create a blessed nation. May God bless you".]

What is interesting in this speech by the church's former leader and grandson of Isaiah Shembe is that the rule against sex before marriage (the importance for girls to keep their virginity), which has been part of the church since its

FIGURE 4.1 *A group of maidens marching with their sticks in the temple (worship area) in eBuhleni. They are heading towards the spot where they will make an imaginary rondavel.* (2009)

FIGURE 4.2 *Maidens creating an imaginary rondavel. (Ebuhleni 2009)*

FIGURE 4.3 *Maidens' leaders running around and hopping in front of the maidens coming to create an imaginary rondavel.* (*Ebuhleni 2009*)

FIGURE 4.4 *Maidens' leader, MaDuma, marching with the maidens. She is wearing a red hat. On her right is another leader who uses the loudspeaker to lead the song.* (*Ebuhleni 2009*)

inception, is interpreted as having been set in place to protect amaNazaretha against HIV/AIDS. It suggests that this issue (HIV/AIDS) had been a concern of the church, of the church's founder at least, and had been prophetically spoken about even before the pandemic actually started. This is an interestingly pragmatic interpretation or rendering of the otherwise ethereal texts of Isaiah Shembe, in which the loss of virginity causes a maiden to be unworthy to stand before God. What is also telling is the fact that the two voices in the text, of *uThingo* and King Goodwill (both revered in the Nazaretha Church), talk about AIDS as a strange disease that is taboo. But *uThingo's* representation of the church's old text allows him to talk about this otherwise avoided subject.

Umgonqo

As stated above, *umgonqo* is ideally a two-month ritual commencing on the 25th of July and running until the 25th of September. During this period, the girls are supposed to be closeted in their area and must have no contact at all with men. This does not happen due to other commitments of the church and of the individual girls. As Mphathi MaDuma states:

> *Kushukuthi umhlaka 25 Julayi uyisango lokungena emgonqweni. Abanye ababe besahamba emva komhlaka 25, bayahlala nje balinde uSeptember. Bavele sebesemgonqweni. Kodwa manje akwenzeki ngoba abanye bayahamba beyolanda ukudla emakhaya ukuze babuye bezohlala la. Manje kunezindawo eziningi uShembe aya kuzo, manje nje uma kuphela uJulayi uzoya kwenye indawo. Futhi akakwazi ukuhamba ngaphandle kokuthi nathi sibe khona. Manje-ke abazohlala lapha yilabo abazoya emakhaya beyolanda ukudla, okothi uma sesibuya nomhlangano sibafice la. Bazobuya bangene emgonqweni. Emgonqweni siyadumisa bese sikhuluma ngomthetho wesonto.*
>
> [It means the 25th of July is like the gate of entering to *umgonqo*. Some don't go back to their homes after the 25th; they just stay and wait for September. They are already in *umgonqo*. But now it doesn't happen because some go to fetch food from their homes to come and stay here. And now there are many places where Shembe goes to, now at the end of July he'll be going somewhere else. And he can't go without us also coming. So the only ones who will be staying are the ones who will go to their homes to get the food, and when we come back here we will find them. They will come back and enter in *umgonqo*. So in *umgonqo* we worship and then we talk about the law of the church.]

Central to *umgonqo* ritual is the biblical narrative of Jephtah, which, to use Gerald West's term, is "re-membered"[17] from the book of Judges 11. It is written thus in the isiZulu version favoured in Ibandla lamaNazaretha:

> *Abahluli 11: 30–40*
> *1. UJafethi wenza isifungo kuJehova, wathi: "Uma uJehova enikela abaka Amoni esandleni sami, lowo oyokuqhamuka kwabendlu yami ukungihlangabeza uma sengibuya empini, uyakuba wumnikelo wokushiswa kaJehova ophuma esandleni sami." Nangempela uJehova wanikela abaka Amoni esandleni sikaJafethi.*
> *2. UJafethi wabuyela emzini wakhe eMizpa, bheka indodakaza yaphuma ukumhlangabeza, iza nezigubhu nokusina, kwakukuphela kwayo, ngaphandle kwayo engenaye omunye umntwana. Wathi ukuba ayibone, wadabula izingubo zakhe, wathi, "Awu, mntanami, uyangithobisa kakhulu, ungowabangihluphayo. Ngivulile umlomo wami kuJehova, ngingebuye.*
> *3. Indodakazi yakhe yathi, "Baba, yenza kimi njengokuba ukhulumile kuJehova, ngoba uJehova unikele izitha zakho esandleni sakho. Ngiyavuma ukuba ngibe wumhlatshelo kaJehova. Kodwa ngicela ungidedele izinyanga ezimbili ukuze ngiye ezintabeni ngililele ubuntombi bami kanye nabangani bami.*
>
> [Judges 11: 30–40
> 1. Jephtah made a vow before Jehovah, saying, "If Jehovah will give the Ammonites into my hand, then whoever comes forth from my house to meet me, when I return victorious from war, shall be a burnt offering to Jehovah from my hand." And indeed, Jehovah gave the Ammonites into the hands of Jephtah.
> 2. Jephtah came back to his home in Mizpah. Behold, his daughter came out to meet him with timbrels and dances. She was his only daughter; besides her he had no children. When he saw her, he tore his clothes and said: "Alas, my daughter! You have brought me down, and you are one of my tormenters. I have opened my mouth to Jehovah and I cannot go back on my word."
> 3. His daughter said: "Father, do to me what you promised Jehovah, for Jehovah has given your enemies into your hands. I agree to be an offering to Jehovah. But, I ask you to let me alone for two months, that I may go to the mountains and lament my virginity together with my companions."]

17 See West (1999 and 2006).

This ritual draws on both the biblical narrative of Jephtah and his daughter, and on the traditional rite called *umgonqo*. It is a commemoration and a lament of the death of Jephtah's daughter. The ritual commences with the virgin girls going to *ezibukweni*.[18] Here too the Jephtah narrative mentioned above is read. After that the girls then travel back to *eBuhleni* where they sing, beat drums, and march around home wearing white gowns (which have collars) called *imiJafethi*, after the biblical character, Jephtah. Perhaps because this dress is linked to lament, the girls change to the traditional dance attire when they go to dance. They do not dance wearing *imiJafethi*. The girls meet again on the 24th of September, and on the 25th they go to *ezibukweni* again. Here the Jephtah text is read after the girls have readied themselves for a return to *eBuhleni* to march around the home as in July. But in September, after marching around *eBuhleni*, the girls do not go change for the sacred dance, rather, they do what is called 'playing the ball', which in effect is an exchange of gifts between the girls and Shembe (even the late Shembes are given gifts). With the R10 donations made at *iNtanda*, the girls buy a gift for Shembe which can be anything they want. But Shembe always gives an ox to the girls. Muller (1999: 189) states wrongly that the ox was given to Shembe by the girls and even goes on to state, in the endnote that, "Kriege (1988 [1950]: 102) mentions in her account that traditionally, a father of the girl in seclusion offers an ox on the day of her coming out. There has obviously been some kind of reversal in terms of the giver and receiver of an ox in the case of Shembe."

Interpreting the *iNtanda* and *Umgonqo* Rituals

It seems to me that these rituals, even though sometimes they are said to lament the death of Jephtah's daughter, are a celebration of the maidens' spiritual virtue. The Judges 11 text on the narrative of Jephtah's daughter is used to denote the strength she displayed both in keeping her virginity and in accepting death so as to allow for the fulfilment of her father's promise to God. This is done to encourage the Nazaretha maidens to follow her example by keeping their virginity until they get married as *uThingo* stated in his talk to the girls. But it is also used to encourage the whole Nazaretha community to have the same spiritual virtue. Isaiah Shembe started his church against a great deal of adversity from the state and the missionaries, and this created in him a belief

18 This is a river in which girls participating in *umgonqo*, both the traditional ritual and that appropriated by Isaiah Shembe; go to bathe to prepare for the public dance. They rise before dawn on the morning of the final day of *umgonqo* and go to the river.

that to be a person of God one needs to persevere and be willing and ready to worship God against the odds.

Hymn No. 38, which is included in the Catechism under the heading, "Rules Concerning the Maidens of Nazaretha on the Sabbath Day, 27 July, 1933" (Papini and Hexham, 2002: 118), calls for such spiritual virtue and bravery. Even though this hymn is included in the section "Concerning the Maidens", it speaks to the whole community and actually deals with death and the difficulties associated with the heavenly journey. Since all the members die, all can learn from the bravery and spiritual commitment displayed by Jephtah's daughter. Thus in the chorus "give me the strength/ Of Jephtah's daughter", the speaker deliberates about the difficulties he or she may face when death comes. It is in such time that s/he will require strength and bravery equal to those of Jephtah's daughter:

Ngiyohamba ngingedwa	I shall travel alone
Esigodini sosizi.	In the valley of sorrow.
Chorus:	Chorus:
Nginikele leso sibindi	Give me that strength
Sentombi kaJafethe	Of Japhtah's daughter.
Futhi ngongena ngingedwa	And I will enter alone
Ethuneni lami.	Into my grave.
Chorus:	
Nginikele leso sibindi	Give me that strength
Sentombi kaJafethe	Of Japhtah's daughter.
Ngiyakusikhala ngingedwa	I will cry alone
Isililo sami	My lament
Ngobe ngingenabani	I will have no one
Mina soni	Me the sinner.
Chorus:	
Nginikele leso sibindi	Give me that strength
Sentombi kaJafethe	Of Japhtah's daughter.
Indlela yethuna iyesabeka	The way of the grave is fearsome
Noma ihanjwa ngabaningi abayithandi.	Although many walk it they don't like it.

Chorus:	
Nginikele leso sibindi	Give me that strength
Sentombi kaJafethe.	Of Japhtah's daughter.

Shembe saw being a person of God as something so difficult it required real strength to persevere. The valley of sorrow refers to the place in the afterlife which is like hell, where those who did not do well on earth will end up.[19] The idea is that through her religious strength in keeping her virginity and in consenting to be a sacrifice to God, Jephtah's daughter must have made it to heaven, and whoever wants to avoid the valley of sorrow, and instead go straight to heaven, must follow her example in being truthful to their faith.

The translation of stanza two in Papini and Hexham (2002: 120), "I too shall go alone/ Into my grave", implies that the speaker here is different from the one in the first stanza and suggests that like Jephtah's daughter the speaker will go alone to his/her grave. But the correct translation of the hymn is "Also, I shall go alone/ Into my grave" (*Futhi ngongena ngingedwa/ Ethuneni lami*) emphasising the fact that this hymn is about the afterlife and the hardships one is likely to encounter on one's journey. The message put across in Hymn No. 38 is the same as the one in Hymn No. 143, for instance, which points to the difficulty of being a Nazaretha and calls on all who want to join the faith to have religious strength because the Nazaretha way is difficult. According to the speaker in the hymn, being a Nazaretha is like a slippery rock on which most people cannot manage to walk:

Ukukholwa kwethu	Our faith
Kulobu buNazaretha	In this Nazaretha
Kuyidwala elibushelelezi	It is a slippery rock
Lehlula abaningi.	It beats many people.
Wena uyathanda ukusilandela	If you like to follow us
Lapha siya khona	Where we are going
Uboqala uthenge isibindi	You must first buy valour
Lapha siya khona.	Where we are headed.

In terms of the actual practice of these rituals, especially *iNtanda*, they celebrate the virginity of the girls and they look forward to or anticipate the fact that these girls are going to get married. The performance of the leaders, where

19 The valley of distress is also mentioned in Hymn No. 218 which also talks about the difficulty of the laws of Shembe and the suffering of those who failed to keep those laws.

they run-hop in front of the girls and jump and then say "*Nang'umntwana!*" (literally meaning, "here is the child" but actually saying, "here is the bride"), suggests that these are the future wives. "*Umntwana*" is used in weddings to refer to the bride.[20] The imaginary rondavel they create with their sticks points to the fact that they are meant to build the homes of the men they are going to marry. In the Nazaretha Church, as in Nguni society more broadly, when men propose they say they want the girl to 'build a home' (*ukwakha umuzi*) or to 're-build a home' (*ukuvusa umuzi*) of their fathers. The suggestion by Muller that Shembe protects the *amakhosazane* at the cost of the denial of sexual desire (1999: xix) is an overstatement and creates an impression that these girls are urged or even encouraged to remain virgins forever. The truth here is that they are urged to wait until they get married (as *uThingo* was saying above); in fact not getting married is so discouraged that those who choose to stay unmarried forever are regarded as depriving their homesteads of the cattle they would have received in the form of *lobola*. In the 2013 *Ntanda* ritual, the present leader, Unyazi, also addressed virgin girls when they had finished their performances. Even though the address was meant for the maidens, all members who had been watching the activities, including myself, were sitted inside the temple as uNyazi made his address. In his speech, uNyazi praised the virgin girls for abstaining from pre-marital sexual activities; told them how significant they were in the life of Ibandla lamaNazaretha; and concluded by wishing them prosperous marriages:

> *Ngike ngezwa uMvangeli uNgcobo walapha ekhaya ethi ningcwele nina makhosazane eniseNtanda. (Ameni, uyingcwele, Ameni) Kushukuthi bekufanele uMvangeli akhulume kanje ngoba lo mkhosi enisiqalele wona uyisiqalo somhlangano kaJulayi. (Ameni, uyingcwele, Ameni.) Isihlabelelo salayikhaya siyasho sithi "imikhosi emikhulu ngeyabangcwele"; ningcwele makhosazane! (Ameni, uyingcwele, Ameni.) Nize ningaboni ubungcwele benu. (Ameni...) NgesiZulu uma uyintombi nto, uphelele, usuke ungcwele (Ameni...) ngoba usuke ukwazile ukubekezela wehlukana nezinto ezenziwa emgaqweni, ezenza umuntu egcine engasazi noma uwusisi noma uwumama noma ungusisi-makoti. (Ameni...) Abaningi bayafisa ukuba yinina (Ameni...) kodwa akuselula, baqala ngokugcinwa ngakho. (Ameni...) Nginifisela imendo emihle makhosazane! (Ameni...)*

20 When a bride is about to come to the groom's home for the wedding, she is heralded by a group of young men who go to the home singing. This is called *ukubikaumntwana* (announcing the bride).

> I heard Evangelist Ngcobo of this Temple saying you maidens who have gone to Ntanda are holy. (Amen. You are holy, Amen.) It was necessary for the evangelist to speak like this, because this festival you have started for us is the beginning of the July festival. (Amen. You are holy, Amen.) One of our hymns says that "great festivals are for the holy ones"; you are holy, you maidens. (Amen…) Do not spoil your holiness. (Amen…) In Zulu if you are a (complete) virgin, you are holy (Amen…) because you have been able to persevere and stayed away from what is done in the streets, which makes a person end up not knowing if it is a sister, or mother, or sister-wife. (Amen…) Many wish to be you (Amen…) but it is no longer easy, they started with what comes at the end. (Amen…) I wish you beautiful marriages, maidens! (Amen, You are holy, Amen.)
>
> INKOSI MDUDUZI SHEMBE, *Ebuhleni*, 8 July 2013

Participating in these rituals as well as other performances like the sacred dance – all of which are considered worship – provides the space for the girls to move closer to God spiritually, and they use this space to pray for marriage, among other things. One of the virgin girls who attended the *iNtanda* ritual in 2009 was my wife Nokwanda MaCele Sithole. While she was at *iNtanda*, she had a dream in which she saw Shembe, *uThingo*, offering her a gift. She did not know what the gift was since it was wrapped. But when she was 'chosen'[21] she interpreted the dream to mean that the gift was a husband or marriage. This belief was strengthened by another virgin girl's vision which she saw on the last Sabbath of July (after which proposals happen). This girl is one of Nokwanda's companions, and her name is Sindi. During the Sabbath service they were some distance apart. Sindi told Nokwanda that as the service was progressing, she saw a vision in which *u-anti* (literally meaning 'aunt', but referring to those women who did not get married who are now leaders of the maidens) approached them with a small sitting mat (*isicephu*). She could see that there was something wrapped in the sitting mat. The Aunt placed the sitting mat in front of Sindi and the other girls who were next to her. But

21 As stated in chapter two, the way men are supposed to get married is that they choose the girl they would like to marry and, in the process called "*ukucela ebhentshini*", they propose to the girl, having ascertained her details (name, place where she lives and temple). If a girl is proposed to and she accepts, she says, "I have been chosen" (*Ngikhethiwe*). It was at the end of the July 2010 meeting that Nokwanda and I were 'engaged'. The initial wedding, called *ukuhlanganisa*, took place in October 2010 in the Temple Judea near Gingindlovu, and the final wedding took place at my home in Hlathikhulu near Estcourt in December of the same year.

in the vision she felt as if at her side was not the girl who was actually there but Nokwanda. Thus, she said, "Open it, Nokwanda, because it's yours." When Nokwanda opened the sitting mat, in it there was a piece of beadwork (she did not know what beadwork it was but they interpreted it as "*ucu*", a beadwork piece given by the bride to her groom on the day of the initial wedding taking place in the church site); the ring; and the blue *inansook* (worn by recently-married virgin girls).

So if *amakhosazane* do lament their sexual loneliness, it is not during the *Ntanda* and *umgonqo* rituals. Being a virgin in the Nazaretha Church is something to be proud of, and there is no better place to show off one's virginity than by taking part in the virginity testing, *iNtanda* and *umgonqo* rituals and the sacred dance. The hope that the virgin girls dance with in Hymn No. 92 comes from the knowledge that being true virgins they are worthy to stand before Jehovah. The hope is that they will be appreciated by both God and the Nazaretha community for keeping their virginity. Again, the translation in Papini and Hexham (2002: 120) is inaccurate. The maiden of Nazaretha shall not fear nothing because she is 'perfect' but because she is 'complete' (*Angiyukwesaba lutho/ Ngoba mina ngiphelele*): *ukuphelela* means to be complete, not to be perfect, and in the case of *inkosazane* it means she is a virgin. The "We" in the second stanza can be misconstrued as referring to the maidens like the "I" in stanza one. But in stanza two the speaker is the Nazaretha community who confirm that they also trust the singing maiden in stanza one. They trust that she is a 'complete' virgin girl as she claims:

Ngiyosina nginethemba	I shall dance with hope
Ngiyintombi yomnazaretha	Being a maiden of Nazaretha
Angiyikwesaba lutho	I shall fear nothing
Ngoba mina ngiphelele.	For I am complete.
Nathi siyakwethemba	We too trust you
Nayizolo besikwethemba	Even yesterday we trusted you
Nanamuhla siyakwethemba	And today we trust you
Nakusasa siyokwethemba.	And tomorrow we shall trust you.

Virgin Girls and the Sacred Dance

As stated above, the maidens in the Nazaretha Church have their special dance after the *Ntanda* ritual. This dance is like a herald to the sacred dance of all people because before this girls-only dance, the dance for all the people cannot take place. It is this dance that other members of the church, married women and men, can watch because during its performance they are not supposed to be performing their own sacred dance.[22] It is mainly during this dance that Nazaretha men search for potential wives. The duration of this dance is ideally five days, and that is because there are five types of dance attire that the maidens have to wear. Only when they have worn all the five types of dance attire can the sacred dance of all people start.[23] This dance is similar to any other dance the girls perform except that their attire is mainly Western, with occasional use of some beads from the *isidwaba* dance attire. Thus it is called *imvunulo yesilungu* (English/Western attire).

The first of the *isilungu* outfits is called *upinki* (pink), from the colour of the long blouses the dancers wear. The skirt and the top of this blouse are linked at the waist by a white coloured cloth. With this the maidens wear hair nets on their heads, with a white belt in front. They also wear white gloves. The second *isilungu* outfit is *iveyili* (veil). This consists of red pleated skirts, with a thin black line at the bottom, and blue shirts on the top. The dancers wear purple hats with long veils of the same colour covering the face. On the upper arm they wear white beads. A third form of *isilungu* attire is called *isikotshi* (scotch). These are red checked skirts with red tops, and are worn with all the beads associated with the 'traditional' attire (this is explained in more detail in Chapter Six). The fourth outfit resembles that worn by members of the Church of England (*Sheshi*), comprising black skirts with white tops. This attire is called *igwababa*. The fifth one is called *insephe*. This consists of black skirts and pink tops. On the head they wear the same as they do with *upinki* above.

If the point made in the previous chapter about some dancers creating their own personal vernaculars in the sacred dance applies to virgin girls, it is not immediately clear to the onlooker. While for virgin girls as well the sacred dance does provide a space to define the self as is the case with some men,

22 One of the rules for the sacred dance (though it is not strictly adhered to) is that the sacred dance is never watched by members of the church because they are supposed to be taking part in it. Those who do not have the necessary attire to participate and those who are 'incomplete' are supposed to join the dancers and sing with them and beat the drums and blow the trumpets for them.

23 In special circumstances the sacred dance of all people happens even before the girls have completed their own dance. In 2009, for instance, the girls returned from eNtanda on Wednesday and started the dance on Thursday. They used two types of dance attire a day on Thursday and Friday, and were left with one more. But on Sunday the sacred dance of all people took place and the girls finished their own dance on Monday. This was done because, had the dance for all people not started then, there would have been much less time for it because it would have to start the following week which was to be the last one.

FIGURE 4.5 *Maidens wearing* upinki.

FIGURE 4.6 *Maidens wearing* isikotshi.

FIGURE 4.7 *Maidens wearing* insephe.

FIGURE 4.8 *Maidens wearing* iveyili.

FIGURE 4.9 *Maidens wearing* igwababa.

and they do to an extent create "difference through competition" as was discussed in chapter three, this is less pronounced. Instead of defining the self, virgin girls mainly use the space afforded by the sacred dance to present themselves to God, Shembe, ancestors and especially to potential husbands. It is the last point – presenting themselves to potential husbands – that necessitates a kind of competition in the sacred dance for virgin girls. In an interview I had with about ten virgin girls at the University of Zululand on 14 March 2015, they agreed that there is competition or self-differentiation in the sacred dance for girls, even though it is not as pronounced as in the competitions. According to one of the virgin girls, Andile Gumede, dancers try to outperform others especially if they know that they 'have spectators'. This happens when someone is engaged and knows that her in-laws would be watching the sacred dance. But, another virgin girl called Mpume Mlambo, in the same interview as Andile Gumede, also mentioned that there are virgin girls who have made their names by dancing so well that people would just go to the dance to watch them (Mlambo and Gumede, Interview, University of Zululand, 14 March 2015).

It is usually in the sacred dance that a man will choose a girl to marry and many men when watching the sacred dance of virgin girls are not interested in how they dance but in how they look, for most men watching are looking for potential wives. While there are comments about a girl who dances well, most of the comments male spectators make are about the beauty of the girl, some even going so far as to search for the particulars of a specific girl if they think they might want to propose to her at the end of the meeting.

It is therefore not common in the sacred dance for virgin girls to fight for positions in the centre of the line.[24] The centre is reserved for older maidens who have been dancing for many years. The rule is that, as years pass by and the person participates in the dance, that person moves closer to the centre. This happens because other girls get married or, unfortunately, fall pregnant, leaving their spaces open for other girls further from the centre to occupy. And the lines are much longer than those one finds in men's dances, perhaps three times as long. Mpanza maintains that the sacred dance for virgin girls is the same as that of married women and men:

> *Umgidi uyefana, ngisho angabe owamakhosikazi, uma sikhuluma ngomgidi sisuke sikhuluma ngomgidi osuke wenziwa emhlanganweni ongcwele. Uyabo? So umgidi noma ngabe owamakhosikazi noma ngabe owamakhosazane noma angabe owamakhosana uyafana. I-value yawo iyafana.*
>
> [The sacred dance is the same, be it for women [or other groups], because here we are talking about the sacred dance that takes place in the holy congregation. You see? So the sacred dance is the same, be it for married women, for virgin girls or for men. Its value [significance] is the same.]
>
> MTHEMBENI MPANZA, *Interview*, 13 August 2009

In spite of this assertion by Mpanza, there are some differences in terms of what actually happens in the performance, rather than what is supposed to happen. Some of these differences are mentioned above, but perhaps the most important one relates to the point made earlier that the sacred dance does not allow virgin girls a space to create their own personal vernaculars, but rather that it provides them with the space in which they can present themselves as potential wives. So the actual performance of the sacred dance for virgin girls

24 These days, because the number of girls who participate in the sacred dance has increased dramatically, one does witness some shoving and pushing for positions. But it is normally for girls trying to avoid being at the far ends rather than trying to secure spaces in the centre as such. The problem of the increasing number of girls participating is compounded by the fact that the number of lines and regiments does not increase with the number of dancers as is the case with men and married women.

is without the force noticeable in men's and, to a lesser extent, in the married women's dance. Their performance is characterised by the stealth of movement and the softness of their beatings on the ground. As for the steps, they are the same for them as for the married women and for men.

On the 10th July 2008, a group of virgin girls was wearing *isikotshi* dance attire for their post-*iNtanda* dance. They danced for hymn No. 6, *Sakubona Kuphakama* (Greeting *Kuphakama*). Gunner says this about this hymn: "Hymn 6, an early work, speaks vocatively, as if addressing the bearer of a praise poem, to both the Holy City (*eKuphakameni*) and northern Judea, near Gingindlovu" (2002: 29). These are the first two verses of the hymn that the virgin girls sang interchangeably:

Sakubona Kuphakama	Greetings Kuphakama
Sakubona Judiya	Greetings Judea
Ubabekephi abafowethu	Where did you leave my brothers
Ababethunyelwe kuwe.	Who were sent to you.
Babalekile bakushiya	They ran and left you behind
Baxoshwa wubungcwele.	They were chased by holiness.
Masango okuphakama	Gates of Kuphakama
Phakamani singene.	Rise up so we can enter.

While the hymn does speak vocatively as Gunner asserts, when choosing a hymn for performance in the sacred dance, it is not the meaning or the words that are important but the way that particular hymn is performed in the dance. This hymn is not one of the common ones in the sacred dance, but it is one of the most favoured by those who know how to perform it. It is one of those hymns that encourage liveliness on the part of the dancers when they perform it. Even the virgin girls when dancing for this hymn (and others like it) tend to move to the point of commitment and feeling to the extent that one can say they are "mesmerised" by the performance. They give themselves to the dance, so much so that it is as if they are in a kind of 'trance'.

Yet even though they have given themselves to the dance, that softness of touch to the ground and refusal to succumb to complete agility still remains. The forty or more girls who were performing in the girls-only dance on the 10th of July 2008 reached this point of flowing with the dance when the tune had changed to the second stanza. This entailed changing from the step of the first stanza, which is characterised by the double beats of the left and right foot, with the right foot moving forward and back and the rising and falling of the shields at certain particular intervals. In the second stanza the move changes: the girls still do the double step but this is different from the one performed earlier. Here the raising and lowering of the shields is not controlled by the hymn but is at the discretion of the dance leader or *umshayindweba* (flute blower).

However, new developments like the establishment of dance competitions by NABACHU and NATESA in which girls also take part has made it important for participating girls to dance in such a way as to differentiate themselves from others. In the dance competition that took place in October 2008 on the Pietermaritzburg campus of UKZN, the competition was divided between that of *inhlalisuthi* (men) and that of (*intabayepheza*) virgin girls. Although the criteria used for judging were the same, girls' groups were competing with each other, while the young men of the church were pitted against those of their own sex. Most importantly perhaps, the song used by *intabayepheza* in their competition was different from that of *inhlalisuthi*. The girls danced for hymn No. 18 "*Amaqhawe kaThixo*" (God's Victors). What comes out prominently with regards to this dance is the force of the performance, which is uncharacteristic of the virgin girls' dance. The first group, from the host campus UKZN Pietermaritzburg, were the ones whose performance was most agile; and the ones who won the competition! In their performance they raised their legs in a way uncharacteristic of the virgin girls' dance and their stamping on the ground was harder. (See the picture below.)

The Pietermaritzburg girls' group comprised four girls, three of whom wore black skirts and white shirts, and one who wore a black skirt and black shirt. The one with the black shirt was the lead singer, and her difference in dress from the others reminded one of *isicathamiya* groups where the leader always dressed differently from the others. This is not surprising considering the fact that these competitions are influenced by *isicathamiya* competitions. It is important to note also that this kind of difference on the part of the leader does not occur in the sacred dance taking place within the church. Another difference with the girls dancing in the formal sacred dance is that here the dancers start the song themselves. In the case of the Pietermaritzburg group, the song leader sang at quite a high pitch and speed, and this leads the instrument players (trumpets and drums) to follow suit, thus creating a kind of experience to the knowing audience that is both similar to and different from the usual sacred dance that takes place in the church.

Except for the high pitch and speed, the song they danced for was performed in a way similar to that done in the church context. But it was when the tune changed, from the first part of stanza one to the third part, which marked the change of step as well, that the pitch and speed of song were markedly higher than usual. The hymn is represented as follows in the hymn-book:

Amaqhawe kaThixo ayazikhethela	The Lord's heroes make their own choices
Asuke ashiye umlaza	They tend to leave *umlaza*
Ngokwanele abangcwele.	As befits the holy ones.
Ngamukele ngethemba	Accept me with hope
Gcwalisa inhliziyo yami.	Fulfil my heart.
Sengihlanjululwe nguwe wedwa Nkosi	I've been cleansed by you alone Lord
Angisamdingi omunye futhi.	I do not need anyone anymore.
Ngamukele ngethemba	Accept me with hope
Gcwalisa inhliziyo yami.	Fulfil my heart.

In terms of performance, this can be represented as follows:

1. Lead Singer:	*Amaqhawee kaThixo, akaThixo Aya…*
2. Group:	*Ayazi…*
3. Lead Singer:	*Awu ayazi* (*khethela*)
4. Group:	…*Khethela.*
1. Lead Singer:	*Ayazikhethela, amaqhawe*
2. Group:	*Amaqhawe akaThixo*
3. Lead Singer:	*O kaThixo aya*
4. Group:	*Ayazi…*
5. Lead Singer:	*Awu ayazi* (*khethela*)
6. Group:	…*Khethela.*
[1. Lead Singer:	The heroes of Jehovah, [those] of Jehovah they…
2. Group:	They…
3. Lead Singer:	*Awu* They (make their choices)
4. Group:	Make their choices
1. Lead Singer:	They make their choices, the heroes
2. Group:	The heroes of Jehovah
3. Lead Singer:	Of Jehovah they…
4. Group:	They…
5. Lead Singer:	*Awu* They (make their choices)
6. Group:	Make their choices.]

FIGURE 4.10 *Maidens from* UKZN, PMB.

The part from 1 to 4 serves as a prelude, in which the performers, as well as those who play the drums and the trumpets, prepare themselves to commence the dance. It is when the song starts again that the drums start to beat, the trumpets blow and dancing begins. The dancing and the singing start more slowly, with the dancers performing double beats with each foot, and during this first step each beat takes about three seconds to be accomplished. The foot is raised to about twenty-five centimetres from the ground (in the sacred dance taking place in congregations, the foot is raised to about ten centimetres or less) and the whole body rises and falls with each beat. This rise and fall is this group's own improvisation that is meant to 'spice up' their performance, setting them apart from the other groups. As I stated with regards to the girls' performance within the church, that the girls seem to be presenting themselves as potential wives (in addition to praising God), the performance here redirects the attention of the audience, especially the judges, to the performance itself.

This setting here is one of those few occasions where males and females in the Nazaretha Church share the same performance space. While this sharing of space is welcome, it comes with the price of time constraints and having prematurely to change the tune to allow space for not only other girls but for boys as well. Thus, after only two minutes thirty seconds the performance changes to the next step. The song changes to the last part or the last two lines of the first stanza, ("I have been cleansed by you alone/I do not want another one") but the singing is the same as above. The second part of stanza one ("They tend to omit *umlaza*/ As befits the holy ones") is omitted because it does not lend itself well to performance. Here the momentum increases and the pitch of the song, especially the lead singer's, rises. The step comprises alternative turnings to the right and to the left, with alternating hard and soft beats. The hard beats are executed with the right foot when facing the right and with the left foot when facing left. These hard beats are repeated three times before changing to the other foot. As each foot hits, the heel of the other leg is raised, leaving only the front part of the foot touching the ground. This is also not part of this step's church choreography, but is brought by this group to bear on their performance to differentiate them from others.

The third step is performed with the fastest speed, and offers the girls a last chance to make a mark or to impress the audience and the judges. With this step it is the agility and the liveliness the dancers give to the dance that matter. The step is the easiest to perform in terms of the beat, which is one step with each foot. But this is performed with a kind of playfulness that is interesting to watch. While here the performer makes use of her whole body (more than in the previous steps where the focus was on the stamping of the foot), it is the hands that take centre stage. The girls play with the shields and umbrellas, moving left and right, back and forth as they do. Sometimes they raise their shields and charge forward, as if going to a fight, and then they lower them and revert to their former position. Sometimes when they are a few metres from the judges they turn and go back to the *isigcawu* (dancing space) in a similar movement or performance. Sometimes they imitate a stabbing action with their umbrellas, the right hands carrying the shields moving forward and backward, and as they do this they march forward in the direction of the judges. When they have turned they march back to the *isigcawu*, and here they make a few turns, and then leave the stage to give others the chance. One of the judges, Evangelist Mngwengwe, used the interval to give advice to the drumbeaters:

> *Anilalele la, nina abashaya izigubhu. Niyezwa nina abashaya izigubhu, qaphelisisani ukuba ningashiyani. Ngoba uma nishiyana niyabaphazamisa. Isandla senu asishaye kanyekanye. Ngale kwalokho niyeke kusale oyedwa.*
>
> [Listen here you drumbeaters. Do you hear, you who are beating the drums, make sure that you do not beat in disharmony. Because if you do, you disturb them. Your hands should hit at the same time. Or else you should quit and let one person beat the drum.]

FIGURE 4.11 *Maidens from* DUT (PMB).

FIGURE 4.12 *Maidens from* DUT (DBN).

After this the second group started dancing and, though their performance was not exactly the same as the previous one, the differences are so minor that they do not merit close examination. The point that one can make here is that these were less confident about their performance, and they lacked the zest that characterised the preceding group. The third group to compete performed better than the second, and maybe better even than the first group, although they attained second place. Their performance was not so far removed from the usual sacred dance for virgin girls. It was characterised by the stealth and sluggishness which is so absorbing when done with the kind of adeptness that the girls of Durban University of Technology (Pietermaritzburg) displayed in their performance. But an interesting point to make with regards to this group is that while they worked as a team trying to win the competition, there was another kind of competition internal within the group. The group was doing the same thing while at the same time each dancer was doing her own thing. This kind of competition within the group was also happening with regards to the first group where one member seemed bent on outperforming the others. But, as the first group collectively spiced up their dance, with the third group the little details of performing that spiced up the dance were done individually, each girl setting herself apart from the others.

Conclusion

This chapter has looked at the question of gender and identity in the Nazaretha Church, dealing specifically with virgin girls' performances and rituals that demonstrate the significant role they play in the life of the church. I have argued that Muller's claim that virgin girls have to sacrifice their sexual desire in order to obtain Shembe's protection is exaggerated because it creates an impression that the virgin girls are encouraged to stay virgins for ever. In reality, what is emphasised is abstinence till one is married, and this goes for both virgin girls and men. While the church is itself not egalitarian in terms of leadership especially, when it comes to performance virgin girls seem to take centre stage. This says something about their position in the church since these religious performances, especially the sacred dance, are very important for members of the church, men included. I have also dealt with the maidens' sacred dance in two different contexts, showing how the introduction of virgin girls to dance competitions has influenced the way they dance and the motivation for taking part in the dance, or the purpose of performing the sacred dance.

CHAPTER 5

Male Circumcision, Marriage and the Notion of (In)Completeness

Introduction

Because the sacred dance is regarded as a form of worship in Ibandla lamaNazaretha, participation in it is exclusive to those members of the church who are considered ritually clean. This exclusivity only involves the sacred dance in great meetings where the congregants meet in the presence of the church's leader, Shembe. This dance is referred to as "*umgidi wabantu bonke*" (the dance of all people) which the leader announces following the afternoon service of the Sabbath[1] preceding the Sunday of the dance. If the sacred dance is to be on Tuesday or Thursday, the evangelist who is the speaker of the church (or of the church's leader) announces it after the evening prayer of the day before the dance. Because the word for this dance can only come from the leader, he announces it on Shembe's behalf, saying: *Lithi izwi leNkosi, umgidi wabantu bonke kusasa.* (The word of the iNkosi says it's the sacred dance of all people tomorrow). This means it is the dance of all the three divisional groupings in the church: *inhlalisuthi* (men); *intaba yepheza* (virgin girls); and *ujamengweni* (married women).

Women who have husbands but are not 'properly' married to them, and girls who are no longer virgins (nowadays it is doubtful that all the girls who take part in the sacred dance are virgins, but those who do, do it unlawfully), and men who are not properly married to their wives or have children outside marriage are not supposed to dress in the dance attire of their group and to dance with them. They can only join the group to help with singing, hand clapping and playing the instruments. But in the overnight meetings of *u*-23 (for men), *u*-14 (for women) and *u*-25 (for the maidens), in weddings and in *vukanathi* (wake up with us) meetings (where members of the church are invited to a particular home for the morning service, usually there is a sacred dance after these services), this law of limitation does not apply.

This law of exclusion is maintained because the sacred dance is believed to yoke together the physical and the spiritual realms. As Mthethwa states, when the sacred dance has been announced (he is talking about the "sacred dance

1 The Sabbath for the Nazarites is on Saturday.

 | DOI 10.1163/9789004320628_007

of all people"), it cannot be cancelled because "the call is made to both the living and the deceased members of the church. Once invited, they cannot be denied" (Mthethwa, 1996: 1). For this reason those who take part in the sacred dance of all people have to be complete, to be without blemish. In this chapter I look at two ritual forms that are related to the notion of completeness, namely, male circumcision and marriage.

One of the misrepresentations in Muller's book that this study aims to correct is her claim that the "denial of sexual desire" is exclusive to virgin girls:

> The prophet Isaiah Shembe used his knowledge of the mission bible and the mythical power of virgin girls to win his battles against the racist state. Political struggle assumed form as spiritual and moral warfare, with the virgin girls as the frontline warriors. The cost of this protection of female adherents, however, was the denial of sexual desire. In this context, sacrifice was reinvented in terms of an innovative combination of Old Testament and Nguni traditional practice, and located in the purity of young women's bodies. (1999: xix)

With regards to her emphasis on Isaiah Shembe using women's performances and rituals to "win his battles against the state", West has challenged Muller, maintaining that, "Within the literary liturgical setting of the Rule, the enemies of Jephthah/Israel/Shembe/Ibandla lamaNazaretha are not given prominence. What is given prominence is the integral relationship between members of the community, specifically, Shembe, the Nazarite maidens, their parents, the coming generations, the indirectly invoked biblical witness of Moses, David, Jesus and the apostles, the directly cited presence of Jephthah and his daughter, and God" (West, 2006: 504). The purpose of this chapter is to demonstrate that in fact the sacrifice of sexual desire obtains in both women and men, and has to do with ritual performances having a physical and spiritual significance, the performers performing for the audience of both the living and the dead. I argue that Muller's claim regarding the role these rituals and performances of young women (and men, in some cases) play in 'political struggle' is unfounded and that her misreading emanates from the fact that she ignores the actual motivation for those who perform those rituals.

The Sacrifice of Flesh and Blood: Male Circumcision

I stated elsewhere (Sithole, 2005) that some of the stories (I was referring to the narratives of near-death experiences) in Ibandla lamaNazaretha, once told, cease to belong to the people who experienced them, and become part of the church's cultural capital that circulates within the church in sermons and conversations. Some dream experiences take that form, depending on what they are about. One such a dream narrative is about a man who had gone to be circumcised and when he came back he had a dream. He saw himself in a wild area where he was following a group of people he did not recognise. A voice asked him if he knew the people and he said he did not. The voice then told him that the people he saw were the spirits of his dead relatives. They had been 'living' in the cave for many years because the man's uncle had *thwala*-ed with them (an act of witchcraft which is like sacrificing people to the evil spirits, so that a dead person's soul does not go to heaven or to its ancestors but is kept and used by the person who did *ukuthwala*). But because this man had gone to be circumcised, he had freed them from his uncle's hold and they were now on the way to heaven.[2]

As this story shows, dreams occupy an important role in the lives of amaNazaretha, and many of them are regarded as a form of communication with the ancestors. But this story also points to the sense in which through ritual practice (circumcision in this case) the divide between the physical and the spiritual realms is removed, so that the sacrifice of blood and flesh of a living person can bring about the liberation of the spiritual beings in their own realm. I suggest that here lies an important motivation for Nazaretha men, through a very painful experience, to sacrifice their own blood and flesh. They do it because they hope to create a heaven for their own relatives who have passed on and at the same time create a heaven for themselves. As the voice in the story mentioned above added: "You too will see heaven if you keep the rules of God".

However, circumcision in Ibandla lama Nazaretha is also explained in terms of Abraham's covenant with God in the book of Genesis in the Old Testament. In the 'old' Zulu version favoured in the church, published in 1883 (West, 2007), Genesis 17 verse 10–14 details this covenant as follows:

> *Lesi siyisivumelwano sami phakati kwami nawe nenzalo yako emva kwako, eni ya kusi gcina: Baya kusokwa bonke abesilisa bakini. 11 Niya kusoka inyama yejwabu lenu; ku be upau lwesivumelwano pakati kwami nani. 12 U ya kusokwa lowo wakini onezinsuku eziyisishiyagalombili, bonke abesilisa ezizukulwaneni zenu, lowo ozaliweyo endhlini, na lowo otengiweyo ngemali kubafokazi bonke, e ngesiyo inzalo yako. 13 U yakusokwa nokusokwa yena*

2 I first heard this dream narrative in 1997 in the sermon preached by Minister A. Ngema in the Temple called Maqhaweni in Soweto, Gauteng.

> *ozalwe endlini no tengwe ngemali yenu, si be yisivumelwano esinganqamukiyo. 14 Owesilisa o nga sokiwe, o nga soki inyama yejwabu lake, lo muntu u ya kukitywa kubantu ba kubo, weqe isivumelwano sami.*
>
> [This is my covenant between me and you and your posterity after you, which you will keep: All of your males will be circumcised. 11 You will circumcise the flesh of your foreskin; to be a symbol of the covenant between you and me. 12 He will be circumcised that of you who is eight days old, all the males in your posterity, the one born in the house, and the one bought with money from all foreigners, not being of your offspring. 13 He will be circumcised he who is born in the house and the one bought with your money, it will be a covenant that cannot break. 14 A male person who is not circumcised, who does not circumcise the flesh of his foreskin, this person will be removed from his people, he broke my covenant.]

Muller has noted that Shembe combined "his deep knowledge of the mission bible with his respect for traditional Nguni ways, and with some knowledge of commodity capitalism, he constituted a new and hybrid regime of religious truth (Foucault, 1980) in competition with ideologies of the state and Christian mission" (1999: 19). Circumcision is one form of ritual practice that Shembe appropriated and gave new meaning. As the biblical text above shows, circumcision in Israel was meant to be a symbol of a covenant between a person and God, and boys had to be circumcised at the age of eight days. In Ibandla lamaNazaretha the youngest boy circumcised is at least ten years old (which itself is very rare), but it is mostly matured young men (and adult men) who go for circumcision. This is because this ritual is not just an appropriation of the biblical text but it is also part of an African traditional rite. In pre-Shakan Zulu society young men used to be circumcised in the 'African' way. Here, circumcision was a rite of passage in which young men of a certain age would go to the bush to be circumcised and taught the ways of the tribe, and then come back as men. Shaka thought this practice was weakening young men whom he wanted to conscript for his regiments and therefore he put an end to this tradition. As Funani puts it, "Shaka, having placed Zulu people on the war footing, could not afford to have armies incapacitated by circumcision and stopped it. But, great psychologist that he was, he substituted service in *amabutho* as a condition of entry into manhood. Note that Shaka and his generation were all circumcised" (Funani, 1990: vi). So in introducing circumcision Shembe was both importing a ritual practice from Israel and at the same time reinstituting a tradition that had been lost in the time of Shaka.

In Ibandla lama Nazaretha circumcision is a new hybrid form that does not fit either the kind of circumcision practised in Israel or the kind practised in pre-Shakan Zulu society and in the present day South African societies that still practise it. As the story mentioned above of a Nazaretha young man who went for circumcision and had a dream shows, circumcision in Ibandla lamaNazaretha is linked to African religion in a way that pre-Shakan circumcision and circumcision in other African societies was (and is) not. The next section of this chapter looks at circumcision in pre-colonial African society.

Circumcision among the South African Communities

Although there is not enough information about its distribution, circumcision in southern African societies was (and is) more of a social practice than a religious one. Writing in 1936, Krige had this to say about the distribution of circumcision in South Africa: "The present distribution of circumcision cannot be fully plotted out, owing to complete lack of information on many tribes" (Quoted in van der Vliet: 1974: 228). She goes on to list ethnic groups that still practised it. Among these are Xhosa, Thembu, Fingo and Bomvana, some of the Tswana tribes, the Southern Sotho, and the Pedi, to mention but a few. As for the Zulus, van der Vliet mentions that "the Zulu cut the string under the foreskin at about nine years of age, but this is not a ritual occasion" (228).

In most of the African societies in the subcontinent that practised it, circumcision was perceived to be the rite of passage through which a boy becomes a man. As Funani states, "In Africa circumcision is associated with male initiation into manhood" (1990: 22). Nelson Mandela, in *Long Walk to Freedom*, emphasises the same fact about the role of circumcision among the Xhosa:

> When I was sixteen, the regent decided that it was time that I became a man. In Xhosa tradition, this is achieved through one means only: circumcision. In my tradition, an uncircumcised male cannot be heir to his father's wealth, cannot marry or officiate in tribal rituals. An uncircumcised Xhosa man is a contradiction in terms, for he is not considered a man at all, but a boy. For the Xhosa people, circumcision represents the formal incorporation of males into society. It is not just a surgical procedure, but a lengthy and elaborate ritual in preparation for manhood. As a Xhosa, I count my years as a man from the date of my circumcision. (1994: 24)

Because circumcision represented incorporation into manhood, Mandela and his fellow initiates were urged to cry, "*Ndiyindoda*!" (I am a man!), after the actual operation and it was considered a disgrace (at least Nelson Mandela felt this way) if one succumbed to pain. Mandela admits that the pain he felt was so intense that it took seconds before he remembered to utter the word "*Ndiyindoda*" and this hurt his feelings: "But I felt ashamed because the other boys seemed much stronger and firmer than I had been; they had called out more promptly than I had. I was distressed that I was disabled, however briefly, by the pain, and I did my best to hide my agony. A boy may cry; a man conceals his pain" (1994: 26). And also the novices were subjected to different kinds of hardships and ordeals to test resilience against the trials of life and at the same time strengthen them for their future duties of manhood. These hardships included beatings, sleeping on the floor, bathing with cold water (the initiations were normally held in winter to ensure that the wounds healed quickly) and others.

Jean Comaroff states about initiation among the Tswana that, "On the evening when the moon of *Mophitlho* (March) was seen all the boys to be initiated proceeded in ward groups to the chief's court, where they spent the night in song and dance" (1985: 89–90). In the morning the boys were escorted to their lodge in the bush where they were circumcised on the day of arrival. No woman or uninitiated man was allowed even to see the lodge and their presence was considered defiling. Those who did come to the lodge were required to refrain from sexual intercourse for the duration of the initiation because "it was critical that initiates be kept away from the heat generated by adult sexuality" (90). Another important feature of initiation was the education bestowed on the novices. For the Sotho groups, including the Tswana, van der Vliet states that the education emphasized loyalty to the tribe and the values, rights and obligations of citizenship (1974).

Circumcision in Ibandla lamaNazaretha

In Ibandla lamaNazaretha, apart from the link it creates between the physical and the ancestral worlds, circumcision is also a mode of personal cleansing and of creating a way to heaven. This understanding does not tally with either the biblical text mentioned above or circumcision in Xhosa and Tswana traditions. In both the Israelite and African traditions no link is made between circumcision and entering heaven, even though in the case of the Israelites it signifies a covenant between them and God. But since the Bible has a significant place in the church of amaNazaretha, and Isaiah Shembe "seized and reconstituted the bible" as much as it also took hold of him and drew him (and his followers, I argue) to its narrative (West, 2007: 494), and because African tradition plays an important role in the church, the question of whether circumcision should be explained in African terms or in biblical terms is a complex one that is hard to resolve. Some members of the church view this practice as a biblical one and want it to be practised according to scripture. As a man called Mlaba said in an *u*-23 meeting of February 2008 held in the homestead of the Chunu Chief of Mandleni in Mdubuzweni area near Mooi River:

> *Njengoba silapha sengathi uNkulunkulu engasisiza siphelele. Bese siya ebhekinqola. Kukhona into eshiwo ngabantu kodwa uNkulunkulu akayishongo. Uma ngabe sifunda incwadi kaGenesisi, uthi uGenesisi ingane uma ngabe kweyomfana iyozalwa, kuphele izinsuku zibe wuseveni, ngalolu luka eyithi, uthi ayihambe iye ebhekinqola iyosokwa. Usho njalo uNkulunkulu kodwa abantu bathi ayize ibe ndala. Bathi ayifanele ukuthi ingane iye lapha. Okwethu-ke lokho, okwabantu. Ziyaya nje izingane sezindala laphaya? Azifuni, sezazi namalungelo. Sinayo nje ingqekana le ngeke usho ukuthi ayiye le. Kodwa ingane uma iseyingane… akekho zinsizwa njengoba silapha onelungelo lokwenza isono ngoba akayile ebhekinqola. Kukhona yini lapho kushiwo khona wuShembe lokho ukuthi uma umuntu engakayi ebhekinqola yena ukhululekile ukuthi akenze izono? Hhayi, asimusukhohlisana. Asiyenzeni lento, njengoba uNkulunkulu eshilo. Uthi uNkulunkulu yenza uphawu lube yisivumelwane sakhe. Uma le ngane ingasabi ndala? Uthi uNkulunkulu ingane ayizalwe wuNkosikazi, izinsuku eziwuseveni, ngalolu luka eyithi, ayihambe iyokhula. Kodwa-ke okwethu thina bantu wukuthi ingane ayibe ndala.*
>
> [As we are here I wish God can help us be complete. And go to Bhekinqola (a place of circumcision in Ibandla lama Nazaretha). There is something that is said by people but God did not say it. If we read Genesis, Genesis says if a child is born a boy, he will be born, and after seven days, in this eighth one, He says [the child] should go to Bhekinqola to be circumcised. That is what God says, our people say [the child] needs to be grown. They say a child is not supposed to go there. That is ours [the opinion], it's of the people. Do the children when they are grown go there? They do not want, now that they have rights. We do have these gangs of children but you cannot tell them to go there. But if a child is still a child… there is no one, young men, as we are here who has a right to commit sin because

> he has not gone to Bhekinqola. Is it there where Shembe says that if a man has not gone to Bhekinqola he is free to commit sin? No. Let's not lie to each other, let's do this thing as God said. God says create a symbol to be His covenant. What if this child does not get old? God says a child be borne by a woman, seven days, and in this eighth one, [the child] must go to *khula* (to grow up). But ours, we people, is that the child must be grown up.]

But even in this formulation of Mlaba's the role of circumcision is still linked to the traditional practice of circumcision. His comments about circumcision, for instance, are prefaced by a statement that links circumcision to the notion of completeness that obtains in both the African and the Nazaretha ways of understanding: that if a man has not been circumcised, he is not a man, he is still a boy and he is incomplete. He also refers to it as *ukukhula*, meaning to grow up, also showing that this practice is seen as a rite of passage through which a boy becomes a man. This shifting understanding of circumcision, from the biblical to the traditional, is common in Ibandla lamaNazaretha. In an *u*-23 meeting of April 2008, Moses Hadebe of Nkonzenjani Temple in Ntabamhlophe near Estcourt also talked about circumcision as something that Shembe appropriated from the Bible. But in his formulation he also relates circumcision to its significance as an African ritual practice:

> *Imithetho yalayikhaya inzima kabi ngoba sisenkolweni kaJesu. UShembe wazosifaka ngaphansi kwenkolo kaJesu kodwa abanye abazi ukuthi uShembe wazosifaka ngaphansi kwenkolo kaJesu. Izinkolo lezi eziningi azazi ukuthi safakwa ngaphansi komthetho kaJesu. UJesu wenziwa klini ene seven days. Enezinsuku eziwuseveni wase useyenziwa-ke lowo mthetho. Nathi-ke uthe uma efika uShembe wasibuyisela kulowo mthetho. Wokuthi asibuyele emthethweni kaJesu ngoba singaphansi kwenkolo kaJesu. Ngokufika kwalo mthetho ubungavumi ukuthi noma wubani afunde umbhedesho weSabatha. Kwakufuneka umuntu okhulile. Kukhona ukukhula okwenziwayo kule nkonzo ngoba kuthiwa nenkosi uBabamkhulu watholakala esehleli le lapha kuya khona izinsizwa. Kukhona indawana lapha kuya khona izinsizwa, ziyaqiniswa ukhakhayi ukuba zibe yizinsizwa saka. Manje-ke sasithi uma sifika kwenye indawo eGoli ethi amaXhosa uyoze ufe uyikhwenkwe njengoyihlo. Manje-ke sesiyawaphikisa sithi "cha noma ningasho nithi niyoze nife ningamakhwenkwe njengoyihlo kodwa ubaba akalona ikhwenkwe futhi nami angiselona ngoba kwafika uShembe wathi asenze kanje."*

> [The laws of this home are difficult because we are in Jesus' religion. Shembe came to put us under Jesus' religion but others do not know that Shembe came to put us under Jesus' religion. Jesus was made clean (was circumcised) when he was seven days old. When he was seven days then this law was performed. Here also when Shembe came he returned us to that law which means we should return to Jesus' law because we are under Jesus' law. Because of the coming of this law it was not allowed for just anyone to read the Sabbath service text. It had to be somebody who is grown up (circumcised). There is *ukukhula* that is done here, you Nazaretha, in this church because it is said that the *inkosi Babamkhulu* was found sitting there where the young men go. Now when we used to arrive in another place in Johannesburg the amaXhosa would say "you will die boys (*amakhwenkwe*) as your fathers". Now we negate them saying, "no you can say we will die boys as our fathers, but our fathers are not boys and I also am no longer a boy because Shembe arrived and said we should do like this."]

The last comment Hadebe made about the Xhosa and their circumcision is interesting here and may point us to one possible explanation for Shembe's reincorporation of circumcision in Ibandla lama Nazaretha. It is clear from Mandela's account, and others, that circumcision among the people who performed it was very important in the constitution of masculine identities, and an uncircumcised man was relegated to boyhood. So, for Shembe who was born a Zulu but grew up in the Free State among the Sotho who still practised circumcision, it is possible that he himself grew up under scorn as someone whose father was a boy and who himself would die a boy as happened to Hadebe and his fellow Zulus in Johannesburg.

In Ibandla lamaNazaretha, as is the case with the Xhosa according to Mandela, there are certain rituals that exclude everyone who is uncircumcised. Hadebe mentions one of these as reading the prayer in the hymnal. The communion is another ritual for only complete people, and this, for men, means both being properly married and being circumcised. Also, one is not allowed to take part in a number of chores in the church including the slaughtering of cows for the meeting if one is not circumcised.

But what seems to be unique in Ibandla lamaNazaretha is circumcision as ritual cleansing. The reason why Mlaba emphasises that no one is allowed to commit sin even if one is not circumcised is that it is considered worse to commit sin when you have been circumcised because when you are circumcised you are believed to be cleansed. You are cleansing yourself and your ancestors, and therefore defiling yourself defiles your ancestors as well because, as I mentioned earlier, the ritual of circumcision is believed to bridge the gap between the physical and the ancestral worlds. One way a man can defile himself and his ancestors is by sleeping with a woman he is not married to. This is called *ukuhlobonga* and is prohibited for any man in the church, but the prohibition is especially emphasised for those who have been circumcised. If a circumcised man engages in pre-marital sex, his sanctity attained through circumcision is lost. It is equal to "uncircumcising" oneself. As Minister Mthethwa said, drawing on the biblical narrative of Samson:

> *USamsoni wagundwa wuDelila. Yingakho kungafanele umfana walapha ekhaya alale nokadebenetha. Ngoba uma uke walala nokade benetha uzobuthatha bonke ubustrongi balesi sihluthu, ukade benetha. Abuthathe ahambe. Nokusokwa kwakho kuzospaya. Walala nje nokade benetha, finishindaba yakho! Ushaywa wumuntu ngempama uwe. Ulale nokade benetha.*
>
> [Samson's hair was cut by Delilah. That is why boys of this church/home should not sleep with *kadebenetha* (women who are not members of the church) because if he sleeps with *kadebenetha* she will take away all the strength of his long hair. *Kadebenetha* will take it and leave. And his circumcision too will be expired. If you sleep with *kadebenetha* you are finished. You will be slapped by a person in the face and you will fall. You slept with *kadebenetha.*] (Minister Mthethwa, Interview, 12 July 2008).

Hymn No. 18 in the hymnal also talks about circumcision and links it with ritual cleansing and paving the path to heaven:

Amaqhawe kaThixo ayazikhethela	The Lord's heroes make their own choices
Asuke ashiye umlaza	They tend to avoid *umlaza*
Ngokwenele abangcwele.	As befits the holy ones.
Ngamukele ngethemba	Receive me with hope
Gcwalisa inhliziyo yami.	Fulfil my heart.
Sengihlanjululwe nguwe wedwa	I have been cleansed by you alone
Angisamdingi omunye futhi.	I do not need anyone anymore.
Ngamukele ngethemba	Receive me with hope
Gcwalisa inhliziyo yami	Fulfil my heart.

Abasokwa ngokwanele	Those circumcised adequately
Ngokuyithanda inkosi	Because of their love for *iNkosi*
Bachaba indlela eya ekhaya	They weed the path towards home.
Ngamukele ngethemba	Receive me with hope
Gcwalisa inhliziyo yami.	Fulfil my heart.
Wesihambi mawungesabi	You traveller, don't be afraid
Uzobelethwa nguThixo	The Lord will carry you on His back
Ngemihla yokuqala neyokuphela.	During the first days and the last ones.
Ngamukele ngethemba	Receive me with hope
Gcwalisa inhliziyo yami.	Fulfil my heart.

According to this hymn, being circumcised makes one a hero because it is a very painful experience and one has to overcome fear before one can be circumcised (some people succumb to fear and return from Bhekinqola uncircumcised). But circumcised people are also heroes because if you get circumcised you commit yourself to living a holy life. Living a holy life means you do not eat unclean food like pork; you do not drink alcohol; you do not cut your hair; but most importantly, you do not sleep with a woman who is not your wife. As Mthethwa said above, engaging in pre- or extra-marital sex undoes ("expires it", in his words) your being circumcised, and many people have been circumcised more than once because they had pre- or extra-marital sex and had to redo circumcision.

Those who join the church already circumcised have to be circumcised again in the Nazaretha way because in being circumcised outside the church they were not cleansed by Him (God of the Nazaretha) as the above hymn says. This (cleansing in Ibandla lamaNazaretha) is the ultimate cleansing after which one does not need another cleanser. But one must confess before being circumcised so that all his sins (and those of his ancestors) will be cleansed. Thus when we were to be circumcised in 1999 (I was not doing it for research!) we had to start by confessing. We were told to wear our prayer gowns and one after the other we went to the circumciser, who was sitting few metres away from us, for confessions. Unlike normal confession where you volunteer what wrong you committed, here the circumciser asked me (and the others I presume) if I had ever slept with another man's wife; if I had ever slept with a white person (or a person of another race)[3]; if I had ever engaged in pre-marital sex; if I had ever slept with another man; and lastly he asked if I had ever masturbated.

3 Inter-racial sexual relationships and marriages are prohibited in Ibandla lamaNazaretha.

Where I answered in the negative, he said "God bless you", and if I responded in the affirmative I had to pay a fine of between two and six rand. Then he ritually cleansed me. I had come with a flower and a container, which was an empty milk container, with water. I had to hold my hands together and he poured water on them twice, each time telling me to spill it. On the third time he told me to wash my hands. Then I had to hold the flower with both my hands and he held my hands in his and started praying. After this he said "God bless you" and I was ready to go and wait for the final moment.

Cleansing ensures that God is able to come closer to the person and even to carry him/her over to the next life. The metaphor of a traveller, also in the hymn quoted above, works in two related ways. The first one is that we as living people are only here on earth on a temporary basis, that at some point we will pass on to another realm. This is echoed in hymn No. 137:

Kuhle inyama yami ihlupheke	It is fitting that my flesh suffers
Ukuze inhliziyo ikhumbule	So that my heart will remember
Ukuthi akusilo ikhaya leli	That this is not my home
Kuyidokodo lomhambi.	It is a makeshift room of a traveller.

But even while we are still here on earth, if we are cleansed by "him alone" we are ensured an easier and better life in which God will carry our burdens and hardships. Related to this sense is the notion of a traveller in heaven. One of the tropes that characterises the narratives of near-death experiences in Ibandla lamaNazaretha is 'the journey' in which the person having a near-death experience sees/feels him- or herself travelling, sometimes through green pastures and sometimes having to cross rivers and climb mountains. So according to stanza four, if you are cleansed the spirit of God will carry your spirit on the way to heaven. But if you are defiled, you cannot be in close proximity with God. Not even with Shembe.[4]

Now I complete this section by telling the rest of my story of circumcision, hoping to show how this practice is similar to and different from circumcision in African society.[5] So after cleansing it was time for the actual operation

4 There is a story of a girl of Dlamini near Estcourt who passed away for a few hours and then was resurrected. It is said that she called her father and told everyone there that she had passed away and had seen Shembe on the other side. Shembe said he was going to show her jails in heaven but he ordered her to maintain a distance from him because he said she was unclean (she had two illegitimate children).

5 Note especially the uttering of the words "Stay here boy I am now a man" when burying the foreskin, and the way this is similar to what Mandela and other Xhosas said immediately after the operation.

which is the most challenging part of the process. There were only four of us because it was Tuesday and many had been circumcised on Saturday afternoon. We enviously watched these moving up and down, limping, due to their wounds, and wearing their towels. Reflecting on that experience now, and each time I visit the initiates at Bhekinqola, I am fascinated by the commitment and determination one has to command in order to stay there till the end. When we went to our initiator to receive two bandages each, one fastened around the waist and the other anointed with some antiseptic that we were to take to the 'place of operation', I could feel my heart pounding and my legs felt as if they were going to collapse.

If those who undergo circumcision do it for the love of their *iNkosi* as suggested by stanza three, it means their love is really strong. And this love is indeed for the *iNkosi* of heaven whom they are hoping to meet when they pass away. As you are standing there waiting for your turn, you think about pain, you think about death, you think about running away! But the heroes of God make their own choices. The four of us, like the thousands who had gone before us, chose to stay and face whatever was coming. The three of us were singing as one man had gone into the little forest where our circumciser was waiting for us with his razor blade.

When it was my turn (I went in second) I had not thought about safety measures and diseases like AIDS that one can contract if cut with a razor blade that had cut a person who had it. But I was pleasantly surprised when I saw our initiator wearing clean gloves and putting away those that he had worn while 'working' on the man who went in first. He also took out a new razor blade. By this time I had lost control of my body. I was very tense and even today I do not know why, and how was it that I was smiling. All I know is that it was not me!

The cutting was so fast and sharp that for a second I did not feel the pain. When it did come it was so intense it felt as if it was not just coming from the cutting of the foreskin, it was as if my body was cut in half. But it lasted for a surprisingly short time. As he was bandaging me, I was feeling the pain one feels from a normal cut. Then, covered in a white cloth that had red spots of my own blood, our initiator gave me my foreskin. I went out of the forest, and as told, looked for little holes that had been dug just outside the forest. I found them and chose one that was to be the grave of my foreskin. I buried it, and as my initiator had instructed me, I said: *Sala mfana sengiyindoda!* [Stay here boy I am now a man!] And indeed I felt like a man as I went to join the other initiates who had already been circumcised. As I went, with my legs wider apart than usual, I was thinking about God. I was thinking about God the creator who created all things and all that is in the world. I was thinking about

God who created me and my parents and my grandparents and theirs. I thought about a group of many spirits who might be saved as a result of my pain. I felt spiritually empowered. I was a complete *Nazaretha* man!

Marriage and Completeness

Marriage is important in Ibandla lamaNazaretha both as an institution and as a ritual. It is through marriage that men and women can become complete. Not being married does not mean that one cannot take part in the sacred dance or the holy communion, as long as one does not engage in sexual activities. If a woman and a man have a child out of wedlock, or are living together but not properly married, then they are considered unfit to take part in those holy gatherings. Also, the way in which a man who has a child with a woman he is not married to or a woman who has a child out of wedlock can become complete is to get married. This becomes harder for women because a decision to get married or to initiate marriage rests with men. If a man has a child with a woman, all he needs are the resources necessary for marriage to happen: he has to have cattle or money, or both. But a woman on the other hand depends on a man who made her pregnant to be willing to marry her, and if not, she can only hope that another man will propose to her. In the sermon on 18 April 2015, Minister Mlungwana talked about this in his sermon at Mdubuzweni. He told the story of two girls who went to the late leader of the church, UThingo, to complain about their situation.

> *Zithi Baba, sasiyizingane zika 25 sase sihlangana nezinsizwa sase sibuyiselwa eceleni. Manje inhliziyo yethu ibuhlungu ngoba asigidi futhi asiyi esimayweni. Ithi iNkosi manje uma inhliziyo yenu ibuhlungu nicabanga ukwenzenjani? Zithi Nkosi, sizocela umendo, noma usinike abantu siphindele kuJehova.*
>
> [They said, Father, we used to be the children of twenty-five then we met young men and then we were put aside. Now our hearts are hurting because we don't take part in the sacred dance and we don't partake in the holy communion. The iNkosi says now if your hearts are hurting, what do you intend to do? They said Nkosi, we have come to ask for marriage; that you give us men so that we can get back to Jehovah.]

In the following section I examine the institution of marriage as it happened in Zulu society before *ubuNazaretha*. The reason for this is that such an examination can help us understand what Shembe appropriated from the 'traditional' marriage and maybe from the 'Western' one.

Appropriating the Pre-Colonial Marriage

Muller (1999) states, drawing on Jeff Guy's work, that the institution of marriage played an important role in the African precolonial homestead economy. She quotes at length Guy's description of this African precolonial homestead economy:

> The homestead was made up of a man, his cattle, and small stock, his wife or wives and their children, grouped in their different houses, each with its own arable land. Materially these homesteads were self-sufficient, subsisting on the cereals produced by the agricultural labour of women as well as the milk products of the homestead's herd. Animal husbandry was the domain of men, most of the labour time being expended by boys in herding. There was a clear sexual division of labour under the control of the husband/father, who allocated arable land for the use of various houses to which his wives belonged, on which they worked with their children for their own support and for that of the homestead. [Guy, 1990: 34] (Muller, 1999: 27)

For Guy, even the word 'marriage' is inappropriate for the kind of union that took place between a man and a woman, even though he concedes that this union was an essential element of the homestead: "Working backwards in the search for analytical priorities, we have to note that marriage presupposed the pledge or the passing of cattle from husband's father's homestead to wife's father" (1990: 36). The transfer of cattle from the home of the prospective husband to the home of the wife is called *ilobolo* (bride price/bride wealth) in isiZulu. It is the bride price that Guy sees as important in understanding the oppression of women in African precolonial Nguni society. He accuses other observers/critics who have written about this transaction of bride wealth of failing to note that *ilobolo* "united two great male concerns – the control of women and of cattle – in a dynamic totality" (36). He goes on to argue that this failure to see the link between bride wealth and the two above-mentioned male concerns resulted in them [the observers] being "unable to show *why* bride wealth was so important, or to understand its role in appropriation and exploitation of women" (36).

Important in Guy's formulation is the concept of labour power which he acknowledges Marx used to explain capitalism. Some scholars view this concept as inappropriate in analysing precolonial societies. But for Guy, the concept of labour power is "an applicable, indeed essential, concept for understanding these societies" (1990: 38). He says labour power is a concept devised and used by Marx in referring to the productive and creative potential of people. It is realised "in productive activity and in the products of labour" (38). Marriage then was a social institution devised by men in order to control the labour power as well as reproductive power of women as it was important that a man's wife be physically fit to produce agriculturally as well as to give birth to children who would also work for him and, if they were girls, whom he would exchange for cattle. The cattle were an object of accumulation in these societies, but with a clear gender dimension in that "cattle [were] the means by which men acquired and accumulated the labour power of women" (1990: 40).

However, it seems to me that Guy overemphasises the role of cattle in bride wealth and ignores the fact that it was only towards the end of the precolonial period (with an increase in cattle raids and the giving of cattle to honour heroism in battle) that cattle became the main means of giving bride wealth. Before this, the Zulu people gave anything as *ilobolo*, as Krige states: "There was, before the codification of the Zulu law, no fixed amount of *lobola*, and when the husband's people had no cattle they could even produce two or three stones, and their suit could not be refused on this account" (1950 [1936]: 121). It was an honour though to *lobola* with many cattle. But by many cattle it is meant about four or five head of cattle, only half of what had to be given after bride wealth was fixed during the colonial period. This fixing only happened during Shepstone's rule under his Natives' Customary Law (Msimang, 1975). It was then that the number of cattle for a daughter of a common man was set at ten; sixteen for a headman; twenty for a chief; while for the king's daughter, especially the first born, they amounted to fifty.

Also disturbing about Guy's formulation is that he tries to explain an institution which involved a long process, but limits his discussion to what he can manipulate for his own purpose. Even when bride price was fixed and it became a debt that could be paid even after marriage, it was still a decision between a man and a woman to be married that presupposed marriage. While it is true that sometimes parents did influence their sons' and daughters' choices about whom to marry, forced marriages, if they happened at all, were not the norm. What did happen was a lengthy process and rituals that culminated in a wedding ceremony. This process started with the girls' being given permission firstly to respond to and secondly to accept suitors (*ukujutshwa*) they liked and the whole act of "courting" and the rituals that went with accepted proposals.[6] Guy also chooses to ignore the spiritual side of marriage ceremonies and the rituals that were meant to join the marrying woman to the ancestors of the husband's family. What follows here is an examination of marriage in Ibandla lamaNazaretha and how it is linked (or not linked) to precolonial marriage and to the notion of completeness and the sacred dance.

The Marriage Process in Ibandla LamaNazaretha

On the 14th September 2008, the Nazareth's Tertiary Students' Association (NATESA) of the University of KwaZulu-Natal (UKZN), Pietermaritzburg, hosted a workshop in which Minister Mvubu and Evangelist Mpanza spoke about the overnight meetings of *u*-23, *u*-25 and *u*-14. The sacred dance competition followed later. One of the things that Mvubu talked about was the problem of male leaders who ignore young boys in their teaching and preaching in these religious meetings. He said his younger brother complained to him one day that he was not interested in going to *u*-23 meetings because the people who preach there always talk about completing the men's marriages and going to *Bhekinqola* (to be circumcised); he said that nothing relevant for him as a young boy is ever talked about. My own experience has been that what Mvubu's brother has said about completing marriages and being circumcised is true, but also it is quite rare to attend an overnight meeting for men and not to hear that a Nazaretha man does not pursue or court women, does not have an affair. In other words, young Nazaretha men are taught to sacrifice their sexual desire as is the case with young women. The following excerpt from an *u*-23 meeting of August 2008 in Ntokozweni Temple in Ntabamhlophe near Estcourt (on the opening day, 22) serves as an example:

> *...Lapha eKuphakameni side sikhuluma njalo ukuthi insizwa yaseKuphakameni iyahamba iye ebhentshini iyocela. Ayimi emakhonini maNazaretha. Insizwa ka 23 ithatha inkosazane ishade. Kubonakale ukuthi kuthathe isosha elisha. Uma-ke uyinsizwa, uhamba uyothatha endaweni yamakhehla, asazi ukuthi nawe uyikhehla yini. Ngoba kufanele uthathe umuntu ozothi uma eqhamuka la abantu babone ukuthi cha lensizwa ithathile. Bakubongele abantu, nabakini abangasekho bayabonga ukuthi wenze into enhle.* (Nhlalisuthi Memela)

6 For a discussion of these processes see Krige (1936) and Msimang (1975).

> [Here at eKuphakameni we always talk about it that the young man of eKuphakameni goes to *ebhentshini* to get engaged. He does not stand on the corners you Nazaretha. The young man of twenty-three takes the girl and gets married. It becomes clear that it's a young soldier who married. Now if you are a young man, and go to get your wife where the old men should, we do not know whether you are also an old man.[7] Because you have to marry someone who, if you appear with her people will see that no this young man is really married. People should congratulate you, and your ancestors thank you that you did the right thing.]

As the above passage shows, what is emphasised is that young men should choose girls they like from the *amakhosazane* (virgin girls) and propose to them in what is called *ukucela ebhentshini*. This is a process headed by *Abaphathi* (girls' leaders), who are Shembe's appropriation of what in Nguni society was called *amaqhikiza*. These were older girls who acted as teachers/advisers to and leaders of other girls. If a girl wanted to accept a young man, she told the *amaqhikiza* and they were the ones who gave the girl's lover a bead called *ucu*, which was a symbol of love. However, in Ibandla lamaNazaretha a man is not allowed to approach the girl directly. While in Zulu society the girls were given permission at some point to talk to the young men who courted them, and at another time given permission to accept those they like, and young men who had reached puberty were allowed to court girls (*ukushela*), in Ibandla lamaNazaretha 'courting' is not allowed.

What is allowed is *ukucela ebhentshini* which goes as follows: A man who has seen the girl he would like to marry approaches *abaphathi* or *o-anti* (literally meaning aunts, but referring to the adult women who never married) on the evening of the last Sabbath[8] of the meeting (These can be any of the big meetings, January, July, and October, or any of the smaller ones around the year where the leader is present) or on the following Sunday, and writes the girl's name and temple and his name and his temple on the list of prospective engagements. For this he pays a fee which had increased from R20 to R50 in July 2014 which is unrefundable if the maiden does not show up or refuses.[9] After this, contrary to what Muller says, that the leaders fetch the girl to the

---

7 This refers to a young man who marries a woman who is no longer a virgin. Those who have lost their virginity are considered suitable for marriage by older men, who have married virgins before.

8 The new leader, UNyazi, has put an end to proposals happening on the Sabbath evenings, now they can only happen on Sunday of the weekend in which the meeting came to a close.

9 If she accepts the proposal the groom has to pay another R50.

girl's enclosure (*Esipholi*), it is the man's duty to ensure that the girl comes to the girl's enclosure. The man brings the sitting mat that they are both to sit on and then the leader speaks to the girl on behalf of the man. As a rule, the girl need not know the man, or that he intends to marry her, until this day. As one of the leaders, MaDuma, said, "a man must see a flower from a distance and pick it up without it knowing" (Personal communication, July 2008). But sadly for MaDuma, most prospective couples come to *ebhentshini* having agreed among themselves. They only go there as a routine and MaDuma claims that such a deed is a sin and it is equal to lying to God.

In her account of this process, Muller says, "I was told that the girl had an option of refusing the man, although it seems to me to be an extremely charged situation – one in which it would be difficult to say no" (1999: 206–207). Muller is correct about it being difficult for girls to refuse men, but the girls do have other options. Perhaps the most effective one is for a girl simply to refuse to go there. Since it is up to the man and his helpers to ensure that the girl comes to *esipholi*, if a girl does not want to marry that man she just refuses to go there at all. This, and the fact that prospective husbands prefer to talk to the girls before they go to *ebhentshini* (this tends to be done because it is very humiliating to be refused in that very public situation, and it is preferred by most men to go there knowing that they will be accepted), explains why Muller did not see any man being refused.

But if it does happen that a girl cannot evade going to *ebhentshini* and maybe she is pressured to accept the proposal, one other option she has is to accept a man in *ebhentshini* and then reject him later on. In one such case a girl accepted because of the pressure and tried to reject the man, but he kept sending his marriage negotiators, showing that he did not accept her rejection. The girl then decided to fall pregnant, in which case the man had no option but to let her go. There are so many engagements that get annulled in the church that a minister (for a long time it was Minister Ntombela) has been appointed just to announce those annulments. As a rule, if a man gets engaged in the church and he takes too long to pay *ilobolo* and other things he may be required to pay, the girl may reject him. To do this, she and her parent (usually the mother) should consult the Minister of that man and tell him how many years have passed and what the man had done or had not done. If the Minister thinks the claim is justified, he writes a letter which the girl and her parent take to Minister Ntombela who will then read it in the temple (another huge disgrace).

Previously, the annulments had been announced in the same way: that such and such a girl is now free to be engaged because such and such a man has failed to pay the required *ilobolo* and other things. Usually they would say the number of years that have passed since the couple got engaged. But what has happened in the last few years is that there have been complaints by men that the announcements are always about men who fail to pay *ilobolo*, while in many cases couples are parted because the girl was found to be having an affair or became pregnant by another man (mainly caused by the fact that engaged couples are not supposed to talk to each other, let alone spend some time together). Now, although the majority of the annulments are still those of men who fail to pay *ilobolo*, there are those that happen because of the reasons mentioned above. Sometimes if the parents do not like a man or perhaps their daughter complains that she does not like him, they can simply demand too much *lobolo* and *izibizo* [gifts] so that the man cannot afford to pay.[10] The point I am making here is that, while this institution of *ukucela ebhentshini* may seem to be unfairly in favour of male suitors, there is a great deal that happens behind the scenes before and after the proposals.

However, most engagements that happen in *ibhentshi* do end in marriage. The time that passes between the engagement in *ibhentshi* and the actual wedding varies from three months to five years, depending on how well prepared the groom was when getting engaged. The two years suggested by Muller may be reliable as an average. Muller also describes Ibandla lama Nazaretha's wedding ceremonies in so much detail that it would be redundant to repeat the process here. But of greater interest for this project is what she does not include at all (probably due to her being ignorant about it): the final wedding ceremony that takes place in the groom's home.

But before I look at this ceremony, it is necessary to comment on an important question Muller raises concerning what she calls "a fascinating twist to Isaiah's formulation of the Nazarite marriage rite" (1999: 209). This "fascinating twist" is that Isaiah Shembe had no state authority to perform legal marriages, but he remarried all the converts who had been married by the missionaries. An interesting question for Muller (and for me) is "why would people want or need to remarry if they had been married by state approved marriage officers?" (209). Her 'simple' answer, that people needed to remarry because "marriage by state officials was characterised by cultural inappropriateness" (209), is correct. But her point that "Isaiah Shembe refashioned marriage after his own image, an image that reincorporated both the religious dance and drumming", and that both "the drum and the dance are believed to embody the spirit and patterns of the ancestors [and in] this context the dancing and the drumming constitute a musical metaphor for the unification of the ancestral lineage

10 A man I know had clashes with his fiancé and his in-laws, which led to the couple getting separated. The parents of the girl reported the matter to the ministers and the man was forced to continue with the marriage and then the in-laws demanded R39 000 *lobolo*.

believed to occur in the sacralisation of marriage", does not fully explain why Nazaretha converts remarried (and still remarry) if they had been married by the state's marriage officers.

Muller's point is based on Mthethwa's statement that "no religious rite is complete without its culmination in *ukusina*, the sacred dance by means of which the ancestors meet with living Nazarite members" (1999: 206), and that "it is not so much the speaking of vows and the laying of hands on the bible that solemnize the marriage as it is the moment in which the bride and groom dance the festival dance accompanied by the beating of the drum" (Muller, 1999: 209). While the importance of the sacred dance cannot be overstated, it is not the dance that (for lack of a better word) finishes the marriage. In other words, when dealing with the question of completeness, the question asked is not whether the bride (or groom) danced or not, but the question asked is whether a cow called *umqhoyiso* (also called *umqholiso*) has been or was slaughtered for the bride/wife. A woman for whom *umqhoyiso* has not been slaughtered is considered incomplete and cannot participate in the sacred dance, in the communion and most importantly, she cannot wear a black belt worn by women on their waist over their prayer gowns. Similarly, a man who has not slaughtered *umqhoyiso* for his wife is considered incomplete and cannot take part in some of the holy rituals in the church.

My contention here then is that the answer to Muller's question of why it was (is) that people married by officers authorised by the state still needed to remarry when they joined Ibandla lamaNazaretha is that if you join the church having been married but *umqholiso* has not been slaughtered then you are considered incomplete. In contrast people who were married in a mixed Western and African wedding, in which case they are wedded by the state's marriage officers, and they wore Western kinds of dress (veils and suits) but the necessary slaughtering, especially *umqholiso*, happens, are not expected to remarry because they are considered complete even if they did not dance the sacred dance or any traditional dance that might connect the living people being married with the ancestral realm.

The rest of this chapter explores a wedding of iNkosi Nduna Mchunu which took place on the 7th of August 2008 in the Mandleni Homestead in Mdubuzweni near Mooi River. The reason why I chose this wedding in particular is because I was present when it happened. The groom is my maternal cousin, and I was one of the 'groom's men' who were dancing with him when it was time to dance. Most importantly, I use this because I also recorded it especially for my research, and was therefore able to explore it further.

I am looking at this wedding as both singular and representative of Nazaretha marriage. I choose to explore in detail one wedding ceremony instead of talking about marriage in general because I hope in this way my work can avoid the trap of writing about 'the other' in the timeless present tense, thus denying them "coevalness" (Fabian 1990). I also want to emphasise the fact that most of the time marriages have their own particularities so that it is better to talk about an individual marriage than to talk about marriage in general. This is because there is a great deal that happens 'behind the scenes' that informs what happens in the wedding (or the marriage itself). As mentioned earlier, the marriage process is long and involves extensive negotiations before the final wedding. But the following description begins with the final wedding ceremony itself.

Saturday evening, 06/09/08 10: 49 PM

The bridal party arrives. It is the bride and a group of about twenty girls accompanying her. They sing hymn No. 153 *"Nanti ilizwi elomemo/ Liyamema bonke abantu/ alikhethi noma munye/ Liyamema bonke abantu."* [Here is the word of invitation/ It invites all the people/ It does not exclude anyone/ It invites all the people.] The song is sung in the dancing style and the bridal party is beating the drum and blowing the *imbomu* (kudu horn) as they enter. The girls accompanying the bride escort her to the room where her 'mothers' are staying.[11] As they enter, the members of the chief's family collect the grass from an old demolished hut and they burn it to create light so they can see the bridal party. The bride is to spend the night with these women who have been appointed by the bride's mother who herself is not allowed to attend her daughter's wedding. The bride has to stay here with her kist because she cannot be separated from it. The other girls move to another rondavel where they sing and dance for the most part of what is left of the night.

Sunday morning: 07/09/08 05: 45

The bride moves around the homestead performing *isigwiyo*, leading a group of young men from her side of the family. The performance goes like this:

Bride: *Hebe!*
Party: *WuSuthu!*
Bride: *Hebe!*
Party: *WuSuthu!*
Bride: *Babengaphi?*
Party: *Babengapha singapha!*
Bride: *Babengaphi?*
Party: *Babengapha singapha!*

11 These women escorting the bride arrived a little earlier, at about eight.

[Bride:	Hebe!
Party:	It's uSuthu
Bride:	Hebe!
Party:	It's uSuthu
Bride:	Which side were they on?
Party:	They were this side we were that side!
Bride:	Which side were they on?
Party:	They were this side we were that side!]

Having circled the homestead they leave. The bride goes back to the river where her bridesmaids are.

06:30

The women and girls are called to the kraal to be shown the cow that is being given to the bride as *umqholiso.* (By this time, the men with the bridal party are already skinning the cow referred to as the cow of the bride's father. This should have been slaughtered on the previous day so it is the first thing they did when they woke up.) The women, all wearing shawls, give thanks to the chief who is the one pointing at the cow. They then go back to their place and the girls remain to watch as the negotiator stabs their sister's cow (their cow). There is a fine (it is negotiable between the girls and the negotiator) for every wound he stabs after the first one, therefore the girls shout, "*Vuka Nkomo*" [Wake up Cow] as he stabs it.[12] The cow falls down and dies after the third wound and, having decided that the fine will be ten rand, the girls go back to the river to join the bride and other girls who remained with her.

08:42

In the kraal the *umqholiso* cow has been skinned and its legs cut off (leaving the thighs) but everything else untouched. The bride comes from the river with her group, singing hymn No. 106, "*Thixo Nkosi yamakhosi*" [Lord, King of Kings]. She is dressed in a black skin-skirt. On top she wears a white t-shirt and a top-knot on her head. She carries a knife in her right hand and a string of white beadwork which is about one metre in length. At the gate of the kraal the group stops and the bride enters with two girls from her group. They walk to where the skinned cow is. She kneels down when she is next to the cow and moves towards it on her knees. She places the knife on the chest line of the cow and moves it down to the stomach. As she does this, the women in the homestead ululate, some saying, "the wife is entering the home!"

12 In most cases the sisters and other girls on the groom's side would sing, "*Lala Nkomo*" [Fall Cow] in competition with the bridal party.

She places the beadwork where she moved the knife and then she puts a two rand coin on the cord of the cow. She stands up and with her escorts she leaves the kraal.

12: 48

The bride comes from the river with a group of women and girls, singing hymn No. 153 "*Nanti ilizwi elomemo*" [Here is the Word of Invitation]. She, as well as four bridesmaids, is wearing a black skin-skirt, white t-shirt and top-knot covered with coloured beads. On their waists, on top of the t-shirts, they wear grass belts called *amaxhama*. On their ankles they wear a bead covering called *amadavathi*. They approach singing the hymn and dancing to it, with the drum beating and the trumpet blowing. They enter the kraal and start dancing. They make a line facing the homestead and continue dancing. The kist, *ibhokisi*, is in front of them as they dance.

As this is happening, the groom is in his house getting dressed. There are eight other men dressing with him (one of them his first-born son from the first wife).

1: 07

The groom's party comes out of the room. One man starts singing hymn No. 106 "*Thixo, Nkosi yamakhosi*" [Lord, King of Kings]. Outside the room three men from the Chunu clan approach the chief and suggest they should sing the Chunu tribal song as they march to the kraal. The Nazaretha hymn is ignored for a while and one non-Nazaretha man starts singing the song of the Chunu clan which is sung in a call-and-response style. It goes like this:

Leader: *Awu! Awu!*
Group: *Uyinsingizi yamakhosi uyinsingizi*
Leader: *Awu! Awu!*
Group: *Uyinsingizi yamakhosi uyinsingizi*

[Leader: Awu! Awu!
Group: You are a *nsingizi*[13] of the chiefs You are *insingizi*.
Leader: Awu! Awu
Group: You are the *insingizi* of the chiefs. You are *insingizi*.

As they sing this song they march slowly, as if counting their footsteps. In front is the praise singer, invoking the spirits of the late Chunu chiefs. When they reach the main rondavel of the homestead, *kwagogo* (at grandmother's),

13 This is a kind of bird associated with royalty.

the leader stops singing the song and starts the performance called *ukukhuza* which is a call-and-response but is not sung, it is shouted:

Leader: *Elavutha!*
Group: *Elavutha! Izul'elavutha*
Leader: *Elavutha!*
Group: *Elavutha! Izul'elavutha*
Leader: *Kwakunjani?*
Group: *Kwakumnyama kuthe bhuqe!*
Leader: *Kwakunjani?*
Group: *Kwakumnyama kuthe bhuqe!*
Leader: *Isibhamu sazo!*
Group: *Isibhamu sazo! Esadubula sathi zhi zhi!*
Leader: *Isibhamu sazo!*
Group: *Isibhamu sazo! Esadubula sathi zhi zhi!*
Leader: *Isibhamu sazo!*
Group: *Isibhamu sazo! Esadubula sathi zhi zhi!*

[Leader: That which burned!
Group: That which burned! The storm that burned!
[Leader: That which burned!
Group: That which burned! The storm that burned!
Leader: Their gun!
Group: Their gun! That fired, and went *zhi zhi*!
Leader: Their gun!
Group: Their gun! That fired, and went *zhi zhi*!
Leader: Their gun!
Group: Their gun! That fired, and went *zhi zhi*!]

Thereafter the groom's party resumes the clan song "*Awu*! *Awu*!". They stride on to the kraal and at the gate the leader stops them and starts *ukukhuza* again. They enter the kraal, turning to the left as they enter, leaving the bridal party (dancing faster now) on the right hand side. They proceed to occupy the northern part of the kraal, near the smaller gate facing the rondavel *kwagogo*. Here, the leader finishes his role by starting the *ukukhuza* again. After this, the Nazaretha resume control of the stage. They sing hymn No. 5 (*Abathanda uku-phila/ Emhlambini kaJesu*) "Those who want to Live/ In Jesus' Flock". Now the bridal party is stopped from their own performance. Temporarily they become part spectators. As the groom's party's dance intensifies, they march forward to the bridal party. They proceed till they reach it. Here, the two groups join to make one. The bride and the groom occupy the centre of the dancing line, with all the women dressed with the bride being on her left hand side and those with the groom on his right. Now the bride is wearing the leopard-skin shoulder covering called *amambatha* over the t-shirt. It is this piece of dress that separates her from the other women dressed in the skin skirts. The hymn is still No. 5.

After dancing to this hymn, the groom leaves the dancing group to sit on the chair near the small gate of the homestead. The bride also leaves to sit next to the goods she has brought to give to her in-laws in the part of the wedding called *umabo* (Giving of gifts). The other women who were with the bride take a background position and now it is only the men who are dancing. Even those not dressed in the sacred dance attire take part. The giving of gifts and the dancing (which now is more akin to entertainment than worship) take place concurrently. In the homestead the food is beginning to be served to those not engaged in the activities.

Interpreting the Chunu Chief's Wedding

Through this wedding of a Chunu chief, I propose to explore marriage in Ibandla lamaNazaretha (and perhaps Zulu/Nguni/African society) as a complex institution that is characterised by conflict and negotiation. The marriage under discussion here is one of the many marriages that are not initiated according to the Nazaretha tradition: where the bride and the groom get engaged in the church. This is not an ideal marriage according to the church. It resulted from an 'illegal' love affair between a member of the church (who was a designated chief) and a woman who was not a member of the church. Chief Nduna Mchunu had been taking part in the sacred dance and after he started the process of getting married to his new wife (the third), who is referred to as MaMajola (Daughter of Majola), he could not take part in the sacred dance before he was properly married, because his love affair made him ritually unclean and his taking part in the sacred dance would make the ancestors unhappy.

The wedding of this kind, which was not initiated in the church and in which the bride is no longer a virgin is not very different from that of a virgin girl.[14] The process described above would have obtained even if this wedding

14 It is, however, very different in terms of status. A woman married as a virgin girl wears a blue shawl, *inansuka eluhlaza*, which symbolises her status as a wife married the 'right' way.

was of an *inkosazane.* The only difference concerns two features of dress: one on the part of the bride and another on the part of the groom. As for the groom, if he had been married through the church, he would have worn a long string of beads across his left shoulder to the right thigh and around his back. This beadwork is called *ucu.* It was used as a symbol of love in pre-colonial Nguni society, and a girl gave her suitor *ucu* as a sign that she was accepting him.

As for the bride, instead of wearing a white t-shirt with a grass belt, *ixhama*, she would have worn only the skin top covering, *amambatha.* There are many animals from whose skins *amambatha* can be made but the leopard skin is the most favoured one. Muller's suggestion that "this leopard skin embodies the relationship between young girls and Shembe, in terms of the praise name for Shembe as the 'leopard' written into the text of Hymn 84, the hymn Isaiah gave to the girls as a reward for their obedience and moral goodness" (1999: 211) is incorrect because it assumes that this "covering" is always made from the leopard skin. Also she does not realise that no girl ever owns *amambatha* but they are always borrowed for the sake of the wedding. This means if they were to embody any relationship it would be between men and Shembe, not virgin girls and Shembe.

I think the reason why a woman who marries as a virgin wears only the skin covering while the one who is not a virgin wears a t-shirt suggests that it is acceptable for a virgin girl to show her upper body, especially the breasts, while it is not acceptable for someone who is not. Put differently, the breasts of a virgin (as well as her body) represent purity and cleanliness and therefore are a public sight, while those of a non-virgin represent uncleanliness and shame. The reason for this is that sex in general is considered defiling. That is why members are expected to abstain from sex in the evenings preceding the days designated for holy gatherings like the Sabbath, overnight meetings of twenty-three, and fourteen; and during the holy monthly meetings of January and July members are not expected to have sex even if they are not in the meeting. It is therefore fitting in Nazaretha belief that virgin girls, whose bodies are not defiled, should wear close to nothing on their upper body, only some beads above the breasts and on the waist, and women, whose bodies are perceived to be defiled by sexual intercourse, must cover all their body, showing only the face, the hands and the feet.

Interestingly, while the main point of the wedding is to incorporate the bride into her groom's family, her position as an outsider is always maintained. This is symbolised by the fact that she has to leave her father's homestead at night and also arrive at the groom's homestead at night. In this case, the night represents both the fact that she herself is being 'stolen' from her own home and also that she comes to this home as a thief, stealing membership of it.[15] A reference to the fact that the wife came at night is always made when members feel the need to invoke her status as an outsider, referring to her as *umafika ebusuku* (the one who came at night). However, this points to the ambiguous position of women in the church in general: that they are regarded as outsiders in their own homes because they are meant to leave and create a home for someone else, while in their home by marriage they are regarded as outsiders because they came (at night) from another home. It is better though to be marginalised as a married woman than to be marginalised as an unmarried one because married wives have their solid position in the home but unmarried women are marginalised even by their sisters in law, saying they should "be married and making laws in their 'own' homes".

What is also noteworthy with regards to the chief's wedding is the contestation of 'public' space between the Nazaretha and the non-Nazaretha, with their different but related expressive forms. This is shown in the way the non-Nazaretha Chunu demanded a Chunu clan song to be sung when the groom was leaving his room for the kraal. Isaiah Shembe's negotiation of traditional and new forms shapes many Nazaretha rituals even today. It was Shembe's embracing of traditional forms that made his ministry appeal to many people. But some traditionalists wanted their forms 'pure' and unchanged, and Shembe's hybrid forms did not appeal to them. The same thing was happening in this wedding. While many people like Ibandla lama Nazaretha for its upholding of African values, those who want their 'pure' precolonial forms felt sidelined and demanded their own space. Had the Nazaretha song been sung, many non-Nazaretha who ended up taking part in the performance would have been mere spectators. But even though the Nazaretha were part of the 'Chunu clan' singing, they occupied a marginal role. This was significant because the wedding was supposed to be a Nazaretha wedding. It was only in the kraal that the Nazaretha and their performance of the sacred dance took centre stage.

Conclusion

In this chapter I have looked at the two important rituals in the Nazaretha Church that deal with completeness, namely male circumcision and marriage. Being complete is important because it enables people to take part in the

15 It is interesting to note that, when a woman is engaged, she is expected to respect her in-laws and present herself as a good wife to be, a practice called *ukuntshontsha izinkomo* (stealing cattle).

sacred dance especially, and in other holy gatherings. Circumcision as a ritual is performed in a way similar in some senses to the way it was/is performed in African societies, but it is explained in terms of the biblical narrative of the covenant between Abraham and God. It is, however, a new form that is unique to the church because of its combination of the two strands and also because it is given another dimension which does not obtain in both the biblical and the African traditional understandings of circumcision. This is circumcision as a way of cleansing and of paving a way to heaven.

I have dealt with marriage as an institution characterised by conflict and negotiation. Members not properly married (those who have partners) are considered unclean and incomplete, and marriage is the only way for a woman and a man who had a child out of wedlock to become complete again. But marriage is supposed to begin with an engagement in the church where a man chooses a virgin and proposes to her in *ebhentshini*. However, not all engagements end in marriage. Sometimes the girl accepts the man because of the pressure in *ebhenshini* but rejects him later on. Sometimes a girl falls pregnant while the man is struggling with the demands of her family: the bride price and gifts (*izibizo*).

CHAPTER 6

Dress Codes and the Poetics of Performance in the Sacred Dance

Introduction

In an obvious challenge to missionary ideology concerning dress and Christianity, Isaiah Shembe asserted to Nelly Wells that, "Natives need not wear clothes nor pass Std VII to get to heaven" (Brown, 1992: 101). This was indeed against the grain of the teaching of the missionaries in Zululand and Natal, who thought that, "if some of the externals of the Christian life were assumed, Christian faith and goodness would follow" (Unterhalter, 1981: 124; quoted in Brown, 1992: 97). As a result of this belief, Unterhalter argues, "Christian life came to be associated with conforming to manners, dress and aspirations of the missionaries" (97). One of the things which characterises Isaiah Shembe's Ibandla lamaNazaretha is its deviation from or its non-conformance with such aspirations of the missionaries in terms of dress and practice. Shembe was critical of the missionaries' equating of dress with Christianity. For Shembe, what mattered was the inside of a person, not the appearance. Thus, he is reported to have told his followers that "You must not think that because you cover your bodies with clothing that you are Christians. You are not. Before you can claim to be a Christian, you must put evil things from you, and live as Christians" (Brown, 1992: 98).

However, despite Shembe's claims about the insignificance of dress in defining Christianity, he dedicated a great deal of time to designing the outfits for his followers to use in church services and especially to use when performing the sacred dance. In this chapter I look at the kind of dress Shembe chose for his followers, its significance and meaning, and how these changed over time. The second part of the chapter looks at the poetics of performing the sacred dance, exploring the different dance styles performed in the Ibandla lamaNazaretha, namely, *isigekle* and *amagxalaba* (Shembe style). I argue that both the dress and the sacred dance are improvisations on the old pre-colonial features. As the accounts of people like M.A. Delegorgue have shown, dance played an important role in the lives of the Africans in the pre-colonial period, and in the Ibandla lamaNazaretha the dance was reconfigured and given new meaning. But that new meaning was/is not political in the sense advocated by Brown and Muller as stated in Chapter Three. In the pre-colonial period dance

 | DOI 10.1163/9789004320628_008

was more of a social phenomenon and in the Ibandla lamaNazaretha it is first and foremost a religious phenomenon. As many members would say, "*Umgidi uyinkonzo*" (Sacred dance is worship).

Dress and the Sacred Dance

In the twenty-three meeting of November 2008, Chief Simakade Mchunu requested the opportunity to give advice to the *inhlayisuthi* (male members) gathered in his homestead in Msinga near Greytown. His talk incorporated the poetics of the sacred dance (although he did not go into the details of how each song is performed) and the importance of dress codes. His speech forms the foundation of this chapter so that it needs to be reproduced at length here:

> *Njengoba kuwu 23 omkhulu ohlale uba khona, ngithi ake ngibeke lokhu. Ngake ngaya emgidini. Uma ungakakwazi ukuzisinela ngokwakho, ungabongena phakathi nendawo. Ufike uwone uwuqede umgidi, ngoba awukakwazi ukuzisinela ngokwakho. Ukuba njengoba lomkhandlu kaNkulunkulu ungaka nje, ungake ushayelwe isigubhu kuhlatshelelwe, bese kuthiwa ake usinele leligama, awukwazi ukuthi uzobukela kubani. Pho manje ungenelani phakathi? Ngoba phela usuzolokhu uzaza nje phakathi. Kahlenini bakwethu. Futhi-ke okunye, sasicelile nhlayisuthi ukuthi izingane zazike ziphathe nezikhumba nje zembeleko. Manje na akubukeki umgidi omkhulu kangaka abanye baphume bheka (ephakamisa isandla)baphakamise izibhakela angathi bayoshayana egroundini. Asikucabange lokho. Kanti futhi kukhona engikubukayo, ukuthi uma uhla luphuma, kulandele ingane, kulandele nabadala baxubane, kuye kuthi uma selumile uhla, into engiyibukayo wukuthi izingane zibe sezima lapho. Akuwona umthetho lowo. Ngisho angabe uyigagu kangakanani akuwona umthetho ukuthi ingane ime phakathi kwamadoda. Okokugcina yilokhu. Ngizocela ukuthi ngisukume nginikhombise (esukuma ephinda umnazaretha awufake ngaphakathi kwebhulukwe). Uthi akubukweni? Yini lena othi ayibukwe njenga wenze nje? Wawungakhacwa kabi yizinsizwa zaseKuphakameni kuqala. Zithi "Owakabani lomfana?" Cha bobo musani ukuthatha iminazaretha niyishutheke la... Yilokho nje ebengithi nami angikubeke, ukuthi ake kulandelwe okunye okwaziwa yithi esibadala. (Amen) Lokhu ukuthi akekho umuntu omdala esontweni... Sikhona! (Bayede!)...*
>
> [As this is an important twenty-three meeting, I want to say this. I once went to the sacred dance. If you are still unable to dance on your own,

do not stay at the centre of a line. If you do that you spoil the dance completely, because you cannot dance on your own. Let us say as this congregation of God is this big, if they beat the drum for you and sing, and you are told to dance for that particular song, but you do not know who to watch from. But now why do you enter the line in the centre? Because you are going to look this way and that way [not knowing what to do]. No, do not, my folks. And another thing, we had requested from you *nhlayisuthi* that the children used to carry the hides of goats. Now it does not look good in this important sacred dance if some enter [the dancing stage] (raising his hand) having their fists raised as if they are going to fight in the play grounds. And again there is something I am observing, that if a line is entering, the children are followed by the adults, they are mixed, when the group is standing, what I have noticed is that the children keep the positions they entered in. That is against the law. No matter how adept you are it is against the law that a child stands in the middle of men. The last thing is this. I want to stand up so I can show you (he folds his *umnazaretha* and shoves it under his trousers on the right hip). What do you want people to see? What is it that you want people to see as you are doing this? In the olden days the men of *eKuphakameni* would have shouted at you, saying "What's the surname of that boy?" No. Do not take your prayer gowns and shove them under your trousers. That is all I wanted to say; that let there be something done that is known by us the older members. (Amen) The saying that there is no old person in the church ... We are there! (*Bayede*)]

The above text opens with perhaps the most important feature of the sacred dance: that each and every hymn has its particular form or style of dance that a person can either know or not know. This means every member has to learn and master the different steps of each song. However, this does not mean that all the 242 hymns in the hymn book have their own styles, but one has to know which songs are performed in a particular way. For instance, hymn No. 4 "*Yiza namuhla*" (Come Today), hymn No. 5 "*Nina abathanda ukuphila*" (Those of you who want to Live), hymn No. 87 "*Inhlanhla yesoni*" (A Sinner's Luck) and a number of other hymns are danced in the same way. This means if one knows how to dance for hymn No. 4, then it follows that one can also dance for hymn No. 5 and No. 87. The only difference is the words of the hymns, but the singing, the pitch of the song, and its performance are the same. So if the group is very large, it happens that people cannot hear what the leader of a song is saying; but by hearing the tune, they know it is one of the hymns that are sung and danced in that particular way. If then the leader sings the first part of hymn

No. 4 and someone in the group cannot hear properly, that person can sing the first part of hymn No. 5 (if he thinks that is what is being sung) and the dance would not be disturbed because the change in words does not mean a change in performance, as long as the rhythm is the same.

I stated elsewhere (Sithole, 2005) that it is every dancer's desire to be in the centre of a line because the centre is the heart of the sacred dance where the lead singer, the drums, the trumpets, and 'audible' singing from the group all converge to help the dancers feel the beat. The centre of a line is thus a locus or domain of the most powerful and adept dancers. Sometimes when the dancing is about to begin there is shoving and pushing among the dancers, all trying to be as close to the centre as they can possibly manage. The young members, the new converts and the un-ordained members are relegated to the far sides of the line, the least fortunate occupying the furthest spot. This spot is called *iqhulu*, and nobody likes it. These issues are incorporated in the first and third points of Chief Mchunu's speech. They have to do with perfecting the sacred dance and the hierarchy in the church where the young and the lowly have always to know their position.

The second and fourth points concern the appearance of the dance or dancers. The shields that Mchunu mentions are part of the features of the sacred dance, along with the umbrellas that, according to Bongani Mthethwa, were added in order to enhance "the visual interest of the dance" (see Brown, 1992: 100). In the twenty-three meeting of January 2008 in Ebuhleni, Minister Magwaza of Nkandla preached about the importance of taking part in the sacred dance and owning the sacred dance shield. According to Magwaza, the shield protects the person and the home of a person who owns and uses it in the sacred dance. He told the male congregants that he had travelled from Durban (where he worked) to JudeaTemple near Gingindlovu with all his dance regalia. On the Saturday night preceding the Sunday on which they were to dance, he had a dream. In the dream a voice he did not know told him to look at the mountain and there he saw his father's homestead with his shield, now extremely large, floating over the homestead. For Magwaza, what the dream meant was that the shield protects not just the person who owns it but also the rest of his or her home against all the evil spirits and things that can befall that given home. He was thus urging members to buy their own shields.

The introduction of umbrellas occurred even earlier, in the 1930s, and Brown claims that "They might have once been considered prestige items – and they also appear in photographs from the 30s of traditionalists in festive dress" (1992: 100). While today the umbrellas are exclusively carried by married women and virgin girls, in the time of Isaiah Shembe men also carried umbrellas.[1] In one

1 Today men carry *amashoba*, (made with a small stick and the skin at the end of the cow's tail).

photograph inserted in the church's calendar of 2003, Isaiah Shembe stands with five men who are dressed in *amabheshu* (loinskins). Isaiah Shembe is clad in his black robe and carries what looks like a basket with flowers in his left hand; his right hand might be carrying something but it is obscured. Three of the five men are carrying umbrellas and one of them is carrying a small shield[2] as well.

An interesting contradiction with regards to dress for the sacred dance and dress in general is that while with the actual dance change is discouraged and criticised by the older leaders of the church, no one postulates a return in the dance regalia to what it was during the time of Isaiah Shembe. But the dance attire has certainly changed over the years. There are even some features of dress that obtained in the time of Isaiah Shembe which are prohibited today. For instance, today a man would not be allowed to dance carrying an umbrella. And the loinskins worn by the men with Isaiah Shembe in the photograph are much shorter than the ones generally worn today. The front parts of the men's loinskins, called *isinene/izinene*, only reach to the middle of the thighs but today men generally wear *izinene* that reach to the knee and the back parts, *amabheshu*, sometimes almost reach to the ankles.

The men in the photograph belong to the group of male dancers called *injobo* in the Ibandla lamaNazaretha. Today's dress for this group is much richer and more complicated than that worn by the men in the time of Isaiah Shembe. Beside the differences mentioned above, there are a number of other features that distinguish what was worn then and what is worn now.[3] The most visible difference is that the men in the photograph wear close to nothing on their torsos while today men of the *injobo* group wear a garment made from cowhide around their shoulders covering the entire chest and a part of the stomach. These are called *amambatha*, and are made from the skins of wild animals, especially those of the cat family like the leopard and the *indlonzi* (cheetah). Around the calves another piece is worn, a band usually made from animal skin called *izikhono*, and around the ankles there is a band made from beads or some plastic material. These are called *izihlakala*. The men in the picture wear thin head-ties, *ongiyane*, which are seldom worn today. Today men wear around their heads thicker head-ties called *imiqhele* usually made from leopard skin, buck skin or *indlonzi* skin. Some also wear a

---

2 A shield like this one is now carried by women. Men carry much larger shields which are designed differently from the one carried by the man in the photograph.

3 This is assuming that what the men are wearing in the photograph is what they would wear for the sacred dance. It is clear that they are not dancing in the photograph, but the fact that they are carrying umbrellas and one is carrying a shield suggests that they would have dressed the same way if they were dancing the sacred dance.

plumed headdress called *isidlodlo* or *idlokolo*. It is difficult to account for these developments in the dance attire, but I think that it has to do with increased communication, with people copying and borrowing from each other, and has also to do with the creativity of the makers of the dance attire, who develop ways to expand their businesses and make the sacred dance attire more attractive to the eye and at the same time more expensive.[4]

An alternative sacred dance attire for men is *isikotshi*.[5] Unlike the dance attire for married women and virgin girls which combine traditional and European features, this is an entirely European attire with not a single precolonial feature. This costume consists of the knee-length pleated cotton kilt and a hip-length, long-sleeved white smock which has a white tasselled border at its hem. On their heads members of this group wear white pith helmets and on their feet wear black and white football socks and black army boots. The younger members of this group, of the adolescent age and younger, wear a pink and white checked kilt and instead of a pith helmet they wear a headband with a pompon motif.

Women in the church are divided into three groups according to age and marital status. The group of young women not of marriageable age (about fifteen years and younger) is called *utubhana*. This group is identified by the bright red, pleated cotton skirt they wear. Another distinguishing feature for this group is that they wear nothing on their heads, except for a little piece of beadwork that is fastened in the hair. The other features of dress worn by this group are the same as those worn by the group of virgin girls and women of marriageable age (I discuss this group below). These consist entirely of beadwork. Fastened around the waist and the chest are thick bands made of three rolls of beadwork and at the hips are equally thin bands but made of nine rolls of beadwork. There are also two flat pieces of beadwork. The smaller one, about five by fifteen centimetres, is fastened below the rolled bands on the chest. This beadwork touches but does not cover the breasts. The bigger flat beadwork starts from the waist, just below the rolled bands, reaching to the bottom of the nine rolled pieces of beadwork covering the hip. Other rolls of beadwork fastened around the hip are made of thinner rolls of beads put together to make rolls thicker than the ones mentioned above. These are of red, blue and yellow colours and are only visible on the sides and back since

4 One thing that separates the dance regalia for *injobo* from that of *isikotshi* is that *injobo* regalia can be very expensive, the full regalia costing up to R 5000 depending on the quality one chooses.

5 This is also a name given to the kind dance or dance style of the group who wear this attire.

in front they are covered by the flat beadwork. There are also thinner bands of beads on the calves, and covering the ankles.

The other group of women and virgin girls of marriageable age is distinguished from the *utubhana* group by the black cotton skirts with layers made of strands of wool overlapping in four to five rows. On their heads these virgin girls wear tight fitting hair-nets around which are headbands with red motifs. This group is sub-divided into the *isidwaba esincane* (small loinskirt) and *isidwaba esikhulu* (big loinskirt). The younger girls, ranging from sixteen to nineteen, belong to *isidwaba esincane,* and older girls and women to *isidwaba esikhulu.* The only feature of dance attire attributable to the pre-colonial period is the shields that are carried by all the dance groups. All female groups carry their shields along with umbrellas.

The last group is of married women called *ujamengweni* or *ingudlungudlu.* Larlham calls this group *ubuhlalu* (1985). This term may have been used at the time he conducted his research but now it is not used. This group wears pleated leather skirts, *izidwaba,* that are precolonial in origin. Worn over the leather skirts is the red cotton wrap called *isicwayo.* This was introduced during the time of J.G. Shembe and covers the entire torso. Another semi-traditional feature in the costume of married women is beadwork called *amagxaba.* This is a black cotton skirt worn over *isidwaba,* and is decorated with beadwork at the hem. The black cotton is covered by the *isicwayo,* so that it is only the beadwork of the *amagxaba* that appears below the *isicwayo* over the *isidwaba.* Over *isicwayo* on the waist is a grass, beaded belt called *ixhama.*

The headdress, *isicholo,* can either be cylindrical or cone-shaped, narrow at the base and broadening to the rim. The former used to be worn by Zululand women while Natal women preferred the latter. However, nowadays that distinction is not as clear as it used to be. Perhaps the reason for this is that all of the Church's accessories are sold by members who travel all over South Africa with the congregation, and one can choose whichever headdress one likes. Fastened around the headdress is a beaded band resembling that which the virgin girls tie over their hairnets. The *ikhulu* (one hundred) is named after the number of strings of beads which make it. This is attached beneath the *isicholo* and hangs over the shoulders. The last feature of dress for married women is called *ibhayi.* This is a long black cotton cloak which is fastened around the neck and hangs down the back to the bottom of *isidwaba.*

What is clearly noticeable from the above discussion is that dress in Isaiah Shembe's Ibandla lamaNazaretha incorporated both precolonial and colonial features. In her article "Dress, Ideology and Practice: Clothing in the Nazareth Baptist Church in the 1920s and 1930s" quoted above, Karen Brown poses the question regarding dress in Ibandla lamaNazaretha: "What was the reason or reasons behind Isaiah Shembe permitting or reintroducing traditional dress?" (1992: 101). A possible answer for Brown is that maybe he wanted to attract new members: "Certainly one cannot deny that it must have been very attractive to prospective members, most of whom were traditionalists living in the rural areas who had suffered severe ruptures to their traditional way of life" (101). There is, indeed, a certain amount of truth in this statement. One of the early converts to Ibandla lamaNazaretha, Mjadu, is reported to have asked Isaiah Shembe if he would make them take off their traditional dress were they to convert to his church. Shembe reassured him, and others, that they did not need to take off their loinskins if they had to join his church (Themba Masinga, undated audio cassette). Also, Chief Silwane Mchunu of Msinga is said to have told his family (in a rather prophetic tone) that a minister who would not require them to take off their traditional dress will arrive in his land. He said he would only convert to the church of that man (Interview, Chief Simakade Mchunu, 18 May 2008).

However, I think that the question Brown poses above need not be restricted to the reasons for Shembe permitting traditional dress in his church, but can be expanded to: Why did Shembe, having told Wells that "natives need not wear clothes to be Christians", still insist on designing special clothing for his followers? The answer is in some way similar to the one above: that perhaps Shembe designed these clothes to attract new members, but that he was aiming for people who were living their lives in a way different from that of traditionalists. This is especially true if a police report of 1921 is anything to go by: "Shembe's success in attracting females is the dress and spectacular shows which he arranges, all dress in white, wear a band around the head and carry palm leaves, they then go in procession to the places where the so called religious rites take place accompanied by dancing" (Quoted in Brown, 1992: 98). This point is also supported by Roberts (1936) who suggested that those members who were traditionalists were more likely to wear traditional dress, while the more Westernised members were less likely to do so.

The Poetics of Performing the Sacred Dance

In pre-colonial Zulu society song and dance featured very prominently in cultural and religious life. Even well-known kings like Shaka participated in some of the dances that took place in their kraals. These events were still taking place in the time of Mpande, as M.A. Delegorgue gives a striking account

FIGURE 6.1 *Young men of the Nazaretha Church dancing at eBuhleni in July 2008. Younger boys on the sides wear pink skirts while older ones in the middle wear black ones.*

FIGURE 6.2 *Isaiah Shembe and his followers dressed in loinskins.*

FIGURE 6.3 *Men wearing* injobo *at eKuthuthukeni Temple in Gauteng, April 2008.*

FIGURE 6.4 *Virgin girls wearing* isiZulu *dance attire in eBuhleni, July 2009.*

FIGURE 6.5 *Married women wearing sacred dance attire in eKuthuthukeni, April 2008.*

FIGURE 6.6 Ikhulu *beadwork hanging at the back of a married woman.*

of a performance he witnessed in Mpande's kraal in what he calls a "three day festival of dance and song". Delegorgue reports that it was only on the last day of the festival that Mpande took part in the dance:

> [Mpande] sang marking the beat with both hands alternately, reinforcing it with straight gestures of the arms, directing his assegai in different directions understood by all, lifting it, lowering it, pointing it to the right, then to the left, and his gestures, his words, his movement were identical to those of every participant. The best drilled soldiers do not exercise with such precision; no hand was lifted higher than any other, nor was any tonga tilted more than another, never a delay, nor an error: it was of unequalled uniformity. (Larlham, 1985: 4)

In a similar vein A.F. Gardiner, who visited Zululand in the time of Dingane, offered his own account of the festival of dance and song that he witnessed:

> Each man is provided with a short stick, knobbed at the end, and it is by the direction that he gives to this, the motion of his other hand, and the turns of his body, that the action and pathos of the song is indicated; the correspondence is often very beautiful, while the feet regulate the time, and impart that locomotive effect in which they so much delight; sometimes the feet are merely lifted, to descend with a stamp; sometimes, a leaping stride is taken on either side; at others, a combination of both; but they have yet a more violent gesture; forming four deep, in open order, they make short runs to and fro, leaping, prancing, and crossing each other's paths, brandishing their sticks, and raising such a cloud of dust by the vehemence and rapidity of the exercise, that to a bystander it has all the effect of the wildest battle scene of savage life, and which it is doubtless intended to imitate. (Quoted in Larlham, 1985: 3–4)

Delegorgue's and Gardiner's accounts above describe performances that are not very far removed from the ones performed in Ibandla lamaNazaretha today. This similarity and relatedness between dance and song that took place in pre-colonial period and the sacred dance taking place in Ibandla lamaNazaretha today is important for the argument of this chapter and of the thesis as a whole. The dances that are taking place in Ibandla lamaNazaretha today are improvisations on the dances that took place in the precolonial period and are the same as the ones that took place during the colonial and apartheid periods. So any explanation given for the performances that took place during the time of apartheid and colonialism should in some way be related to (even though not necessarily the same as) the performances that took place before and are taking place after colonialism and apartheid.

With this thought in mind, in this part of the chapter I examine the poetics of performing the sacred dance in Ibandla lamaNazaretha, focusing my attention on the sacred performances of Nazaretha festivals in what is called the sacred dance of all people (*umgidi wabantu bonke*). These are exclusive dances where only the 'complete' members of the church can take part. But the reason for my choosing these performances, instead of the ones taking place in overnight meetings for instance, is that the sacred dance of all people is structured in a way similar to that described by Delegorgue and Gardiner above.

Shembe's Word is Final about the Sacred Dance

Larlham suggests that the massed dancing that took place in the times of Shaka, Dingaan, and Mpande described above "[displayed] the power of the king and the allegiance of his followers" (1985: 4). These dances were organised, especially the one that took place in Shaka's kraal, "to honour and impress the British settlers who had arrived in [Shaka's] land" (4). While in Ibandla lamaNazaretha the dances are part of the Church's life, and are not organised to impress any visitor, they do, however, seem to display the power of the leader and the allegiance of his followers. In Ibandla lamaNazaretha the sacred dance can only take place if the leader has given word that it is to take place. For the bigger Sunday dances, it is the leader himself who announces after the afternoon Sabbath service that there is going to be dancing the following day. This goes like this: "*Umgidi wabantu bonke kusasa.*" [It's the sacred dance of all people tomorrow.] For the dances that take place during the week, on Tuesday and on Thursday, it is the church's announcer who tells the congregation in the evening service of the previous day that there is going to be the sacred dance the following day. This he does on behalf of the leader, saying: "*Lithi izwi leNkosi, umgidi wabantu bonke kusasa.*" [The word of the iNkosi says, it's the sacred dance of all people tomorrow.] On the actual day of the dance, the word has to come from the leader that those prepared to dance can now go to the dancing ground and dance. It is the virgin girls who are sent to announce: "*Lithi izwi leNkosi, ayiphume imigidi*" [The word of the iNkosi says the dancers can go to dance (literally: let the dancers leave).] In all this total allegiance to the leader is encouraged and emphasised. Even in sermons this allegiance to the leader, embodied in abiding by the rules of the sacred dance, is preached.

Preaching about disobedience in the Church as a whole, but especially against Shembe and ordained members who are said to be Shembe's right-hand men (and women), Minister Mthethwa in his sermon of July 2008 travelled back in time to the years of J.G. Shembe, better known to his followers as *iLanga* (Sun). He preached about the sacredness of the dance and other rituals, and the importance of Shembe and his word in all that is done in the Church, especially the sacred dance. Below I present an extract from Mthethwa's sermon. It is lengthy but very important for our understanding of power relations in the Church and the role of the sacred dance in negotiating power relations:

> *Imigidi lena iyingcwele, yingakho beqeqeshwa abantu ngaphambi kokuba baye emgidini. Uma laphaya uMathunjwa kuqeqeshwe abantu. Abanye bese bethi "Hhawu uMathunjwa uyasibambezela." Ha ha ha! Ngangikhona Masina eKuphakameni! Ngangikhona. Mhla kudalek'umonakalo. Umkhokheli uNtombela ethi uyakhuluma ethunywa yiNkosi iLanga, lithi iLanga lithuma umphathi uNtombela uHlalekudeni lithi "Hamba ungibuzele kulabafana baseThekwini nabaseGoli ukuthi izintshebe lezi zishonephi. Ubusubabekela umthetho uthi ngithe lezintshebe namakhanda abawaphungula eGoli naseThekwini abangisize bakhe amakopi katinjam bawabhobose ngapha nangapha abe nebambo, bese uma beshefa bafake uboya phakathi nalobu ababuphungula emakhanda babufake phakathi bese beza nabo lapha ngoJulayi ngoba buyangihlupha lobu boya lobu. Kwaqhamuk'oyedwa namanje ngeke ngimkhombe. Kwaqhamuka oyedwa phakathi esijwini wathi kuNtombela, "Hhawu, kanti uyabheda lo?" Kwakuqala ngqa kulelibandla... Yilelo langa-ke lapho kwaqhamuka khona izimpempe zokusinisa. Kanti sihleli nje izimpempe sezigcwele amaphakethe kuwowonke umuntu. Bafuna nje ukusinisa. Kuthiwa uteleke nemfengwane. 'Shaya imfengwane wena sobanibani sambe. Wabe eseyishaya omunye pepe pe base bemlandela. Sasala nabanye bahamba baya phesheya bayosina... Lase lifika iSabatha elingaliyo. Lase lima, liwakhipha amehlo. Lase lithi iLanga "Sekunogalajane laph'ekhaya. Sekunogalajane." Lase lithi "Lensangu kodwa eniyibhemayo, izophela." Lase lithi, "Kukhona abafana lapha asebehlubukile."... Labe selithi, "Labafana kusasa wumgidi wabo. Niyophuma ngokubona kwenu, nifike nisine ngokubona kwenu, nihlale phansi ngokubona kwenu. Uma kuthi buyani niyobuya ngokubona kwenu. Bathi "Amen!"... Kwase kungena inyanga yeZulu. Ithi iNyanga yeZulu siseLinda, iqhamuka sithi shaya imfengwane ngoba sesijwayele phela "Shayimfengwane wena! Shayimfengwane sambe." Sasingasadli kanti sijahe ukuya edimonini. Yathi "Wowu!" Kusho iNyanga yeZulu. Yathi*

"Yini le ethi pepepe?" Yase ithi "Ha ha ha! Namanje noma sengikhona nisahlubukile? Nisalandela izwi lesiqalekiso leli inkosi eyaniduba? Namanje ngikhona nifuna ukuzenzela umathanda?" Yase ithi "Kusukela namhlanje ngingaphinde ngiyizwe into ethi pepepe. Nihambela uNkulunkulu phambili. Ubani othe sinani? Anisaphethwe ngezwi?... Kwathi ngo 11 o'clock kwaqhamuk'uMamashi iNkosazane. Asimuzwa ukuthi uthini wayengenalo izwi uMamashi. Kanti uthi, "Lithi izwi leNkosi, ayiphume imigidi." Njengoba nizwa kwenzeka nanamuhla lokhu nje.

[These dances are sacred, that is why people are trained before going to dance. Mathunjwa stands there and trains people. Then others say "*Hhawu*, Mathunjwa is delaying us." Ha ha ha! I was there Masina in eKuphakameni. I was there when chaos was started. When Leader Ntombela tried to speak, having been sent by *iLanga*. *ILanga* said, sending Leader Ntombela, Hlalekudeni (his first name) saying, "Go and ask for me from the boys who live in Durban and Johannesburg where their beards are? Then set the rule for them, say these beards and heads they cut in Johannesburg and Durban they must help me by making tins from "tinjam" and make holes on either side of them to make handles. When they shave, they should put the hair inside and the hair they cut from their heads they should put inside and then bring them to me in July because that hair worries me." One man appeared and even now I will not point at him. One man appeared in the middle of the group and said to Leader Ntombela, "*Hawu*, he is talking nonsense!" It was for the very first time in this Church. It was that day that there appeared flutes for directing the sacred dance. We did not know them. [We did not know] that as we were staying, there were flutes in people's pockets. All because they wanted to lead the dance. They were saying he is refusing with the flute. "This man is talking nonsense. Blow the flute you so and so and let us go." Then another one blew the flute *pepepe* and they left. We remained with the others and they went over there to dance. Then the Sabbath came. The *iLanga* stood, opened his eyes and then said, "There are now crooks here at home." Then he said, "But this *dagga* of yours you are smoking will be finished." Then he said "There are boys here who have fallen away."... Then he said "These boys tomorrow it's their sacred dance. You will leave as you see fit, dance as you see fit, rest as you see fit. And come back as you see fit." They said, "Amen!" Then *iLanga* passed away and *iNyanga YeZulu* came. The *iNyanga* said when we were at eLinda, saying "blow the flute" because now we were used to it. "Blow the flute

> and let us go." Then *iNyanga* appeared with the ministers. When he appeared, by then we were no longer eating, we were on the rush to the demon. He said "*Hawu!*" *iNyanga YeZulu* said. "What is it that says *pepepe*? Ministers, what is saying pe pe pe?" Then he said, "Ha ha ha! Even when I am here you are still dissenting? You are still following the word of the curse the *iNkosi* gave you? Even now that I am here you still want to do as you please?" Then he said, "As of today, let me not hear anything saying *pepepe* again. Who told you to dance? Aren't you led by the word now? Stop! Go back and eat!"... Then at eleven o'clock there appeared Mamashi, the virgin girl. We did not hear what she was saying. She had an inaudible voice. What is this *inkosazane* saying? She was saying, "The word of the *iNkosi* says, let the dances start!" As you hear it happens even today. The dancing does not start without the word.]

This text shows that if the sacred dance in Ibandla lamaNazaretha displays the power of the leader, Shembe, as Larlham claims was the case with regards to the Zulu Kings, Shaka, Dingaan and Mpande, that power is highly contested in Ibandla lamaNazaretha. The above text is characterised by conflict which obtains in Ibandla lamaNazaretha between the church's leaders, J.G. Shembe and Amos Shembe on the one hand and the members (or some of them) on the other. The conflict is also between ordained members and ordinary members. In both cases the issue is power and control. In both cases the leaders try to exert their power over their subjects, and the subjects challenge the leaders' attempts. The sacred dance becomes a locus in which this power game is played out. The point Mthethwa makes is that the dance is sacred so the minister, the leader, has to teach people about it. But some people see Mathunjwa's admonitions as a waste of time because for them the sacred dance represents something else. That is why they do not attend to his teachings, and in a way they challenge him.

The more interesting case, however, is that of *iLanga* and the members. After the incident between Ntombela and the members, the power is swayed in favour of the members. At first it seems as if it is Ntombela who is defied, but the reality is that he was bringing the word of *iLanga*; he was *iLanga's* messenger. That is why *iLanga* felt insulted and told the men to do as they pleased, thus openly giving his power away to them. An intended or hoped-for response was remorse, but the congregation responded with a huge "Amen", which meant they welcomed the news.[6] The power and control that were lost by

---

6 Mthethwa says this in a negative way, implying that they (the congregation) should not have said "Amen", that it was like accepting a curse.

ILanga were only regained in the time of *INyanga YeZulu*, when he confronted the men at eLinda and told them not to do as they please. This, I hope, puts into perspective Larlham's statement that, "All decisions – where the dancing is to take place or whether it is to take place at all – are made by the leader" (1985: 36).

Perhaps one of the reasons why the sacred dance has been viewed as a form of resistance against colonialism and apartheid is that the dancing groups are arranged in regiments that resemble the 'war regiments' of pre-colonial society. One striking feature of the two accounts above is that the performances he described could be 'war dances' performed by warriors going to war or they could be peaceful dances performed at certain rituals. Or they could be both.

Two Main Styles of Sacred Dance

There are two main styles or types of sacred dance in Ibandla lamaNazaretha. The first is *isigekle*, which is performed by the men's groups in the second part of the dance, (*umgidi wantambama*/ the afternoon dance), and by the girls in the first part of the dance. The second style is *amagxalaba* and the men's groups can only perform this style in the first section of the sacred dance and the girls in the second. This means there are songs that are danced in a particular way called *isigekle* and *amagxalaba*, but these also have certain little variations depending on which group is performing. For instance, the way *isikotshi* dancers would dance an *isigekle* song is not exactly the same as the way the *injobo* group would. The singing and the speed in movements are different.

Isigekle

Isigekle is the style of dance in Ibandla lamaNazaretha that is closely linked to the traditional Zulu dance that was witnessed by the Europeans who first came to Zululand. Isaiah Shembe adopted *isigekle* from the isiZulu dance of the same name. Mthembeni Mpanza had this to say about *isigekle*:

> *Isigekle amaculo aqalwa wubabamkhulu esathathelwa esiZulwini. Igama elithi isigekle lalivele likhona esiZulwini. Amaculo awuBunazaretha kodwa asinwa kakhulu njengamaculo esiZulu. Ngisho ukuhlabelela kwakhona kuhlatshelelwa njengamaculo esiZulu ngisho ukusinwa kwakhona. Uma uke ubabone abantu abangamabhinca besina, uyabona uma ungake uye emaNgwaneni ufike kusinwa khona, amaNgwane asina njengamaNazaretha, asina isigekle. Ngisho amadoda akhona ngisho amakhosikazi asina ngempela njengoba kusuke kusina amaNazaretha. Umehluko phakathi*

> *kwesigekle sakwaShembe nesakwaZulu yi meaning yegama. Kodwa i-rhythm, isitayela sokuhlabelela kufana nokwesiZulu. Kodwa okwehlukayo yi-message. I-message i-heavenly.*
>
> [*Isigekle* are songs composed by Isaiah Shembe adopting them from isiZulu. The name *isigekle* has always been there in isiZulu. These are Nazaretha songs that are danced like Zulu songs. Even their singing is like that of Zulu songs and even the dancing. If you have ever seen non-believers dancing, you see if you can go to maNgwaneni and find dancing taking place there, the amaNgwane dance like amaNazaretha, they dance *isigekle*. Even the men there and the women they really dance as you would see amaNazaretha dancing. The difference between the *isigekle* of the Zulu and that of amaNazaretha is the meaning of the song. But the rhythm, the style of singing, is like that of Zulu. What differs is the message. The message [of Nazaretha songs] is heavenly. (Interview, Durban, 13 August 2009)

While this gives a sense of where *isigekle* comes from, Mpanza claims he cannot put into words the actual movement and actions of the dancers of *isigekle*, or even that of *amagxalaba* (he calls this the Shembe style). For the purposes of this chapter, I will give an account of the dancing that took place in Ebuhleni on Sunday 13 July 2008. The group of men had been divided into about ten regiments, called *izigcawu*. One of the regiments known for its perfection of the sacred dance, especially *isigekle*, is called *Mbelebeleni* (after the hostel in kwaMashu where most of the dancers stay and where they practise the sacred dance) or *Magumbomane*, (All the Corners of the Earth, because people who dance there come from different areas). The time is 12: 25, which means it is still the first part of the sacred dance, before lunch. All the men's groups are dancing *amagxalaba* style, but this group is dancing *isigekle*. It is their favourite and they know that no other group perfects *isigekle* like they do. So they dance it even when it is time to dance the *amagxalaba* style. There are many spectators who want to see uMbelebele dancing *isigekle*!

When I come to record them, the line that is dancing is in the final step, the one with the highest momentum and which interests both the dancers and the spectators the most. The dancers are more agile and lively, their agility enhanced by the sounds of approval from the audience. It is now that they can bring their own particular flavour or their personal vernacular to bear. As they dance, they are more aware that their time of prominence is almost over. Soon the next group will take over. So they should leave a mark in the minds of the spectators, even if these could be the beings of heaven as well as of this earth. The dancers commit themselves body and soul to the dance. Every part of the body has a role to play. The positioning of the head; the facial expression, the smile; the left hand playing with the shield; the right hand playing with *ishoba*; sometimes they stand still and only move their toes up and down with their torso moving sideways. Then they start dragging their feet forward, to land down with a stamp. Left, right, left, right, and forward they move. Sometimes as the one foot hits the ground, the other is immediately lifted, to be held dangling until its turn of hitting/beating the ground. They march forward and sideways, their shields and *amashoba* being raised and lowered, raised and lowered, sometimes held high up while the feet are stamping and dangling.

As all this is happening, the next group to dance moves in the line led by the leader of this *isigcawu*. They march from the left of the regiment towards the direction of the spectators, creating a circle as they move to join in front of the dancing line from the right hand side. They move in the rhythm of the song and its accompanying instruments: the drums and the kudu-horn trumpets (*izimbomu*). When the leader has reached the far left, where the entering line started, he comes to the centre and leads the new line forward towards the spectators, still in the high momentum of the line they are substituting. They come back to the starting position of dance. Here the leader plays his flute and all the singing and the instruments stop to give way to the new song for the new line. This is another *isigekle* song. It is called "*Lwaduma ulwandle*" (The Sea Rumbles). It is one of those hymns/songs that do not appear in the hymn book, perhaps because of its potentially political undertones. It is based on the biblical story of the exodus of the Israelites from Egypt:

Lead Singer: *Wo lwaduma ulwandle*
Group: *Nang' uFaro*
Lead Singer: *Olubomvu*
Group: *Eshon' emfuleni*
Lead Singer: *Emfulen'uzobuya*
Group: *Nempi yakhe*
Lead singer: *Oh nempi yakhe*
Group: *Nenqola zomlilo*

[Lead Singer: Oh the sea rumbles
Group: Here is Pharaoh
Lead Singer: That which is red
Group: He is heading towards the river

Lead Singer:	From the river he will return
Group:	With his army
Lead Singer:	Oh! With his army
Group:	And the wagons of fire.]

The song is sung in a call-and-response style. Most of the time the lead singer says something and the group say something else. Or put differently, what the lead singer is saying can be taken apart to make its own sense, and what the group says makes its own sense or meaning. This is more noticeable in the songs that are written in the hymn book and have two or more stanzas. While each stanza has its own 'independent' meaning, the leader will sing from either the first or the second stanza and the group will respond by singing the lines from whichever stanza the leader did not sing. For instance, Hymn No. 207 "*Thuthuka Thuthuka*" [Develop! Develop!] is sung and performed exactly like the above hymn. In the hymn book it is written as follows:

Thuthuka Thuthuka	Develop! Develop!
WebuNazaretha	You Nazaretha
Thuthuka nazi	Develop, here are
Izizwe zomile	The thirsty nations.
Sizwa ngendaba	We hear rumours
Besitshela bethi	They tell us that
ENazaretha	At Nazaretha
Sokholwa sichichime.	We will saturate with faith

The hymn will be performed like this in the sacred dance:

Lead Singer:	*Thuthuka Thuthuka*
Group:	*Sizwa ngendaba*
LS:	*WebuNazaretha*
Group:	*Besitshela bethi*
LS:	*Thuthuka nazi*
Group:	*ENazaretha*
LS:	*Izizwe zomile*
Group:	*Sokholwa sichichime.*
[Lead Singer:	Develop! Develop!
Group:	We hear rumours
Lead Singer:	You Nazaretha

Group:	They tell us that
Lead Singer:	Develop [because] here are
Group:	In Nazaretha
Lead Singer:	The thirsty nations
Group:	We will saturate with faith.]

As mentioned above, the above songs/hymns are performed alike. They have a similar 'basic step'. It is this basic step that makes it possible for sacred dancers from different places to be able to participate in the same dance performance. It is when the dancers stray away from this basic step that they run the risk of "going to hell because of their dancing" (Mthembeni Mpanza, Speech, 14 September 2008). The performance of most *isigekle* songs/hymns comprises four basic steps. The second step, which is a much slower version of the final one, is omitted in the main sacred dance performances where there are many people who need to give each other a chance. The first step is important in that it is the one that differentiates between the dancing of hymns like the ones above and others like hymn No. 210 "*Waqala izitha*" [You've Annoyed the Enemies] and "*Vuk'umkhalele uZulu*" [Wake up and Wail for the Zulus] which do not appear in the hymn book. The second, third and fourth steps for these hymns are the same, but the first step of the former two, "*Thuthuka! Thuthuka!*" and "*Lwaduma ulwandle*" is different from that of either "*Waqala izitha*" or "*Vuk'umkhalele uZulu*". The latter two hymns have their own particular styles for performing the first step. In other words one can tell which hymn is being performed by looking at the first step, but after the first step one cannot tell by looking at the performance because it can be either of the above hymns.

An important characteristic of the sacred dance is that each move the dancers make is in time to the song. This is more the case with the first step of every song (especially *isigekle* songs) than with the subsequent steps. In the case of the song sung by the Mbelebele group, "*Lwaduma ulwandle*" [The Sea Rumbles], the dancers beat right left (with the right foot and then with the left one) with their shields down (and *amashoba* held up) in tune to the first two lines of the song, and then repeat the same beats with the shields up (the *amashoba* are still up but are behind the shields, it is the shields that are given prominence) in tune to the third and fourth lines. The right foot beats coincide with the parts sung by the lead singer while the left foot beats coincide with the part sung by the group. During the fifth line, sung by the lead singer, "*Uzobuya*" [He will return], the beat is with the right foot, and here the *ishoba* is projected forward and held up, while the shield is down. In the sixth line, the beat is on the left foot, with both the *ishoba* and the shield held down

FIGURE 6.7 *Shows* inhlalisuthi *from Mbelebeleni dancing* isigekle. *Note the right hands holding* amashoba *and the left hands with the shields down. This position shows that they are in the first two lines of the hymn. But the same position obtains if the song is in line five as well.*

FIGURE 6.8 *Note that the shields are up and projected forward while the* amashoba *are held back. Here the song is in line three and four.*

FIGURE 6.9 *The shields are down, just ahead of the knees and the* amashoba *a little higher than the shields. The song is in line six.*

just in front of the knees. From this, in the seventh line, there is a pause on the part of the dancers, with only a retreating movement of the torso, getting ready for the next move which coincides with line eight sung by the group. Here, the dancers lean their heads to the right and then to the left with the shield and *ishoba* pushed to whichever direction the head leans to. After this the song begins again and the same steps are repeated as many times as the regiment leader (*umsinisi*) allows the dancers, taking into consideration the time left for the other steps and for other 'lines' still to perform.

The second, third and fourth steps are much simpler and the moves are not performed in time to the song the way it is done with the first step above. In other words, one cannot look at the performance or movement of the dancers and tell the exact words the dancers are singing at that particular moment. As mentioned above, the second step is a slower version of the fourth step. This involves slow right left beats that are sometimes followed by a small tap of the heel before the beat of the other leg. The dancers move forward and backwards as well as sideways, raising and lowering their shields according to the lead dancer's decisions rather than the song itself. In the third step the forward-backward moves are the same, but sometimes in the side moves each dancer places his *ishoba* on the right shoulder of the person in front of him. Here the momentum is more than in the first and second steps, with double beats of each foot comprising of forward backward, forward backward beats of each foot. The fourth and final step is characterised by the highest momentum and liveliness of the dancers. As described above, at this stage what is important is the movement of the whole body, but the basic step is a much faster right left right left beat.

Amagxalaba (or Shembe style)

While *isigekle* is actually a Zulu traditional dance style which Isaiah Shembe 'borrowed' and used in performing his own religious songs (also sung in old *isigekle* form), *amagxalaba* is his own style developed from and influenced by other emerging forms like *indlamu* dance. There are a number of hymns and variations of *amagxalaba* style as there are of *isigekle*. The difference between *isigekle* and *amagxalaba* is not that marked, and an onlooker who does not know the sacred dance will not be able to tell that these are different choreographies. Identifying the exact features that differentiate the two choreographies is not easy for even the most experienced dancers, even though they can easily tell you whether this is *isigekle* or *amagxalaba* being performed. The difference between the two has to do with the minor details about the style of singing, the pace, the changes and the movement as well as the shields and *amashoba*. While with *amagxalaba* too one can say that the singing is the call-and-response style, as the voices of the lead singer and of the group are clearly separate, it is not the kind that one finds in *isigekle*. In *amagxalaba* the lead singer leads and the group follows with the same words the leader sings and at some point the singing is unified, unlike in *isigekle* where the leader and the group almost always say different things.

In the sacred dance of July 2009, one of the dancing regiments danced for hymn No. 155 which reads as follows:

Ngilandela ngemuva	I am lagging behind
Indlela yinde kangaka	The journey is so long
Ngophelelwa ngamandla	I'll run out of strength
Okuya eKuphakameni.	To get to eKuphakameni.
Abaningi bangishiyile	Many have left me behind
Ngidinga ngeswele	I have nothing, I am needy
Ngosizwa ngubani	Who will help me
Ngiye eKuphakameni.	Go to eKuphakameni.

This is sung as follows:

Lead singer:	*O ngemuva ngilandela*
Group:	*Ngilandela ngemuva*

Lead singer: *Ngemuva indlela*
Group: *Indlela inde kangaka*
Lead singer: *Ngophelelwa*
Group: *Ngophelelwa ngamandla*
Lead singer: *Ngophela mandla okuya*
Group: *Okuya eKuphakameni.*
Lead singer: *Abaningi*
Group: *Abaningi bangishiyile*
Lead singer: *Bangishiyile ngidinga*
Group: *Ngidinga wo ngeswele*
Lead singer: *Wo ngeswele ngosizwa*
Group: *Ngosizwa ngubani*
Lead singer: *Sizwa ngubani ngiye*
Group: *Ngiye eKuphakameni*

[Lead Singer: Oh Behind, I follow
Group: I lag behind
Lead Singer: Behind, The way
Goup: The way is so long
Lead Singer: I will run out
Group: I will run out of strength
Lead Singer: I'll lose the strength to go
Group: Of heading to eKuphakameni.

Lead Singer: The many
Group: The many have left me
Lead Singer: They left me, I am in need
Group: I'm in need and I want
Lead Singer: Oh, I'm wanting, I'be helped
Group: I'll be helped by whom?
Lead Singer: Helped by whom, to go
Group: To go to eKuphakameni.]

In *amagxalaba* the shields are held up for the duration of the verse of the song, except when the verse ends. They are used as markers of the ending of the verse and signal the *start* of a similar verse or the beginning of the new step. It is this style that is more open to improvisation and group's and individuals' creation of own vernaculars. This was visible in one of the regiments dancing in July 2009 in eBuhleni. The dancing group or line is one of the latest ones in which only the young men dance. This line is charged with competition among the individual dancers, each trying to beat the others, to present themselves as the best, or one of the best, and attracting the attention of the audience. This competitive individuality is most noticeable in the centre of the line, among the four central dancers. While the first step here is characterised by the double beats of each foot, the first being softer and the second harder, the central four dancers of this group add to this their own particular formations that differentiate each one of them from the others. In contrast with the Mbelebeleni regiment it was clear that even though they added their own personal vernacular, what they did they did as a group. As a group that meets on regular basis to practise, their performance was characterised by the advanced kind of uniformity.

Even though dancers in this group or line all follow the same basic step, there is a way in which each dancer does his own thing. The double beats with each foot, which characterise the basic first step, are meant to be done in the same spot, with dancers only taking one or two steps forward at the turn of or the ending of the verse.[7] But some dancers execute this beat by performing a soft beat first (which is the norm) and then charge forward in a leap to land with a harder stamp for the second beat (which is not the norm). At first the two dancers who do this only do it when the verse ends, but as the performance progresses they do it more often.

After 9min 22sec the first part of the song comes to an end, and the second verse and second step starts. This is supposed to be a faster version of the first step, except when the tune ends and is to start again. Here the dancers execute four soft beats with the left foot and then one right and one left, which is then followed by the double beats starting from the right foot. However, comprising young men who must recently have been dancing in *isikotshi* or some of them are still dancing in both *injobo* and *isikotshi*, this line performs in a slower than usual pace for *injobo*, a pace characteristic of *isikotshi*. When the leader of all Nazaretha men, Mathunjwa, notices how they dance, he stops the dance and joins the line in the centre, to teach and guide the young men as to the correct way of performing this part of the song. I suspect that he was not happy with the first step either but let them continue, only to realise he could not take it anymore when they were in the second step. Under Mathunjwa's guidance, the song is started again, with the drums now beating a little faster than before and the dance following the new beat of drums. After 4min the dancers have moved forward and back. Now they start the same verse in an even faster beat,

7 This is only done because the dancers are supposed to move forward and then come back to their original spot. It is when they have returned to their original position that they change to the next step.

the drums also following suit. The beat is still the same double beat but now the dancers turn to the right and to the left as they dance.

When the fourth and final step commences, Mathunjwa leaves the dancers. The movement for this part of the dance is very swift and Mathunjwa realises that he cannot keep pace with the younger dancers. This is the most popular part of the song with the liveliness and agility it calls for on the part of the dancers. The name for this choreography, *amagxalaba*, comes from this part of the dance. This fourth step is called *amagxalaba*.[8] Dancers, especially younger ones, like this step so much that they perform it even when it is not allowed. In the performance by Mathunjwa's group the final step was the correct one for that particular song. But sometimes, because they like this step so much, some dancers would include it even when dancing for songs like "*Nina abathanda ukuphila*" (Those of You who Like to Live) and others that need not include this step in their performance.

Conclusion

In this chapter I have looked at the poetics of performing the sacred dance as well as the nature of, meaning and importance of dress in the sacred dance. I have argued with regards to dress that even though Isaiah Shembe was ostensibly concerned with the inside of a person rather than the looks, he dedicated a great deal of time to designing outfits for his followers to wear when performing the sacred dance. I also stated that the kind of dress worn by dancers today is more complex and is richer than what was worn by the dancers in the time of Isaiah Shembe, and that there is no call to change the dress to what it used to be in the times of Isaiah Shembe.

With regards to the poetics of performing the sacred dance, I stated that the sacred dance has a great relation and similarity to the dances that took place in precolonial time, and suggested that the sacred dance is an improvisation to precolonial 'Zulu' dance. While it has been stated that the sacred dance is not performed the way it was in Isaiah Shembe's time, that it has been shifting and changing over the years, such a change cannot be explained in terms of apartheid period and the post-apartheid period. In other words, we cannot say the sacred dance was part of resistance to apartheid during the apartheid period and now it is something else, and base that differentiation on the way it is performed. This then confirms my point that the sacred dance has been

8 *Amagxalaba* are shoulders, and I do not know why this step is called *amagxalaba*.

misconstrued as resistance to colonialism and apartheid. Also, I have argued that in spite of what is ideally the role of the sacred dance – worship – for many members it is an artistic form that they use to define their own personal identities. Many members form groups in which they 'practise' the sacred dance and in those practises they create their own personal vernaculars and dance to create difference from other dancers.

Conclusion

Miracles in Ibandla LamaNazaretha

In the Introduction I mentioned J.G. Shembe's words in one of his sermons where he accused White scholars who have written about Ibandla lamaNazaretha, saying that they only write about the 'outside' and not the 'inside' or spirit that exists in Ibandla lamaNazaretha. In this Conclusion I want to invoke these words again, and further explain what Shembe actually meant by the 'inside' or spirit that exists in Ibandla lamaNazaretha. Throughout this book, I have tried to speak as both an 'insider' and 'outsider', and I think that I have given more space to the 'outsider's voice', an academic's voice, because my intended readers are mainly academics. But now the balance may shift to or fall on the side of the 'insider', as I explore iLanga's words about the inside and outside. In this Conclusion I argue that it is mainly the perception that Shembe is present in this and the other worlds which informs the belief that through the church's expressive forms – the sacred dance and the hymns – the material and the spiritual worlds are integrated. The idea of Shembe existing here on earth and in heaven is best exemplified in the narratives of near-death experiences. These are stories told by people who have been believed to be dead, or have been pronounced dead, but are resurrected after a while and tell of the spiritual journey they had taken through their souls, while their bodies have been lying 'dead', mostly covered in blankets and placed against the wall while a candle is lit as a symbol of the death in the house (See Sithole, 2005; 2009). Below I will refer to one such narrative, by Chief Mfungelwa Mchunu of Mdubuzweni near Mooi River, who happens to be my maternal uncle. But first, more about iLanga's words.

In the sermon in which iLanga spoke about the 'inside' and 'outside', he referred to the project he had initiated, of recording the stories or experiences in which members encountered Shembe and his healing and miraculous powers. In fact the failure to see the 'inside', according to J.G. Shembe, is the failure to understand the miraculous stories the way they are understood in the church. Joel Cabrita has remarked about J.G. Shembe's project that it was "driven by [J.G. Shembe's] need to depict the church to the bureaucratic apartheid state as a literate-documentary institution, and partly prompted by his need to assert a more centralised authority over the Nazaretha congregation" (2010: 62). This book has tried to challenge such assertions as Cabrita's, because they put the 'state' at the centre, and impose "Western authority upon

 | DOI 10.1163/9789004320628_009

a non-Western text" (Sharpe, 1989: 138). According to this view, whatever the black African did in the time of Apartheid, it goes without saying that it was done in response to Apartheid, and the scholar does not have a duty to explain the link that he/she is making. This is an example of what has been termed 'strain theory', in which the actors are seen "as experiencing the complexities of their situations and attempting to solve problems posed by those situations" (Ortner: 1984: 151). According to this theory, greater emphasis is placed on "the analysis of the system itself, the forces in play upon the actors, as a way of understanding where actors, as [they] say, are coming from" (151). I think this problem can be solved if we heed Brown's call for a re-orientation of methodology in African or postcolonial studies: "rather than subjecting inhabitants of the postcolony to scrutiny in terms of postcolonial theory / studies, how can we allow the theory and its assumptions also to be interrogated by the subjects and ideas that it seeks to explain" (2009: 9). This book has tried to do just that.

The second point Cabrita makes, that J.G. Shembe's project was "prompted by his need to assert more centralised authority over the Nazaretha congregation" is not convincing either. It is true that there were many members of Ibandla lamaNazaretha when J.G. Shembe took on the leadership of the church in 1935; it is also true that there was a woman who claimed to be the 'spirit' of Isaiah Shembe and that this might have been considered a threat by J.G. Shembe; and it may be true that in 1940 Amos Shembe, J.G. Shembe's younger brother, broke "away with a rival faction" (2010: 78)[1], but what is not clear, and Cabrita does not care to show, is how documenting stories of Isaiah Shembe's miraculous powers could have helped deal with the challenges that J.G. Shembe faced. And to say that the "effects of having a centralised secretary and a formal church office was that believers' independent textual production – previously epitomised in the activities of scribes – was radically undercut" (79) suggests that she thinks that the stories are tangible objects that you can either keep or give away, and when you have given it away you do not have it anymore. But, the fact that these stories were 'given' to the church's secretary did not mean that those members could no longer use them in their sermons and in other contexts or that they were disallowed to own their personal notebooks containing the stories that have been documented or recorded by Dhlomo, the secretary. Also, members were not prohibited or discouraged from making their own recordings of the sermons, which shows that the intention was not to 'control' the stories, but it was to 'publish' them

[1] There is no evidence for this claim, except that Londa Shembe (J.G. Shembe's son) made this claim in the court case against Amos Shembe (his uncle) in the church's leadership dispute after J.G. Shembe's death.

and make them widely available to the church community. In the 1968 sermon, J.G. Shembe says this about these stories:

> *Ezinye senaziloba. Nazo ziningi kakhulu, seziyabehlula nabalobayo. Abasazi ukuthi bazoqalaphi bagcinephi. Nokuthi uma sekuthiwa azicindezelwe, kuyoqalwaphi kugcinwephi.*
>
> Some you have written. They too are so many, they overwhelm the writers. They do not know where to begin and where to end. And that when it is time to publish them, where they would start and where they would end.

The same is true about the hymnal. Its publication meant that all members, regardless of their levels of literacy, could have access to it. During the time of Isaiah Shembe the hymnal, in the form of the notebooks, was available only to a chosen few who could write and their close relatives, but there were many who did not have access to them. Now that it was mass-produced in eKuphakameni, all the members, even the recently converted, could have the hymnals.

Now to return to the miraculous stories and experiences involving Isaiah Shembe: one of the stories told to the church's secretary in the 1950s is Chief Mfungelwa Mchunu's story that I mentioned above. That the story had been recorded by the church's secretary did not stop Mchunu from telling his story in sermons and in personal conversations with members and non-members. I heard him narrate this story in a sermon twice, and also when I interviewed him for my Masters research in October 2004. (see Sithole, 2005). But when I first heard this story I was much younger, and it was narrated by my mother, Zithulele (known as MaMchunu Sithole), Chief Mchunu's youngest sister. She was there when her brother was pronounced dead and his body was placed against the wall and all that used to happen when a person had died happened. Except that her father, Pewula Mchunu, who was a member of Ibandla lamaNazaretha, vowed that he would never bury his son the following day, Sunday, until he got the word from Shembe, who was now J.G. Shembe (ILanga) himself. The word was to come with Pewula's brother, Jozi, who was sent on the day in which Mfungelwa 'died' to report to iLanga what had happened, and ask him to 'return' Mfungelwa because he was supposed to become a chief after his father. My mother was there when on Sunday morning the following day Mfungelwa was still 'dead' and the men came with picks and shovels to dig his grave, and her father told them to wait because he was not going to bury him until he got a response from Shembe. But before Jozi arrived, at about nine in the morning, and in the words of Mfungelwa himself this time:

Makushay' unayini kwezwala mina ngikhwashaza, kwezwakala mina ngithimula, kwezwakala mina ngikhwehlela ... Ngenkathi-ke beng ... bengivula lapha hhayi..usebhekile lomuntu. Hhaw' iNkos' ubaba-ke waphuma wahalalisa-ke ngob' uyaz' ukuthi yiNkos' eyenze lokhu ... Wasehalalis' ebaleni kwajabula bonk' abantu. Wase kuyikhon' ey' ebandleni-ke elihleli lapha ngenzans' ehlathini ... Ngoba phela umuzi wakithi wawusehlathini ... eseyobika-k' ukuthi "hhayi, sengiyabonga, seningahamba, umntwana usephilile. Babe sebehamba-ke.

When nine struck, I was heard moving, I was heard sneezing, I was heard coughing. The time they ... they opened me [hhayi] ... this person has woken up. Then my father went out and praised because he knew that it was the Lord who did this. He praised in the homestead and everybody was happy. It was then that he went to the group of men who were waiting down in the forest ... our homestead was situated in the forest ... he went to report that "No, I thank you ... you can go now ... the child has woken up." Then they left. (Chief Mfungelwa Mchunu, Interview, 10 October 2004)

Having woken up, Mfungelwa told his family about the spiritual journey he had taken while he was 'dead'. He told them how he had travelled through green pastures and on his way saw something like an eagle flying towards him. When it landed in from of him he realised that it was not an eagle, it was a person; it was Shembe. It was J.G. Shembe.

Ngajabula ngibon'iNkosi! ... ngoba njoba ngangihamba nje ngangikhululekile ... ngingenankinga. Yafika yangibuza-ke iNkosi yathi: "Uyaphi?" Ngathi: "NgiyeZulwini." Yase ithi, "Ehhe ngizele lokho-ke ... Ubaba wakho ubesethumelile ethi uyakucela ukuba ubuye ngoba uwena wedwa umfana." Ubaba wayesho njalo eNkosini yaseKuphakameni kodwa thina ngangazi sasingabafana siwuleveni. NeNkosi yayazi kodwa yayenzela nje ukuthi ngisinde. Yathi ngoba ubusufile isikhathi esingaka awuzukuzwa ezindlebeni izinyanga ezintathu.

I was very pleased when I saw the iNkosi! ... Because as I was travelling I was feeling good inside, I had no problem. The iNkosi came and asked me: "Where are you going?" I said, "I am going to heaven." Then he said, "Yes, that is why I am here. Your father has sent to me saying he requests you to return because you are the only boy." My father had said that to the iNkosi of eKuphakameni but we boys were eleven. And the iNkosi knew

> that but he just wanted to save me. He said because you have been dead for this long you will go blind for three months.

So, according to this story Shembe, iLanga, has an ability to oscillate between this world and heaven. During this encounter with Mfungelwa in his spiritual journey, he was at Msinga in the Temple then called Zondehleka; today it is called Mzimoya. It was here that Jozi, who was sent by Mfungelwa's father Pewula, found him early in the morning on Sunday in which Mfungelwa was resurrected. It was here that iLanga promised Jozi that his brother's son would be resurrected if he did what he told him. What Shembe did was to write a letter in front of Jozi and instructed him to take it and 'post' it under a rock in the small mountain called Ntanyana in Msinga. All Jozi had to do for his nephew to be resurrected was to get to the mountain before nine o' clock that morning and put the letter under the rock. If he arrived there after nine, he would not be resurrected, but if he did he would. These were Shembe's words. So when Shembe said to 'Mfungelwa's spirit' that your father has sent to me asking you to be returned, Jozi had actually talked to him physically and reported the matter.

Chief Mfungelwa Mchunu's story is part of the body of stories of miracles that circulate in the church, and informs the members' beliefs about who Shembe is and about their own sense of identity. This story, and others that I have written about here, pose a serious challenge to me as an academic: the one similar to that Hilary Mantel was confronted with when she dealt with the life of an Italian saint, Gemma Galgani, about whom she asserted that, "When you look at her strange life, you wonder what kind of language you can use to talk about her – through which discipline will you approach her?" (Mantel 2004: 3). In my case I have employed an interdisciplinary approach to examine Isaiah Shembe's hymns and the sacred dance in Ibandla lamaNazaretha as well as the stories of miracles that give sense to the hymns and the sacred dance. As Karin Barber has argued, oral studies are characteristically interdisciplinary:

> There is an obvious and very good reason for taking an interdisciplinary approach to African oral texts, and that is that the texts themselves can combine 'literature', 'history', 'medicine', 'religion' and other things. The unity of these fields in oral texts suggests that the method of interpretation should also be unified. (1989: 13)

Engaging with these texts has required an approach that involves literary studies, religion and theology, anthropology, history, and ethnomusicology.

It would be fallacious to claim that I have done justice to all these disciplines. Like David Coplan I have been no "respecter of academic boundaries", and my work is likely to be "doomed to be praised by reviewers for its coverage of every area except that of their own specialisation" (1994: xvii). My problem was compounded by the fact that I have also been trying to be true to the people who regard these texts as sanctified and miraculous, while at the same time offering an academically challenging piece of work which is critical of such views.

Another man who had a near-death experience, Thulani Kunene, was not a member of the church when he had it, and no one in his immediate family was a member. While I do not intend to deal with his narrative here, I want to refer to two issues in his story that are relevant for this book. Firstly, on his spiritual journey, which is not quite like Mfungelwa's, but has some similar features, he found the people wearing white prayer gowns singing Hymn No. 53, "Here is the Word of Invitation". When he was finally healed and discharged from the hospital, he quit school and went to Durban to look for work. Here he met many members of his Presbyterian Church. But for many years he did not get the job. He says in his tape-recorded sermon that he would be employed only for less than a day, after that the employer would fire him. Then one day, having just been fired from a job, he mistakenly entered a section of the train where amaNazaretha were gathered. They were singing Hymn No. 53. This angered Kunene, who did not understand why these 'barbarians' should sing a song he heard in his spiritual journey. 'How could they know about this song? Who were they to even know it?' Confused as he was, he moved to the section where his fellow Presbyterians were and asked them to pray for him because he had 'entered the section where there are demons'. (Thulani Kunene, Undated Tape-recorded sermon)

The second thing from Kunene's story is that on the same day that he heard amaNazaretha sing the song he had heard from his spiritual journey, he had a dream in which he saw a horse flying in the air, coming his way. He wanted to run away because he was afraid of horses, but a voice said to him: "Kunene's son! Why are you running away? Are you not looking for a job? This is Shembe! *He is coming from heaven to bless the sacred dance there*. You go to him and ask for a job." He did this. But when he woke up, he realised what had happened. He then spit and said: "Pew! Go away from me, Shembe! Go! Just because I entered the section of your people now you come to me?"

But in the morning he received a call from a white man he had asked a job from about four years before. Then a little later he received another one. He chose one and worked there till the company was closed due to financial problems. But he had worked there for a number of years.

As this book has shown, the above stories of Chief Mfungelwa Mchunu and Thulani Kunene are common narratives in Ibandla lamaNazaretha and they represent the supernatural, the spiritual, and the sacred. They testify to Shembe's healing and messianic powers. But what is significant in Kunene's story for the purposes of my argument here is that, while in Mfungelwa's story we see Shembe (iLanga) present in this world and in heaven, Kunene found amaNazaretha singing the song he heard from his spiritual journey. The hymn is present and performed here on earth and in heaven. It seems as if he expected this song to be sung only in 'heaven', by the spirits, not here on earth. Another thing, perhaps more important, is that in his dream he saw a person called Shembe and was told that he was coming from heaven to 'bless' the sacred dance. Through these narratives we can see how in Ibandla lamaNazaretha the divide between this world and heaven is broken. The hymns, the sacred dance and Shembe exist here and in heaven. Sometimes at the same time!

The main argument this book has propounded is that what motivates members to take part in the sacred dance is this belief that the sacred dance is celestial; it belongs to the unknown world of the ancestors, Shembe, and God. It belongs to the other world as well as to this one. They hold the view that participating in the sacred dance appeases their late relatives, and that the sacred dance takes place both in the physical and the ancestral realms. Closely linked to this is the belief that the ancestors are able to participate through the bodies of their living relatives. What, then, is the implication of this with regards to the argument that the sacred dance is a response to colonialism? It has been argued that not only does this view lead Ibandla lamaNazaretha (and others like it) and its practices to being treated negatively, as a phenomenon of 'independency' and 'separatism', but it also gives undue credit to colonialism itself, making it the centre of everything that happens in the periphery. The problem with the scholars who have proposed such a reading of the sacred dance is that they allow their theories to dictate or to influence their interpretations of what happens in the lives of their subjects.

In pursuing the above argument I have dealt with two prominent rituals in Ibandla lamaNazaretha that relate to completeness and taking part in important religious events, including the sacred dance. These are circumcision and marriage. Both these rituals are linked to the ancestors' presence, and their execution is mainly intended to appease the ancestors and to render the person ritually clean so that he or she may be worthy of participating in the sacred dance, not just for her- or himself but for the ancestors as well, either as spectators or as active, yet invisible, participants. This is exemplified in the story of the man who saw his late brother performing the sacred dance when he had first come to eKuphakameni. In dealing with these phenomena I have sought to correct some of the misconceptions held by Carol Muller especially, particularly her argument that virgin girls have to sacrifice their sexual desire in order to attain Shembe's protection, and her linking this to the central position virgin girls occupy in Ibandla lamaNazaretha. It has been argued in this book that the significance attached to virginity is closely linked with the importance of marriage, so that what is espoused is not celibacy but sexual abstinence before marriage, and this obtains with regards to virgin girls as well as boys and men.

However, it has been my argument here that there is a difference between what is ideal (that the sacred dance is worship and is performed in order to please the God and the ancestors) and what actually happens in practice; not all the members see the sacred dance as simply a form of worship whose audience is God/Shembe and their ancestors. Many members perform the sacred dance as an artistic expression that allows them to define their own identities and to perform in order to please or impress the living audience. However, it is important to note that these two views of the sacred dance – the dance as worship and the dance as an artistic form – are not always mutually exclusive. Most members who take part in the sacred dance recognise that the dance is primarily a form of worship, and it is supposed to please God and the ancestors, but that does not stop them from trying to impress their immediate audience as well. So that if one asked those members who go all the way to 'change' the sacred dance (to spice it so as to impress the audience) about the significance of the sacred dance, they would not hesitate to claim that it is actually worship and they take part in it to please God. And older, high ranking members like Minister Mathunjwa, who is supposedly unhappiest about the spoiling of the sacred dance, once talked excitedly about people who come to the dancing ground specifically to watch him (Minister Mathunjwa, Pre-Dance Advice, 20 July 2008).

Two White Men on the Sacred Dance

Now I want to refer to the comments made by one foreign spectator after he had witnessed the sacred dance. This is a white man who had come to eKuphakameni and witnessed members of the church performing the sacred dance. This man came to have a conversation with J.G. Shembe about his experience. He wanted to know how the sacred dance was choreographed. And when J.G. Shembe informed him that it was his late Father, the founder of the church, who had initiated it, the white man refused to accept that. J.G. Shembe describes their conversation in an undated tape. It goes as follows:

Wathi yena "Hhayi, angizwa kahle uma usho njalo, uthini? Akekho umuntu ongayenza lento. Wayengabe ekuthathaphi konke lokhu?" Wayesho yena ebona abantu bevunule, babeyingcosana ngalelo langa ababefake ingubo emhlaphe. Angazi ukuthi uma engahle afike namhlanje angathini. Kumbe sewafa angazi. Ngoba kwakuyisosha eya empini. Le eJapan. Uthi "Cha bo, ngitshele iqiniso. Ukuthi lento ivelaphi. Ayizange ibekhona into enje emhlabeni. Umhlaba wonke waziwa yimi, ngoba ngihamba nempi. Umhlaba wonke uhanjwa yimi... Wathi ngiyakwazi konke ukusina kwabantu, kodwa angingaze ngingakhala mina. Angize ngingafikelwa wusizi, angize ngingafikelwa yinyembezi. Konke ngiyakwazi nezintombi ngiye ngizibone nezinsizwa ngiye ngizibone, nabantu abavunule ngezimvunulo ezinhle kunalezi ngiye ngibanone. Kodwa lokhu selokhu ngifikile lapha kuthi angikhale. Sengike ngakhala ngaze ngaphuma ngasithela ngale. Ngakhala izinyembezi. Manje-ke uma uthi kwavela kumuntu, hhayi angizwa kahle." Ngathi, "Wayaye athi uma simbuzisisa, kuyazifikela kuvela eZulwini. UNkulunkulu uyaye akulethe noma elele noma ebhekile. Akubone bese kuthiwa Shembe yenza lokhu, abesekwenza. Njengoba ubabona benje nje ekuqaleni kwabo babengayithandi lento laba bantu. Abashumayeli babo bathi uShembe uyahlubuka. Mhlambe uthanda ukubona imizimba yabantu. Kodwa akaze anganaka yena. Waqala kancane, amantombazane amabili amane. Namuhla asemaningi. Uthi-ke lomlungu, "Ngiyezwa-ke uma usho kanjalo. Uthi lendaba ivela ezilwini, ngiyakholwa. Ngoba ayikho into eyenziwayo lapha emhlabeni eke ingifikisele izinyembezi. Noma ngibona abantu befa empini angikhali. Noma ngibona, ngiye ngibone nobukhosi obukhulu bamaNgisi. Namacilongo ngiyawazi nezigubhu ngiyazazi, kodwa angiye ngingakhala. Kodwa le nto eniyenzayo ingifikisela izinyembezi."

[He said, "I don't understand if you say that, what do you say? There is no human being who can create this. Where would he have got this?" He was saying this as he saw people wearing their dance attire. There were few people that day who were wearing white robes. He said, "No, tell me the truth. Where is this thing coming from? Never before has there been something like this in the world. I know the whole world because I travel with the army..." He said, "I know all the dances of people, but I do not cry. I never feel sorrow and shed tears [when I see it]. I know it all, the maidens, I have seen them, the young men, I have seen them, and even people who adorn themselves in better attire than this I have seen them. But this, ever since I arrived here I have been feeling like crying. I have even cried and went on the side and shed tears. Now if you say this came with a human being, I don't understand." I said [to him]

> "He [Isaiah Shembe] used to tell us when we asked him that this comes on its own accord. It comes from heaven. God brings it, sometimes when he is asleep, sometimes when he is awake. He would see it and then be told, 'Shembe do this.' And he would do it. As you see them looking like this, at first they did not like it. Their preachers said Shembe is deserting. Perhaps [they said] he likes to see people's bodies. But he did not mind them. He started small; there were two or four girls. But today there are many of them." This white man then said, "I do hear if you say so, that this thing comes from heaven because I believe that. Because there is nothing that is done here on earth that makes me cry. Even when I see people die, I do not cry. I have seen the big kingdom of the English but I never cry. I have seen saxophones and I have seen drums, but I never cry. But this thing you are doing here makes me feel emotional.]

This conversation between J.G. Shembe and the white man casts some light on the reasons for the belief that the hymns were created from heaven. In one sense the sacred dance is unprecedented and ineffable, and thus it can only be explained in celestial terms. The white man found himself in a position that he had never before found himself. He had thought that he had seen it all because he had travelled the world, but when he came to *eKuphakameni* and witnessed the sacred dance, his response was mindboggling even to him. He had seen better things and worse things, but he had never cried. He claims that he had witnessed all the dances that were more 'sophisticated' than the sacred dance and had perceived dancers dressed more elegantly than the Nazaretha dancers, but he had not cried. He had not been affected the way he was when he saw the Nazaretha perform the sacred dance. This man was confronted with something that he did not know how to make sense of; he did not know in what language he could talk about the sacred dance so he elevated it (or should I say he relegated it?) to the celestial, to the unknown.

In a more recent encounter, Robert Young was also struck by the sacred dance and looked at it in academic terms:

> What the Shembe experience brought sharply home to me is that outside the issue of linguistic translation there are issues of cultural translation that hardly feature in Western forms of postcolonial studies ... the neglect of the power of spirituality ... (Quoted in Chapman 2006a: 207–8)

The "power of spirituality" Young invokes here, I suspect, is what overwhelmed the man in conversation with J.G. Shembe above and caused him to cry in spite of himself. But, more importantly, I hope this project has succeeded, to a certain extent, to provide the cultural translation Young calls for. For in my case, in dealing with these sacred texts, I have attempted to strike a balance between what they seem like to the outsider (mostly scholars who have looked at these in relation to colonialism and how these can be seen to be a response to colonialism) and to the members of the church who perceive them to be miraculous texts that came with the messengers of heaven. However, the above conversation between J.G. Shembe and the white man shows that this insider/outsider divide is not always as marked as it may seem to be. If anything, the fact that someone outside the church sees these as nothing but heavenly inspired performances serves to confirm the importance of not disregarding the inside perceptions regarding these texts. And I believe the suggestion I have put forward that blindly accepting the idea that the hymns came with the messengers of heaven entails an injustice against Isaiah Shembe's creativity and agency still holds.

Bibliography

Primary Sources Interviews

Interview with Mphathi (Ma)Duma, EBuhleni. 8 July 2008.
Interview with Andile Gumede and Nompilo Mngadi, Univ of Zululand. 14 March 2015.
Interview with Minister Khumalo, Nhlangakazi. 10 January 2008.
Interview with Slindile Malinga, Phindile Dube and Nqobile Buthelezi, University of Zululand. 17 August 2013.
Interview with Themba Masinga, EBuhleni. 18 July 2009.
Interview with Minister Mathunjwa, Nhlangakazi. 10 January 2008.
Interview with Bhekinkosi Mchunu, Estcourt. 15 November 2008.
Interview with Bhekinkosi Mchunu, EBuhleni. 14 July 2015.
Interview with Inkosi Simakade Mchunu, Msinga. 18 May 2008.
Interview with Inkosi Mfungelwa Mchunu, Mdubuzweni. 10 October 2004.
Interview with Nompilo Mdletshe, Empangeni. 16 December 2013.
Interview with Bhekinkosi Mhlongo, Estcourt. 16 December 2008.
Interview with MaNtanzi Mhlongo, Estcourt. 14 August 2009.
Interview with Evangelist Mkhize, Pine Town. April 2009.
Interview with Evangelist Mpanza, Durban. 13 August 2009.
Interview with Minister Mthethwa , EBuhleni. 10 July 2008.

Cassette, CD and Video Recordings of Sermons, Advices, Speeches Cited in the Book

Thulani Kunene, Cassette, Sermon, Untitled, Undated.
Themba Masinga. CD, *Babonani Abalandela UShembe*? Durban, Undated.
Minister Mathunjwa. Advice, Nhlangakazi, January 2008.
MaDlomo Mchunu. Cassette, Sermon, Mdubuzweni, 1990.
Evangelist Mngwengwe, Speech at the NATESA meeting, PMBurg, 14 Sep 2008.
Evangelist Mpanza, Speech at the NATESA meeting, PMBurg, 14 Sep 2008.
Minister Mthethwa. Sermon, EBuhleni, July 2008.
Shembe A.K. Cassette, Sermon, Untitled, Undated.
Shembe J.G. Audio CD, Sermon, *Sayuli* Ekuphakameni, 1968.
Shembe J.G. Audio CD, Sermon, *INkosi iLanga eKuphakameni*, Undated.
Shembe J.G. Cassette, Sermon, Untitled, Undated.
Shembe M.V. Sermon. Judea (Eshowe), 28 October 2008.

Shembe Mduduzi. Address to the Maidens. Ebuhleni, 8 July 2013.
Twenty-three Meeting, EMdubuzweni. February 2008.
———, KwaDlamini. April 2008.
———, Ntabamhlophe and KwaDlamini. May 2008.
———, Ntabamhlophe. August 2008.
———, Weneen. November 2008.

Secondary Sources

Awonoor, K. "The Weaver Bird", in H. Moffet and E. Mphahlele (eds.), *Seasons Come to Pass: A Poetry Anthology for Southern African Students*, Cape Town, Oxford University Press, 2002.

Bal, M. *Death and Dissymmetry: The Politics of Coherence in the Book of Judges*. Chicago: Chicago University Press, 1988.

Barber, K. "Popular Arts in Africa". *African Studies Review* 30(3) 1987: 1–78.

Barber, K and Furniss, G. "African-Language Literature", *Research in African Literatures* 37 (3), 1–14: 2006.

Barber, Karin and P.F. de Moraes Farias (eds). *Discourse and its Disguises: The Interpretation of African Oral Texts.* Birmingham: Centre of West African Studies, University of Birmingham, 1989.

——— "Obscurity and Exegesis in African Oral Praise Poetry". In: Duncan Brown (ed). *Oral Literature and Performance in Southern Africa.* Oxford: James Currey; Cape Town: David Philip; Athens: Ohio University Press, 1999: 27–49.

——— *I Could Speak until Tomorrow: Oriki, Women and the Past in the Yoruba Town.* Washington DC: Smithsonian Institute Press, 1991.

Bassnett, S. and Travedi, H. (eds). *Post-colonial Translation: Theory and Practice.* London/ New York: Routledge, 1999.

Bauman R. and Briggs, C.L. "Poetics and Performance as Critical Perspectives on Language and Social Life". *Annual Review of Anthropology* 19 1990: 50–88.

Becken, H.J. (Intro) in Oosthuizen G.C. and Hexham, I. (eds). *The Story of Isaiah Shembe: History and Traditions Centred at EKuphakameni and Mount Nhlangakazi.* (Vol. 1) (Trans. H.J. Becken) Lewiston/ Queenstown/ Lampeter: Edwin Mellen Press, 1996.

——— "EKuphakameni Revisited: Recent Developments within the Nazaretha Church in South Africa". *Journal of Religion in Africa* 9 (3) 1978: 161–172.

——— "The Nazareth Baptist Church of Shembe". In: *Our Approach to the Independent Church Movement in South Africa.* Maphumulo: Missiological Institute, 1966.

——— "On the Holy Mountain: A Visit to the Years Festival of the Nazaretha Church on Mount Nhlangakazi, January 14, 1978". *Journal of Religion in Africa* 1 1967: 138–149.

Bediako, N. *Christianity in Africa: The Renewal of a Non-Western Religion.* Edinburg: Edinburg University Press, 1995.

Beinart, W. and Bundy, C. (eds). *Hidden Struggles in Rural South Africa: Politics and Popular Movements in the Transkei and Eastern Cape 1890–1930.* London: James Currey, 1987.

——— and Dubow, S. (eds.) *Segregation and Apartheid in Twentieth Century South Africa.* London: Routledge, 1995.

Berglund, A. *Zulu Thought Patterns and Symbolism.* London: C. Hurst, 1976.

Blakeley, T.D. and van Beek, W. (eds.) *Religion in Africa: Experience and Expression.* London: James Currey, 1994.

Biesele, M. *Women Like Meat: The Folklore and Foraging Ideology of the Kalahari Ju/. hoan.* Bloomington and Indianapolis: Indiana University Press. Johannesburg: Witwatersrand University Press, 1993.

——— "Different People Just Have Different Minds": A Personal Attempt to Understand Ju/.hoan Storytelling Aesthetics". In: Duncan Brown (ed). *Oral Literature and Performance in Southern Africa.* Oxford: James Currey; Cape Town: David Philip, 1999: 161–175.

Boesak, A. *Black Theology, Black Power.* London: SCM, 1978.

Bonner, P. (ed.) *Holding their Ground: Class, Locality and Culture in 19th and 20th Century South Africa.* Johannesburg: Ravan Press, 1989.

Bozzoli, B. *Women of Phokeng: Consciousness, Life Strategy, and Migrancy in South Africa, 1900–1983.* Portsmouth: Heinemann, 1991.

——— *The political Nature of a Ruling Class: Capital and Ideology in South Africa 1890–1933.* London: Routledge and Kegan Paul, 1981.

——— "Marxism, Feminism and African Studies". *Journal of Southern African Studies* 9 (2) 1983: 139–171.

Bredenkamp, H. and Ross, R. (eds.) *Missions and Christianity in South African History.* Johannesburg: Witwatersrand University Press, 1996.

Brown, D. "Orality and Christianity: The Hymns of Isaiah Shembe and the Church of the Nazarites". *Current Writing* 7 (2) 1995: 69–95.

——— *Voicing the Text: South African Oral Poetry and Performance.* Oxford: Oxford University Press, 1998.

——— "Orality and Christianity: The Hymns of Isaiah Shembe and the Church of the Nazarites." In: Duncan Brown (ed.) *Oral Literature and Performance in Southern Africa.* Oxford: James Currey; Cape Town: David Philip, 1999: 195–219.

——— (ed.) *Oral Literature and Performance in Southern Africa.* Oxford: James Currey; Cape Town: David Philip, 1999.

——— (ed.) *Religion and Spirituality in South Africa: New Perspectives.* Pietermaritzburg: University of KwaZulu-Natal Press, 2009.

Brown, K. "Dress, Ideology and Practice: Clothing in the Nazareth Baptist Church in the 1920s and 1930s". In: N.J. Coetzee (ed.) *Revised Frameworks and Extended*

Boundaries in Research and Education. Pretoria: South African Association of Art Historians, 1992: 97–106.

Bundy, C. *The Rise and Fall of the South African Peasantry.* London: Heinemann, 1979.

Cabrita, J. "A Theological Biography of Isaiah Shembe c. 1870–1935." PhD Dissertation (University of Cambridge) 2007.

——— "Isaiah Shembe's Theological Nationalism, 1920s–1935." *Journal of Southern African Studies* 35 (3) 2009: 609–625.

——— "Texts, Authority, and Community in the South African 'Ibandla lamaNazaretha' (Church of the Nazaretha), 1910–1976." *Journal of Religion in Africa* 40 2010: 60–95.

——— "Politics and Preaching: Chiefly Converts to the Nazaretha Church, Obedient Subjects, and Sermon Performance in South Africa." *Journal of African History* 51 2010: 21–40.

Callaway, H. *The religious Systems of the AmaZulu.* London: Trubner and co., 1868.

——— *Nursery Tales, Traditions and Histories of the Zulus in their Own Words.* London: Trubner and co., 1868.

Campbell, J.T. *Songs of Zion: The African Methodist Episcopal Church in the United States and South Africa.* Oxford: Oxford University Press, 1995.

Chapman, M. "Postcolonial Studies: A Spiritual Turn". *Current Writing* 20 (2) 2008: 67–76.

——— "Robert C. Young in South Africa: Interview". *English in Africa* 32 (2) 2006a: 199–208.

——— "Postcolonial Studies: A Literary Turn". *English in Africa* 33 (2) 2006b: 7–20.

Chidester, D. *Religions of Africa.* London and New York: Routledge, 1994.

——— *Savage Systems: Colonialism and Comparative Religion in Southern Africa.* Cape Town: University of Cape Town Press, 1996.

Cochrane, J. and de Gruchy, J. (eds.) *Facing the Truth: South African Faith Communities and the Truth and Reconciliation Commission.* Cape Town: David Philip, 1999.

Comaroff, J. *The Meaning of Marriage Payments.* London: Academic Press, 1980.

Comaroff, J. *Body of Power, Spirit of Resistance: The Culture and History of South African People.* Chicago: University of Chicago Press, 1985.

Comaroff, J. and Comaroff, J. *Of Revelation and Revolution: Christianity, Colonialism and Consciousness in South Africa.* Chicago: University of Chicago Press, 1991.

Connerton, P. *How Societies Remember.* Cambridge: Cambridge University Press, 1989.

Cope, N. *To Bind the Nation: Solomon kaDinuzulu and Zulu Nationalism 1913–1933.* Pietermaritzburg: University of Natal Press, 1993.

Coplan, D. *In the Time of Cannibals: The Word Music of South Africa's Basotho Migrants.* Chicago: University of Chicago Press. 1994.

Couzens, T. *The New African: A Study of Life and Work of H.I.E. Dhlomo.* Johannesburg, Ravan Press, 1985.

Daneel, M.L. *Old and New in Southern Shona Independent Churches.* The Hague: Mouton, 1971.

——— *Quest for Belonging: Introduction to a Study of African Independent Churches.* Gweru: Mambo Press, 1987.

De Kock, L. *Civilising the Barbarians: Missionary Narrative and African Textuality.* Johannesburg: Witwatersrand University Press, 1996.

Draper, J. (ed.) *Orality, literature and Colonialism in Southern Africa.* Leiden: Brill, 2004.

Dube, M.W. "Saviour of the World but not of this World: A Postcolonial reading of Spacial Construction in John". In: R S Sugirtharajah (ed.) *The Postcolonial Bible.* Sheffield: Sheffield Academic Press, 1998: 118–35.

Dube, J.L. *UShembe.* Pietermaritzburg: Shuter and Shooter, 1936.

——— "A Zulu Point of View on the Missionaries in Africa". *Christian Express* 1 August 1911: 116–117.

——— *A Talk Upon My Native Land.* New York: R. M Swinburne & co., 1892.

Edgar, R. *The Fifth Seal: Enoch Mgijima, the Israelites and the Bulhoek Massacre, 1921.* Berkeley: University of California Press, 1977.

——— *Because they Chose the Plan of God: The Story of the Bulhoek Massacre.* Johannesburg: Ravan Press, 1988.

——— "The Prophet Motive: Enoch Mgijima, the Israelites and the Background to the Bulhoek Massacre". *International Journal of African Historical Studies* 15 (2) 1982: 401–422.

Elphick, R. and Davenport, R. (eds.) *Christianity in South Africa: A Political, Social and Cultural History.* Oxford: James Currey; Cape Town: David Philip, 1997.

Erlmann, V. *African Stars: Studies in Black South African Performance.* Chicago: University of Chicago Press, 1991.

——— *Nightsong: Performance, Power and Practice in South Africa.* Chicago: University of Chicago Press, 1996.

——— "But Hope does not Kill: Black Popular Music in Durban 1913–1939". In: Mayhem, P. and Edwards I. (eds.) *The People's City: African Life in Twentieth Century Durban.* Pietermaritzburg: University of Natal Press, 1997.

Etherington, N. *Preachers, Peasants and Politics in South East Africa, 1835–1880.* London: Royal Historical Society, 1978.

——— "Recent Trends in the Historiography of Christianity of Black Religion in Africa". *Journal of Southern African Studies* 22 (2) 1996: 201–219.

Fabian, J. "Popular Culture in Africa". *Africa* 48 (4) 1978: 315–34.

——— *Power and Performance.* Madison: University of Wisconsin Press, 1990.

Finnegan, R. *Oral Literature in Africa.* Oxford: Clarendon Press, 1970.

——— *Oral Poetry: Its Nature, Significance and Social Context.* Cambridge: Cambridge University Press; Bloomington: Indiana University Press, 1977/1992.

——— *Literacy and Orality: Studies in the Technology of Communication.* Oxford: Blackwell, 1988.

——— *The Oral and Beyond: Doing Things with Words in Africa.* Oxford: James Currey; Chicago: University of Chicago Press; Pietermaritzburg: University of KwaZulu-Natal Press, 2007.

Funani, L.S. *Circumcision among the Ama-Xhosa: A Medical Investigation.* Johannesburg: Skotaville, 1990.

Furniss, G. *Poetry, Prose and Popular Culture in Hausa.* Edinburg: Edinburg University Press, 1996.

——— *Orality: The Power of the Spoken Word.* Basingstoke: Palgrave Macmillan, 2004.

——— and Gunner, E. (eds.) *Power, Marginality and Oral literature in Africa.* Cambridge: Cambridge University Press, 1995.

Fuze, M.M. *The Black People and Whence They Came: A Zulu View* (trans. Harry Lugg). Pietermaritzburg: University of Natal Press, 1979 (1922).

Gerard, A.S. *Four African Literatures: Zulu, Sotho, Xhosa and Amharic.* Berkeley: University of California Press, 1971.

——— *African Language Literatures: An Introduction to the Literary History of Sub-Saharan Africa.* Harlow: Longman, 1981.

Gilroy, P. *The Black Atlantic: Modernity and Double Consciousness.* Cambridge: Harvard University Press, 1993.

Goba, B. *Agenda for Black Theology: Hermeneutics for Social Change.* Johannesburg: Skotaville Press, 1988.

Golan, D. *Inventing Shaka: Using History in the Construction of Zulu Nationalism.* London: L. Reiner, 1994.

Gunner, E. "New Wine in Old Bottles: Imagery in the Izibongo of a Zulu Zionist Prophet, Isaiah Shembe". *Anthropological Society of Oxford Journal* 13 1982: 99–108.

——— "Testimonies of Dispossession and Repossession: Writing about the South African Prophet, Isaiah Shembe". *Bulletin of the John Rylands University Library of Manchester* 73 (3) 1984: 93–103.

——— "The Word, the Book and the Zulu Church of Nazareth." In: Whitaker, R.A. and Sienaet, E.R. (eds.) *Oral Tradition and Literacy: Changing Visions of the Word.* Durban: University of Natal Documentation and Research Centre, 1986: 179–188.

——— "Power House Prison House – An Oral Genre and its Use in Isaiah Shembe's Nazarite Baptist Church". *Journal of Southern African Studies* 14 (2)1988: 204–227.

——— *The Man of Heaven and the Beautiful Ones of God: Writings from Ibandla lamaNazaretha, a Nazaretha Church.* Leiden/ London/ Köln: Brill; Pietermaritzburg: University of KwaZulu-Natal Press, 2002/2004.

Guy, J. *The Destruction of the Zulu Kingdom: The Civil War in Zululand, 1879–1884.* London: Longman, 1979.

——— "Gender Oppression in Southern Africa's Pre-capitalist Societies. In: Walker, C. (ed.) *Women and Gender in Southern Africa until 1945*. Cape Town: David Philip, 1990.

——— *Remembering the Rebellion: The Zulu Uprising, 1906*. Pietermaritzburg: University of KwaZulu-Natal Press, 2006.

Hamilton, C. "The Character and Objects of Shaka: A Reconsideration of the Making of Shaka as Mfecane Motor". *Journal of African History* 33 (1) 1992: 37–63.

——— *Terrific Majesty: The Power of Shaka Zulu and the Limits of Historical Imagination*. Cambridge, Mass: Harvard University Press, 1998.

Hanks, W.F. *Language and Communicative Practices*. Boulder: Westview Press, 1996.

Hastings, A. *A History of African Christianity, 1950–1975*. Cambridge: Cambridge University Press, 1979.

——— *The Church in Africa, 1450–1950*. Oxford: Clarendon Press, 1994.

——— *The Construction of Nationhood: Ethnicity, Religion and Nationalism*. Cambridge: Cambridge University Press, 1997.

Hexham, I (ed.) *The Scriptures of the AmaNazaretha of Ekuphakameni: Selected Writings of the Zulu Prophets Isaiah and Londa Shembe*. (trans. L. Shembe and H.J. Becken) with an introduction by G.C. Oosthuizen. Calgary: University of Calgary Press, 1994.

——— "Isaiah Shembe, Zulu Religious Leader." *Religion* 27 (4) 1997: 361–373.

Hofmeyr, I. *We Spend Our Years as the Tale that is Told: Oral Historical Narratives in a South African Chiefdom*. Johannesburg: Witwatersrand University Press, 1991.

——— "Making Symmetrical Knowledge Possible: Recent Trends in the Field of Southern African Oral Performance Studies". In: Duncan Brown (ed.) *Oral Literature and Performance in Southern Africa*. Oxford: James Currey; Cape Town: David Philip; Athens: Ohio University Press, 1999: 18–26.

——— *The Portable Bunyan: A Transnational History of the Pilgrim's Progress*. Johannesburg: Witwatersrand University Press, 2004.

——— "Books in Heaven: Dreams, Texts and Conspicuous Circulation". Paper presented in English Studies Research Seminar, UKZN, Pietermaritzburg, October 2004.

James, D. *Songs of Women Migrants: Performance and Identity in South Africa*. Johannesburg: Witwatersrand University Press, 1999.

Jedrej, M.C. and Shaw, R. *Dreaming, Religion and Society in South Africa*. Leiden: Brill, 1992.

Johnson, R. and Dawson, G. "Popular Memory: Theory, Politics, Method." In: Robert Perks and Alistair Thompson (eds.) *The Oral History Reader*. London: Routledge, 1998.

Kivnick, H.Q. *Where is the Way: Song and Struggle in South Africa*. New York: Penguin Books, 1990.

Kriege, E. *The Social System of the Zulus*. London: Greens and Co., 1936.

——— "Girls. Puberty Songs and their Relation to Fertility, Health, Morality and Religion Among the Zulu". *Africa* 36 1968: 173–198.

Kruss, G. *Religion, Class and Culture: Indigenous Churches in South Africa, with Special Reference to Zionist- Apostolics.* Cape Town: University of Cape Town Press, 1985.

La Hausse, P. "Isaiah Shembe's Church". (Book Review) *Journal of African History* 37 (2) 1996: 332–334.

——— *Restless Identities: Signatures of Nationalism, Zulu Ethnicity and History of the Lives of Petros Lamula (c. 1881–1948) and Lymon Maling (1889–1936).* Pietermaritzburg: University of KwaZulu-Natal Press, 2000.

Lambard, M. "Nomkhubulwane: Reinventing a Zulu Goddess" In Benedict Carton, John Laban and Jabulani Sithole (eds.) *Zulu Identities: Being Zulu Past and Present.* Scottsville: University of KwaZulu-Natal Press, 1999: 545–553.

Landau, P.S. *The Realm of the Word: Language, Gender and Christianity in a South African Kingdom.* Portsmouth, NH: Heinemann; London: James Curry; Cape Town: David Philip, 1995.

Larlham, P. "Festivals of the Nazareth Baptist Church". *Drama Review* 25 (4) 1981: 59–74

——— *Black Theatre, Dance and Ritual in South Africa.* Michigan: UMI Research Press, 1985.

Lonsdale, J. "Listen while I Read: Christian Literacy in the Young Kenatta's Making of the Kikuyu". In: de la Gorgendere, L. (ed.) *Ethnicity in Africa: Roots, Meanings and Implications.* Edinburg: Centre of African Studies, University of Edinburg, 1996: 17–53.

Maake, N. "Publishing and Perishing": Books, People and Reading in African Languages in South Africa." In: N Evans and M Seeber (eds). *The Politics of Publishing in South Africa.* London: Holger Ehling Publishing; Pietermaritzburg: University of Natal Press, 2000: 127–59.

Marcus, T. "Virginity Testing: A Backward-looking Response to Sexual Regulation in the HIV/AIDS Crisis". In: Benedict Carton, John Laband and Jabulani Sithole (eds.) *Zulu Identities: Being Zulu Past and Present.* Scottsville: University of KwaZulu-Natal Press, 2009: 536–544.

Maluleke, T.S. "Theological Interests in the AICs and other Grass-root Communities in South Africa: A Review of Methodologies". *Journal of Black Theology in South Africa* 10 (1) 1996: 1–48.

Mandela, N. *Long Walk to Freedom. The Autobiography of Nelson Mandela.* Johannesburg: Macdonald Purnell, 1994.

Mantel, H. "Some Girls Want Out". *London Review of Books* 4 March 2004: 14–18.

Mathuray, M. *On the Sacred in African Literature: Old Gods and New Worlds*, London, Palgrave Macmillan, 2009.

Mayhem, P. and Edwards I. (eds.) *The People's City: African Life in Twentieth Century Durban.* Pietermaritzburg: University of Natal Press, 1997.

Mbali, Z. *The Churches and Racism: A Black South African Perspective*. London: SCM, 1987.

Mbembe, A. "African Modes of Self-writing". *Public Culture* 14 (1) 2002: 239–273.

Mhlambi, I.J. *African-language Literatures: Perspectives on IsiZulu Fiction and Popular Black Television Series.* Johannesburg: Wits University Press, 2012.

Mosala, I. "African Independent Churches: A Study in Socio-Theological Protest". In: Charles Villa-Vilencio and John de Gruchy (eds.) *Resistance and Hope: South African Essays in honour of Beyers Naude.* Cape Town: David Philip; Grand Rapids: Eerdmans, 1985: 103–111.

Mpanza, M. *Izwi Lezulu.* Empangeni: Excellentia Publishers, 1999.

——— *UShembe NobuNazaretha.*(n.d.) Inanda: Durban.

Msimang, C.T. *Kusadliwa Ngoludala.* Pietermaritzburg: Shuter & Shooter, 1975. Mthethwa, B. *The Hymns of the Nazaretha.* Unfinished PhD Thesis. (ed.) Carol Muller, 1996.

Muller, C. "Nazarite Women, Ritual Performance and the Construction of Cultural Truth and Power". *Current Writing* 6 (2) 1994b: 127–138.

——— "Written into the Book of Life: Nazarite Women's Performance Inscribed as spiritual text in *Ibandla lamaNazaretha.*" *Research in African Literatures* 28 (1) 1997: 3–14.

——— *Rituals of Fertility and the Sacrifice of Desire: Nazarite Women's Performances in South Africa.* Chicago/London: University of Chicago Press, 1999.

——— "Making the Book, Performing the words of Izihlabelelo ZamaNazaretha". In: Jonathan Draper (ed.) *Orality, Literacy and Colonialism in Southern Africa.* Leiden: E.J. Brill, 2003: 91–110.

Murray, C. "The Father, the Son and the Holy Spirit: Resistance and Abuse in the Life of Solomon Lion (1908–1987)". *Journal of Religion in Africa* 29(3) 1999: 243–284.

Ntarangwi, M. *Gender, Identity and Performance: Understanding Swahili Cultural Realities through Song.* Trenton/Asmara: Africa World Press, Inc., 2003.

Oosthuizen, G.C. *The Theology of a South African Messiah: An Analysis of the Hymnal of the Church of the Nazarites.* Leiden: Brill, 1967.

——— "Leadership Struggle within the Church of the Nazarites-Ibandla lamaNazaretha." *Religion in Southern Africa* 2 (2) 1981: 12–24.

——— *The Healer Prophet in Afro-Christian Churches.* Leiden/New York/Köln: Brill, 1992.

Oosthuizen, G.C. and Hexham, I (eds.) *The Story of Isaiah Shembe: History and Traditions Centred at Ekuphakameni and Mount Nhlangakazi* (vol. 1) (Trans. H.J. Becken) Lewiston/ Queenstown/ Lampeter: Edwin Mellen Press, 1996.

——— *The Story of Isaiah Shembe: Early Regional Traditions of the Acts of Nazarites.* (vol. 2) (Trans. H.J. Becken) Lewiston/Queenstown/Lampeter: Edwin Mellen Press, 1999.

——— *The Story of Isaiah Shembe:* The Continuing Story of the Sun and the Moon, Oral Testimony and the Sacred History of the AmaNazaretha Under the Leadership of Bishops Johannes Galilee Shembe and Amos Shembe (vol. 3) Lewiston: Edwin Mellen Press, 2001.

Ortner, S.B. "Theory in Anthropology since the Sixties". *Comparative Studies in Society and History.* 26 (1) 1984: 126–66.

Papini, R. "Carl Faye's Transcript of Isaiah Shembe's Testimony of His Early Life and Calling". *Journal of Religion in Africa*. 29 (3) 1999: 243–84.

Papini, R. and I. Hexham. *The Catechism of the Nazarites and Related Writings.* Lewiston: Edwin Mellen Press, 2002.

——— "The Nazaretha Scotch: Dance Uniform as Admonitory Infrapolitics for an Eikonic Zion City in Early Union Natal". *Southern African Humanities* 14 2002: 145–167.

——— "A Source Book for the Study of the Church of Nazareth: A Bilingual Publication Project for the Shembe Protoscriptures". *History and African Studies Seminar Series*, University of Natal. No. 24 1997: 1–30.

Pato, L.L. "The African Independent Churches: A Socio-Cultural Approach". *Journal of Theology for Southern Africa.* 72 (September 1990), 24–35.

Pearse, R.O., Clark, J., Barnes, P.R. And Tatham, G. (eds.) *Langalibalele and the Natal Carbineers: The Story of the Langalibalele Rebellion, 1873*, Ladysmith, Ladysmith Historical Society, 1973.

Peel, J.D.Y. *Religious Encounter and the Making of the Yoruba.* Bloomington: Indiana University Press, 2000.

Perks, R. and Thompson, A. (eds.) *The Oral History Reader.* London: Routledge, 1998.

Petersen, R.M. "The AICs and the TRC: Resistance Redefined". In: James Cochrane et al. (eds.) *Facing the Truth: South African Faith Communities and the truth and Reconciliation Commission.* Cape Town and Athens: David Phillip Publishers/ Ohio University Press, 1999: 114–125.

Petersen, R.M. *Time, Resistance and Reconstruction: A Theology of the Popular and Political.* Maryknoll: Orbis Books; Pietermaritzburg: Cluster Publications, 1999/2000.

Peterson, B. *Monarchs, Missionaries and Intellectuals: African Theatre and the Unmaking of Colonial Marginality.* Johannesburg: Witwatersrand University Press, 1999.

Pike, K.L. "Etic and Emic Standpoints for the Description of Behaviour." In Russell T. McCutcheon (ed.) *The Insider/Outsider Problem in the Study of Religion: A Reader.* London; New York: Cassel, 1999: 28–36.

Said, E. *Orientalism: Western Representation of the Orient.* London: Routledge and Kegan Paul, 1978.

Samuel, R. "Perils of the Transcript." In: Robert Perks and Alistair Thompson (eds.) *The Oral History Reader.* London: Routledge, 1998.

——— *Theatres of Memory: Past and Present in Contemporary Culture.* London: Verso, 1994.

Sanneh, L. *West African Christianity: The Religious Impact.* Maryknoll. New York: Orbis, 1983.

——— *Encountering the West: Christianity and the Global Cultural Process: the African Dimension.* Maryknoll. New York: Orbis, 1993.

Schoffelleers, M. "Ritual Healing and Political Acquiescence: The Case of the Zionist Churches in South Africa". *Africa* 60 (1) 1991: 1–25.

Sharpe, J. "Figures of Colonial Resistance". *Modern Fiction Studies* 35 (1) (Spring 1989): 137–155.

Sithole, N. "Testimony, Identity and Power: Oral Narratives of Near-Death Experiences in the Nazarite Church." MA Thesis, University of KwaZulu-Natal, Pietermaritzburg, 2005.

——— "The Mediation of Public and Private Selves in the Performance of Sermons and Narratives of Near-Death Experiences in the Nazarite Church". In: Duncan Brown (ed.) *Religion and Spirituality in South Africa: New Perspectives.* Pietermaritzburg: University of KwaZulu-Natal Press, 2009: 249–265.

Spivak, G.C. "Can the Subaltern Speak?". In: Cary Nelson and Laurence Grossberg (eds.) *Marxism and the Interpretation of Culture.* London: Macmillan, 1988: 271–313.

Sundkler, B.G.M. *Bantu Prophets in South Africa.* London/ New York/ Toronto: Oxford University Press, 1961 [1948].

——— *Zulu Zion and Some Swazi Zionists.* Oxford: Oxford University Press, 1976.

Thomas, L.E. "African Indigenous Churches as a Source of Socio-Political Transformation in South Africa". *Africa Today* (First Quarter) 1994: 39–56.

Thompson, J. "Shembe Mismanaged?: A Study of Varying Interpretations of the Ibandla lamaNazaretha". *Bulletin of the John Rylands University Library Manchester* 70 (3) 1988: 185–196.

Tishken, J.E. *Isaiah Shembe's Prophetic Uhlanga: The Worldview of the Nazareth Baptist Church in Colonial South Africa.* New York: Peter Lang, 2013.

Vilakazi, A. et al. *Shembe: The Revitalisation of African Society.* Johannesburg: Skotaville Publishers, 1986.

Vilakazi, B.W. *InkondloKaZulu,* Johannesburg, Witwatersrand University Press, 1935.

——— *Amal'ezulu,* Johannesburg, Witwatersrand University Press, 1945.

Walker C. (ed.) *Women and Gender in Southern Africa until 1945.* Cape Town: David Philip, 1990.

West, G. *The Academy of the Poor: Towards a Dialogical Reading of the Bible.* Sheffield: Sheffield Academic Press, (1999) Reprinted 2003. Pietermaritzburg: Cluster Publications.

——— "Reading Shembe Remembering the Bible: Isaiah Shembe's Instructions on Adultery". *Neotestamenica* 40 (1) 2006: 157–184.

——— "The Bible and the Female Body in Ibandla lamaNazaretha: Isaiah Shembe and Jephthah's daughter". *OTE* 20 (2) 2007: 489–509.

——— and Dube Musa (eds.) *The Bible in Africa: Transactions, Trends, and Trajectories.* Leiden: Brill, 2000.

White, L. "Poetic Licence: Oral Poetry and History". In: Barber, Karin and P.F. de Moraes Farias (eds.) *Discourse and its Disguises*: The Interpretation of African Oral Texts. Birmingham: Centre of West African Studies, University of Birmingham, 1989: 34–8.

White, J.B. (ed.) *How Should We Talk about Religion: Perspectives, Contexts, Particularities.* Notre Dame: University of Notre Dame Press, 2006.

Williams, R. *Marxism and Literature.* London: Oxford University Press, 1977.

Wimbush, V.L. "The Bible and African Americans: An Outline of an Interpretive History". In: C.H. Felder (ed.) *Stony the Road We Trod: African American Biblical Interpretation.* Minneapolis: Fortress, 1991: 81–97.

——— "Reading Texts through Words, Words through Texts". *Semia* 62 1993: 129–140.

Index

This index is alphabetically arranged word-by-word. IS refers to Isaiah Shembe; and fn. to footnotes. Page numbers in *italic* indicate illustrations.

Printed in the United States
By Bookmasters